# The Tapestry of Prophecy

by
Douglas Lee

Copyright © 2018 by Douglas Lee

All rights reserved. No part of this publication may be reproduced, distributed, or transmitted in any form or by any means, including photocopying, recording, or other electronic or mechanical methods, without the prior written permission of the publisher, except in the case of brief quotations embodied in critical reviews and certain other noncommercial uses permitted by copyright law.

All scripture is taken from The King James Version unless otherwise noted and is in public domain in the United States.

NIV- THE HOLY BIBLE, NEW INTERNATIONAL VERSION®, NIV® Copyright © 1973, 1978, 1984, 2011 by Biblica, Inc.® Used by permission. All rights reserved worldwide.

NKJV- Scripture taken from the New King James Version®. Copyright © 1982 by Thomas Nelson. Used by permission. All rights reserved.

NLT- Scripture quotations marked NLT are taken from the *Holy Bible*, New Living Translation, copyright © 1996, 2004, 2015 by Tyndale House Foundation. Used by permission of Tyndale House Publishers, Inc., Carol Stream, Illinois 60188. All rights reserved.

NASB- "Scripture taken from the NEW AMERICAN STANDARD BIBLE®, Copyright © 1960,1962,1963,1968,1971,1972,1973,1975,1977,1995 by The Lockman Foundation. Used by permission."

ISBN 978-0-578-42725-6

Independently published.

Printed in the USA

Cover photo credit. John Singleton Copley, *The Ascension*, public domain

The Tapestry of Prophecy is a 501 (c) 3 charitable organization

www.thetapestryofprophecy.org

## Isaiah 46:9-10

⁹ Remember the former things of old: for I am God, and there is none else; I am God, and there is none like me, ¹⁰ "Declaring the end from the beginning, and from ancient times *things* that are not *yet* done, Saying,

'My counsel shall stand, And I will do all My pleasure."

## Luke 21:28

"Now when these things begin to happen, look up and lift up your heads, because your redemption draws near."

# A Word from the Author

What in the world is going on? Europe sees almost weekly attacks by home-radicalized Islamic extremists, turmoil in the Middle East is in the news nightly, and Russia and Iran are up to something in Syria. North Korea is testing intercontinental rockets, while Africa is a breeding ground of war, famine, and disease. World War III is threatening to explode in the Ukraine, Crimea, or China. Meanwhile, America is deeply divided in a great many opposite mindsets philosophically, financial equity, socially, racially, and politically. Random school shootings and death caused by the opioid crisis appear almost daily. In addition, there is a measurable upturn for earthquakes and looming volcanic eruptions around the Pacific ring of fire in frequency and intensity from Indonesia to Alaska. In a September 2013 article in the magazine *The Christian Post*, it reports "4 out of 10 Americans believe we are living in the "end times" published the following report, quote, "A recent poll has found that 41 percent of American adults believe the end times have arrived. The percentage is even higher among certain Christian groups, according to the press release. More than three-quarters of Evangelicals (77 percent) and more than half of Protestants (54 percent) agree that, quote "the world is currently living in the 'end times' as described by prophecies in the Bible. Most Catholics take a different view of the world's current state, with 73 percent of them saying the end times have not arrived, though 45 percent of practicing Catholics say they have" end quote. I am one of them. I wish you could know the sense of security and liberating spirit that can only be found at the Throne of God Almighty. Not by happenstance or coincidence, but by His divine design. If there was ever a time when the world needs Jesus to return so God's end game can begin, it's now.

My passing interest in Bible prophecy became a passionate hunger when I realized that the imminent return of Christ could be in my lifetime, as did the early church fathers. Albert Einstein is credited with the following quotation, "If you can't explain it (any subject) simply, you don't understand it well enough." I have put in many hours of research and study. I drew on the wisdom and teachings of the current best and most well-known Bible prophecy teachers. Satan wants us to stay quiet, don't rock the boat. Jesus wants us to share and spread the good news of His story. It began when He came as a baby, continued throughout His ministry, crucifixion, resurrection, and ascension. The good news is His story doesn't end there. The Bible says He will return, but it will get worse before it gets better. The Bible is very clear on what will happen, who it affects, a timeline from beginning to end where Jesus returns as the conquering King Messiah. The only thing that is not given is a start date. There are those who proclaim to have special instructions from God to set dates or spread fear that the world will end soon. They are demonstrably wrong and biblically ignorant. They lend credence to the false belief that prophecy cannot be known. Certainly, if we can split the atom or map the human genome, we can read and understand what is plainly written in God's word. When Jesus does come, He will make wrongs right, He will bring health and prosperity, and finally He will bring true complete peace. How is that anything other than hopeful?

This intent of this book is to simply put in order what the Bible says about God's Master Plan in an easy to read narrative. It is not meant to disparage or judge the reader. That role belongs to the Holy Spirit to bring conviction and urging in the right direction, but ultimately it is the responsibly of the individual to choose. Also, it is meant to awaken a spirit of joy that those of us who study Bible prophecy enjoy. Imagine how you will live your life today if you believed that Jesus could come back tomorrow. Truly, Jesus' return is a question of WHEN, not IF. As modern-day disciples, it is incumbent upon us to present the whole council of God, not to pick and choose only those topics we like a cafeteria buffet. Prophecy should give us an attitude of expectancy, not complacency. It is my hope that you might find a glimmer of hope and take the conscious, necessary steps towards an eternal life in heaven. If the Bible is correct, and I believe it is, time is short. Never before in history have all the elements of prophecy converged at the same time like they have in recent years. Remember this world is not our home. I hope you will find peace of mind, whether it be pre- or post-trumpet sound.

E'en so Lord Jesus quickly come!

# TABLE OF CONTENTS

Chapter 1....The Ship is Docking..................................................page 10

Chapter 2....And God Said............................................................page 15

Chapter 3....The Covenants..........................................................page 35

Chapter 4....The Prophets.............................................................page 54

Chapter 5....The Bridge.................................................................page 60

Chapter 6....The End of Days.......................................................page 66

Chapter 7....I Am the Vine............................................................page 73

Chapter 8....The Messiah: First Advent......................................page 77

Chapter 9....The Church..............................................................page 115

Chapter 10...The Warning Signs................................................page 123

Chapter 11...Be Not Deceived....................................................page 127

Chapter 12...The Rapture...........................................................page 134

Chapter 13...Our Glorified New Bodies....................................page 140

Chapter 14...The Day of Wrath aka the Tribulation................page 145

Chapter 15...What's Next?.........................................................page 161

Chapter 16...The One World Leader........................................page 175

Chapter 17...The Four Horsemen.............................................page 179

Chapter 18...A Way Out.............................................................page 191

Chapter 19...It Goes from Bad to Worse.................................page 194

Chapter 20...The Return of the King........................................page 201

Chapter 21...The Millennium.....................................................page 204

Chapter 22...Eternity, The Choice is Yours.............................page 222

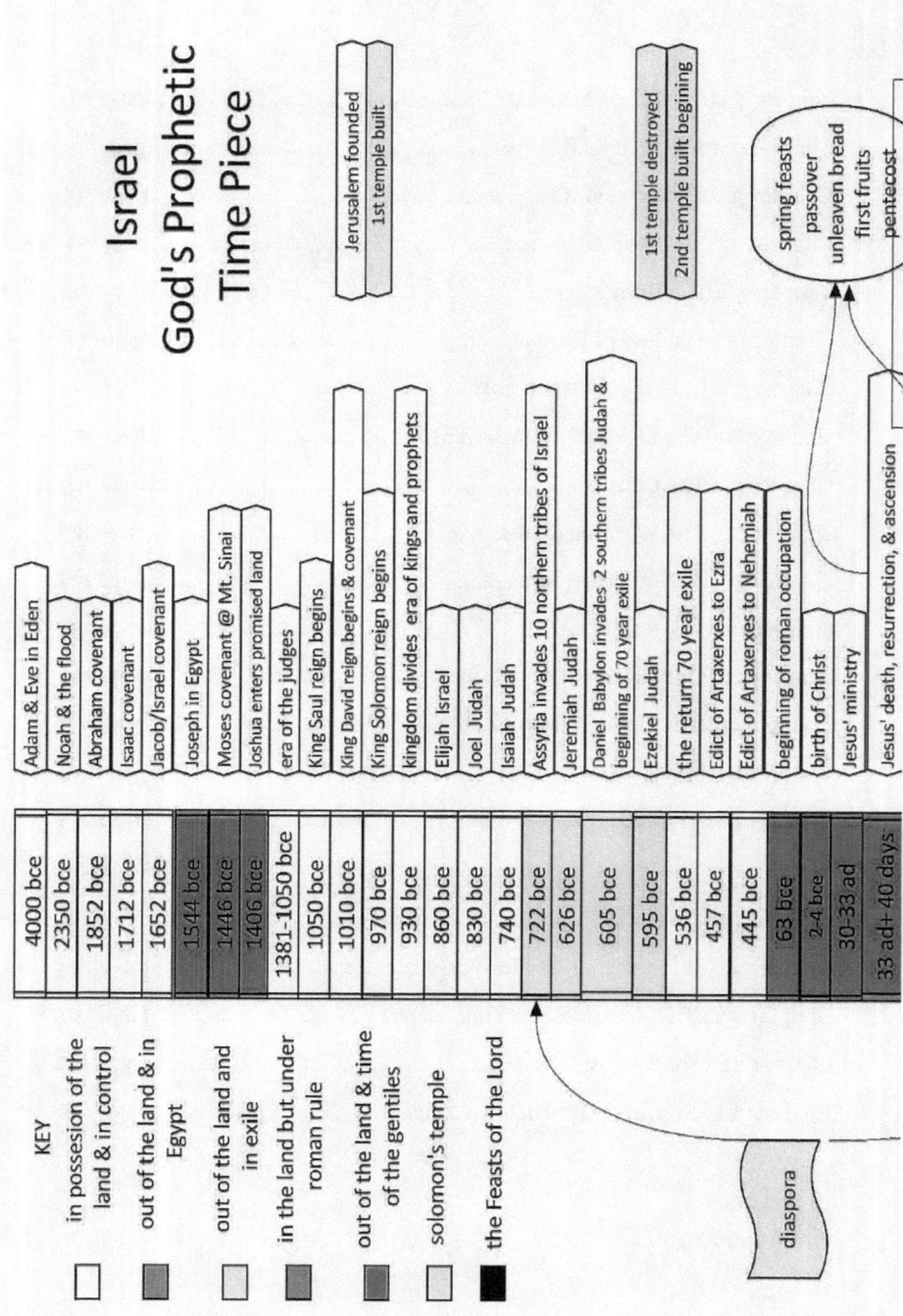

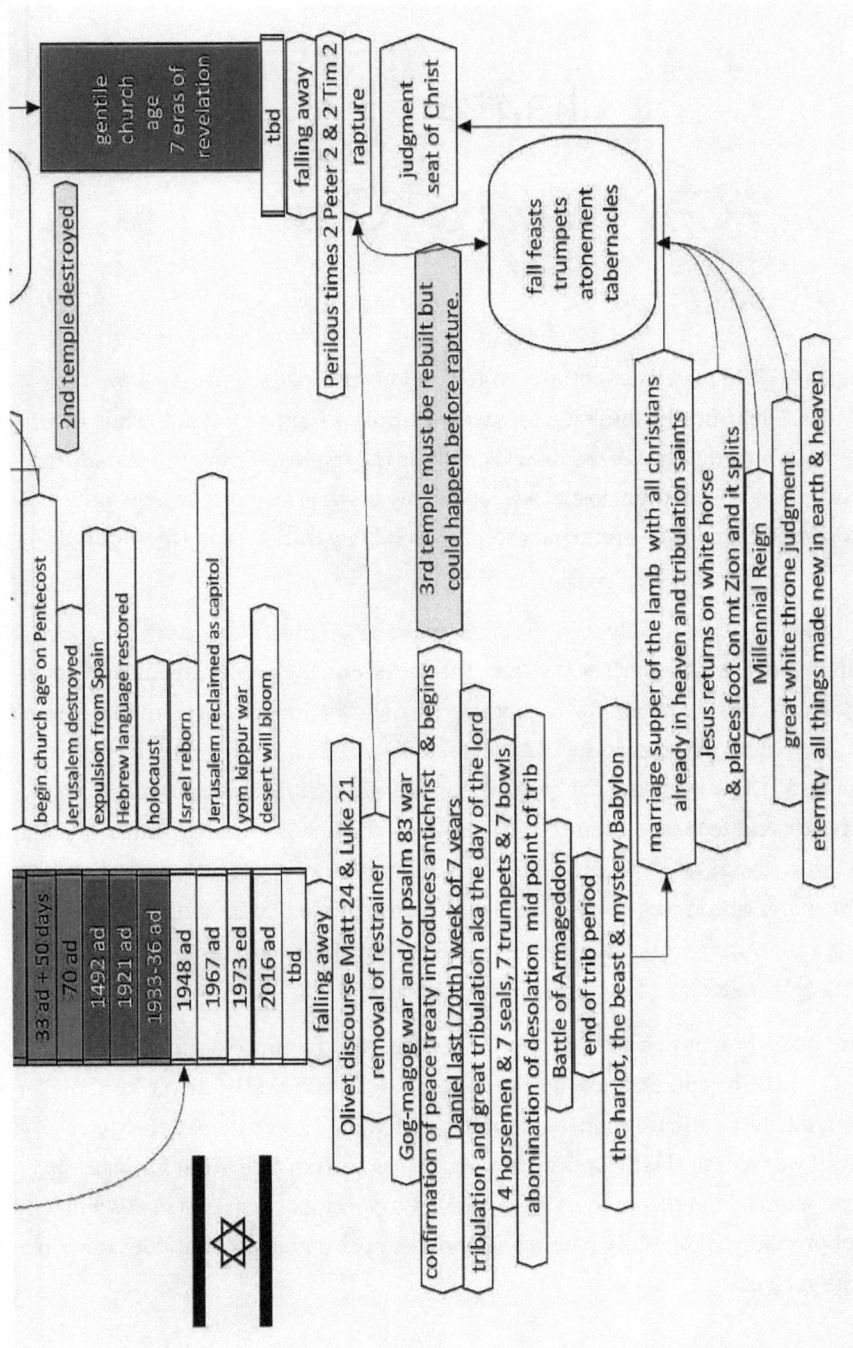

# Chapter 1

# "The Ship is Docking"

In New England, USA, there is a special architectural feature called a "widow's walk" or "widow's watch." Specifically, these features were platforms built on top of the houses of seafarers, upon which their wives would walk daily as they waited for their husbands to return to shore. Ships were often lost at sea, and many of these women consequently became widows. The image of a returning ship is a good illustration as to why study prophecy.

First, on the distant horizon, only the tops of the masts are visible. Then, as they get closer, more details come into view, such as the sails, the decks, and men scurrying up and down the rigging. When the ship enters the harbor, the wife knows time is short and that it won't be much longer before the ship docks and the unloading begins. While preparing to go down to the dock, these women must have been very excited in the anticipation of her husband's return and feeling his embrace. Then, when she finally meets her husband, she is overcome with joy. In this scenario, when Jesus' ship is far off, only little details are known. As it comes closer, more and more signs are recognized and understood. We, who are watching and waiting with anticipation for His arrival, believe that the ship is getting ready to dock and are looking for our savior to come ashore.

Are we there yet? If you have ever traveled with a child, this question was probably asked a multitude of times. They didn't know how to read the signs that tell the driver just how far they are from the destination. Prophecy is similar, in that it is a way to read the signs. Accordingly, if we want to clearly understand what clues to keep an eye out for regarding Jesus' return, we need to tune into His wavelength. Prophecy can be found in His word. The study of prophecy is called Eschatology. So why study Prophecy? What does the Bible say about the subject?

- The Old and New Testaments have books on law, history of the Jews, poetry, Jesus' life and ministry, the formation of the church, the first missionary journeys, promises of future events, and prophecy. Revelation 19:10b (NIV) "For it is the Spirit of prophecy who bears testimony to Jesus." There are 31,124 verses in the Bible. According to *J. Barton Jayne's Encyclopedia of Biblical Prophecy*, prophecy covers 8,352 verses or 27%. Of those verses, the Old Testament encompasses 1,239 prophecies and the New Testament contains 578 prophecies. Jesus' birth, ministry, death, and resurrection as Messiah fulfilled as many as 400 of them as the Associates of Biblical Research website states. That means there are roughly 1,400 prophecies about His return yet to be fulfilled. Do we really what to ignore over ¼ of what God said? God must have thought this was important. We celebrate His birth on Christmas and His sacrifice and resurrection on Easter. We will look more closely at Jesus as the Messiah later in this book. By understanding and showing God's faithfulness to keep His Word in the past, won't it give us hope that He will keep it in the future? We can be assured of the future. Should we not be looking ahead with anticipation for His return!

- It brings blessings and hope. Revelation 1:3 (NKJV) "Blessed is he who reads and those who hear the words of this prophecy and keep those things which are written in it; for the time is near." Titus 2:13 "Looking for that blessed hope and glorious appearing of our great God and Savior Jesus Christ." God is in control and has a plan from the first verse in Genesis to the last verse of Revelation. Revelation 22:7 (NKJV) "Behold, I am coming quickly! Blessed is he who keeps the words of the prophecy of this book." Jeremiah 29:11 (NIV) "For I know the plans I have for you," declares the LORD, "plans to prosper you and not to harm you, plans to give you hope and a future." Nothing surprises him. He knows the end as well as the beginning and has a plan for each of our lives. God has a purpose in everything He does. Nothing is frivolous, inconsequential, or useless. There is no extravagance or waste. God does not need man's permission, cooperation or understanding of His design to do as He pleases. No amount of challenging or denial of His laws will make Him change them. Isaiah 46:9-10 "9 Remember the former things of old, for I am God, and there is none else I am God, and there is none like Me. 10 Declaring the end from the beginning, and from ancient times things that are not yet done, saying, 'My counsel shall stand, and I will do all My pleasure." Psalm 2:4 "He that sitteth in the heavens shall laugh; The Lord shall hold them in derision." 1 Corinthians 2:9 "But as it is written: "Eye hath not seen, nor ear heard, nor have entered into the heart of man the things which God hath prepared for those who love Him."

- It is meant to prepare not to scare. Fear of the unknown may be one of the strongest fears man has. God wants us to know His plan and not be ignorant of it. 1 Thessalonians 4:13-18 "13 But I would not have you to be ignorant, brethren, concerning them which are asleep, that ye sorrow not, even as others which have no hope. 14 For if we believe that Jesus died and rose again, even so them also which sleep in Jesus will God bring with him. 15 For this we say unto you by the word of the Lord, that we which are alive and remain unto the coming of the Lord shall not prevent them which are asleep. 16 For the Lord himself shall descend from heaven with a shout, with the voice of the archangel, and with the trump of God: and the dead in Christ shall rise first: 17 Then we which are alive and remain shall be caught up together with them in the clouds, to meet the Lord in the air: and so shall we ever be with the Lord. 18 Wherefore comfort one another with these words." Jeremiah 33:2-3 (NLT) "2 This is what the LORD says, the LORD who made the earth, who formed and established it, whose name is the LORD. 3 Ask me and I will tell you remarkable secrets you do not know about things to come." Daniel 2:28 (NIV) "But there is a God in heaven who reveals mysteries. He has shown King Nebuchadnezzar what will happen in days to come. Your dream and the visions that passed through your mind as you were lying in bed are these."

- For some Christians, prophecy is confusing and overwhelming. God wants us to be aware of what to look for in regards to Jesus' return. Isaiah 42:8-9 "8 I am the LORD, that is My name; and My glory I will not give to another, neither My praise to raven images. 9 Behold, the former things have come to pass, and new things I declare; before they spring forth I tell you of them." There is a major difference between prediction and prophecy. Prediction is a fancy word for guessing. For instance, if you throw enough darts, you are bound to hit the bullseye once. Prophecy is the sure word of God and hits the mark every time. God left many clues with a myriad of commentators, and like all things, unfamiliarity and ignorance breeds misunderstanding; likewise, repetition and education breeds understanding. Romans 10:17 (NKJV) "So faith comes from hearing and hearing through the word of Christ." God wants us to know of His plan and not be ignorant. Those of us who choose to seek answers will find them. 1 Chronicles 28:9 (NKJV) "As for you, my son Solomon, know the God of your father, and serve Him with a loyal heart and with a willing mind; for the LORD searches all hearts and understands all the intent of the thoughts. If you seek Him, He will be found by you; but if you forsake Him, He will cast you off forever." Jeremiah 29:13 "And ye shall seek Me, and find Me, when ye shall search for Me with all your heart." Matthew 7:7-8 "7 Ask, and it shall be given you; seek, and ye shall find; knock, and it shall be opened unto you: 8 For every one that asketh receiveth; and he that seeketh findeth; and to him that knocketh it shall be opened." Luke 11:9-10 (NKJV) "9 So I say to you, ask, and it will be given to you; seek, and you will find; knock, and it will be opened to you. 10 For everyone who asks receives, and he who seeks finds, and to him who knocks it will be opened." Prophecy is meant to give signs to those who look to what lies ahead and before God acts. God provided clues of what to look for when that would happen so we believers in Christ, would not be caught unaware, unlike those who do not follow Christ will be. Romans 11:25 (NIV) "I do not want you to be ignorant of this mystery, brothers and sisters, so that you may not be conceited: Israel has experienced a hardening in part until the full number of the Gentiles has come in." Only those who look for Him would be able to recognize the signs when they appear much like the three Magi recognized the star in the east as the sign of the Messiah. We should embrace it, not shy away from it.

- Jesus taught about things to come and that He would return. After His resurrection, Jesus told His disciples He would soon be leaving to return to heaven. Remember, they had just seen Him conquer death by rising from the grave, and feeling empowered, they were ready to take on the world. His disciples became greatly distressed when He informed them that He would be leaving. The wind was taken right out of their sails. Jesus said in John 14:1-3 "1 Let not your heart be troubled; ye believe in God, believe also in Me. 2 In My Father's house are many mansions; if it were not so, I would have told you. I go to prepare a place for you. 3 And if I go and prepare a place for you, I will come again and receive you unto Myself; that where I am, there ye may be also." The concept of Christ's return is not foreign to us. How many hymns do we sing where the last verse references God coming in glory. Does this sound familiar? "When Christ shall come with shout of acclamation, to take me home what joy shall fill my heart. Then I shall bow in humble adoration, and there proclaim my God How Great Thou Art!" If He is to come again He first had to leave, but He promised we would not be left by ourselves. The Helper, Advocate, Comforter or Holy Spirit was sent to indwell, inspire, and empower His followers. John 14:16-18 "¹⁶ And I will pray to the Father, and He will give you another Helper, that He may abide with you forever ¹⁷ the Spirit of truth, whom the world cannot receive, because it neither sees Him nor knows Him; but you know Him, for He dwells with you and will be in you. ¹⁸ I will not leave you orphans (comfortless); I will come to you." John 14:26 "But the Comforter, which is the Holy Ghost, whom the Father will send in my name, he shall teach you all things, and bring all things to your remembrance, whatsoever I have said unto you." He also added that in order for the Holy Spirit to come, He would need to leave, which would be an advantage for us. John 16:5-15 "⁵ But now I go my way to him that sent me; and none of you asketh Me, Whither goest thou? ⁶ But because I have said these things unto you, sorrow hath filled your heart. ⁷ Nevertheless I tell you the truth; It is expedient for you that I go away: for if I go not away, the Comforter will not come unto you; but if I depart, I will send him unto you. ⁸ And when he is come, he will reprove the world of sin, and of righteousness, and of judgment: ⁹ Of sin, because they believe not on Me; ¹⁰ Of righteousness, because I go to my Father, and ye see Me no more; ¹¹ Of judgment, because the prince of this world is judged. ¹² I have yet many things to say unto you, but ye cannot bear them now. ¹³ Howbeit when he, the Spirit of truth, is come, he will guide you into all truth: for he shall not speak of himself; but whatsoever he shall hear, that shall he speak: and he will shew you things to come. ¹⁴ He shall glorify Me: for he shall receive of mine, and shall shew it unto you. ¹⁵ All things that the Father hath are Mine: therefore said I, that he shall take of Mine, and shall shew it unto you." John 20:21-22 (NIV) "²¹ Again Jesus said, "Peace be with you! As the Father has sent me, I am sending you." ²² And with that He breathed on them and said, "Receive the Holy Spirit." 2 Peter 1:19-21 "¹⁹ We have also a more sure word of prophecy; whereunto ye do well that ye take heed, as unto a light that shineth in a dark place, until the day dawn, and the day star arise in your hearts: ²⁰ Knowing this first, that no prophecy of the scripture is of any private interpretation. ²¹ For the prophecy came not in old time by the will of man: but holy men of God spake as they were moved by the Holy Ghost." However, the Holy Spirit has a finite period of ministry. He cannot be present when Jesus is on earth just as Jesus was not present when God dwelt among the Israelites when Moses built a tabernacle for Him. We will look at what happens to the Holy Spirit in the "end of days" after we delve into Jesus as the Messiah and a prophet later.

# Chapter 2

## "And God Said"

Before we start to unravel God's tapestry, let's affirm God's authority and trustworthiness by establishing a firm foundation. Let's start our exploration with the question "Can we trust God and His word to be true?" There are the only two options. If God's word is not true, then we can quit right here. If God's word is true, then we must consider that God's truth is complete. He is either all true or none true. One cannot pick and choose in His word what is or is not true like a cafeteria smorgasbord. He is not a God of partial truth. Proverbs 30:5 (NLT) "Every word of God proves true. He is a shield to all who come to Him for protection." We may not understand, comprehend or be able to explain everything but you can rely on that it is true. His truth began at creation to the relationship with the Jewish forefathers to Jesus' birth, life, sacrificial crucifixion, and resurrection, to His promise of redemption and forgiveness, to His return, and finally ending with His living in heaven with Him victorious are all true.

Next, if God does exist, how then does He make Himself known to us, if at all? The Bible says that God spoke directly to Adam and Eve, Noah, Abraham, Isaac, Jacob, Moses, and the prophets. Hebrews 1:1-2 (NKJV) "¹ God, who at various times and in various ways spoke in time past to the fathers by the prophets, ² has in these last days spoken to us by His Son, whom He has appointed heir of all things, through whom also He made the worlds." God spoke through Jesus to the Apostles and the people (Jew and Gentile) who were alive then. When Jesus was on earth, He taught His disciples by speaking directly with them and living by example. They had the benefit of conversing with Jesus face to face. There was no ambiguity. If they had a question or needed clarification on a specific point, they could just ask Him. It was person to person contact. God sent other messengers, such as John the Baptist, Paul, and the 12 Apostles, and the angels Michael and Gabriel. God speaks to us through intercessory prayer, inspiration, and His written word, the Bible. Today God still speaks to us through God's written word and the Holy Spirit. 2 Timothy 3:16-17 (NLT) "¹⁶ All Scripture is inspired by God and is useful to teach us what is true and to make us realize what is wrong in our lives. It corrects us when we are wrong and teaches us to do what is right. ¹⁷ God uses it to prepare and equip his people to do every good work." The Bible gives us insight into God's desire for us and for future generations, regardless of circumstance, stage of life, or station. God communicates with His children. He is not an absentee parent. The Bible is the only written word of God. Deuteronomy 4:2 "Ye shall not add unto the word which I command you, neither shall ye diminish ought from it, that ye may keep the commandments of the Lord your God which I command you." The Bible stands above all others religious writings. The book of Exodus speaks of Moses arrival at Mount Sinai, where he met God on the top of the mountain. Exodus 24:12 "Then the Lord said to Moses, "Come up to Me on the mountain and be there; and I will give you tablets of stone, and the law and commandments which I have written, that thou mayest teach them." God sealed the meeting by God Himself writing with His finger in the rock and gave His Law to Moses to bring to the people.

We also need to consider whether the Bible is either allegorical or literal. An allegory is when a story is told to represent ideas or meaning, but not actual literal events. Our faith system is based on the Bible being true, and therefore, literal. If it is not literal, how could faith in a supremely loving God have lasted so long without man directly experiencing God's workings throughout history? Furthermore, the Bible is all inclusive. Whatever God wanted us to know about prophecy is in there. If God wanted us to have specific information or knowledge, He would have included it. This will become self-evident when we look at the prophets Isaiah, Ezekiel, Daniel, and Jeremiah.

Before we move on, a point about Bible History needs to be explained. The English language Bibles we use today are translations. Remember that old saying, "it loses something in the translation?" Well, it truly does apply. The Bible, as we know it, is not a word by word translation; otherwise, it may be unreadable. Most editions are either a phrase by phrase or a thought by thought translation. It is also an inspired divine act of God to carry on His word to be without error or ambiguity. Remember 2 Timothy 3:16-17 (NLT) "¹⁶ All Scripture is inspired by God and is useful to teach us what is true and to make us realize what is wrong in our lives. It corrects us when we are wrong and teaches us to do what is right. ¹⁷ God uses it to prepare and equip his people to do every good work." When the Bible was written, the original writers used common figures of speech or expressions with which they were familiar. There are some expressions that would have been understood by the Hebrews that the gentile ear does not pick up. These are called idioms. Here is an example of an idiom. When we talk about "Beantown" we all know it is a reference to Boston and not a place where beans are grown. Throughout tis text, we will be referring to several Jewish idioms as we get into some of the phrases that Jesus and the disciples used.

The Old Testament is written primarily in Ancient Hebrew and a small amount of Aramaic. The New Testament is written in the Koine (common) Greek language, which was the basic language used during Christ's time. It replaced Hebrew and Aramaic from when Alexander the Great conquered most of the then known world in the third and fourth centuries BCE. Hebrew was not as well studied, mostly because Hebrew scribes were in decline as a result of being exiled and the increase of Greek as the language of commerce and government. In the second to third centuries BCE, the Old Testament was translated into Greek and was called the Septuagint (70 translators). Latin took over as the dominant language of the church under Emperor Constantine. In the fourth century, St. Jerome translated both the Old and New Testaments, and was called the Latin Vulgate. In 1440 AD the printing press was invented and multiple copies could be made, which was much easier than the old method of one scribe writing one copy at a time by hand. A number of priestly learned men tried to translate and then promote their own editions which caused a great deal of controversy and led to several versions, which were intensely debated. The final draft, with the selected books, of the Roman Catholic Bible was accepted at the Council of Trent (1545–1563). Several other versions were translated beforeo 1611, when King James commissioned an English version. Of course, it was written in old English, which was the language of the day. Today, there are many contemporary versions, which makes it a little easier to read and understand. If there seems to be any contradictions in the text, it is probably a defect of the translation. One other book that is important to understanding the original text is called *Strong's Lexicon or Concordance*. It is considered by many as *the* definitive source that translates the Bible word by word for both the old (Ancient Hebrew and Aramaic) and new (Greek) testaments. It assigns a number to each word which will become apparent as we look at specific words throughout this book.

The Qur'an and Hadith of Muhammad, the writings of Confucius, Buddha, Dalai Lama, Taoism, Gandhi, Hindu, and Shinto were all written by people who considered themselves to be "enlightened," but not God. Those teachings say that one can be rewarded for being a good person in this life or the next, but they do not have the authority or capability to provide eternal life. Men such as Moses, King David, Solomon, all the prophets, the gospels of the Apostles, Paul's letters to the early churches, and John, all did the actual writing, but the Bible was from a direct communication or by inspiration with God. Therefore, the Bible has to be the inerrant, infallible, and indisputable Word of God. Psalm 119:105 "Thy word is a lamp to my feet and a light to my path."

So, if God is true and He communicates with us via the Scriptures, what does His word say about Himself? In no particular order of importance:

- First, He is the creator. Genesis 1:1-2 "¹ In the beginning, God created the heaven and the earth. ² And the earth was without form, and void; and darkness was on the face of the deep. And the Spirit of God moved upon the face of the waters." During the subsequent verses of Genesis 1:3-31 Moses provides a detailed progression that only in the last few years have we been able to comprehend. When these words were written, man did not have the understanding of astrophysics and planetary mechanics that we have today. What do you think the odds are of Moses writing out the exact order of creation in the exact order in which they happened on his own? They would literally be astronomical. The ability to understand and comprehend these complex mathematical concepts comes from God. If we are made in God's image, would He not include the ability to learn to decipher these in time? John 1:1-5 "In the beginning was the Word, and the Word was with God, and the Word was God. ² The same was in the beginning with God. ³ All things were made by him; and without him was not any thing made that was made. ⁴ In him was life; and the life was the light of men. ⁵ And the light shineth in darkness; and the darkness comprehended it not." God created the universe in five days. On the sixth, he created man in his own image, and on the seventh, He rested. When He was finished, He saw that it was good (no sin involved). Genesis 1:31 "And God saw everything that He had made, and behold, it was very good. And evening and the morning were the sixth day." God's ability to physically intervene into our world pales in comparison to the love God has for us by sending His son to pay the ultimate price to redeem us, even though we do not deserve it.

- There is power in the spoken word of God (omnipotent). Genesis1:3-5 "³ And God said, "Let there be light"; and there was light. ⁴ And God saw the light that it was good, and God divided the light from the darkness. ⁵ And God called the light Day, and the darkness He called Night. And the evening and the morning were the first day." Certainly, if He made the earth, He can manipulate it at His pleasure. To illustrate, we only need to read the stories of Noah, Moses at the

Red Sea, caused fiery hail to down from the sky, earthquakes that swallowed Moses' enemies, and the stories of Joshua, Lot, Isaiah, and Daniel. Jeremiah 10:13 "When he uttereth his voice, there is a multitude of waters in the heavens, and he causeth the vapours to ascend from the ends of the earth; he maketh lightnings with rain, and bringeth forth the wind out of his treasures." These examples demonstrate God CAN supernaturally affect the physical world. With His same breath that He generated life into man. Genesis 2:7 "And the LORD God formed man of the dust of the ground, and breathed into his nostrils the breath of life; and man became a living soul." Hebrews 4:12 "For the word of God is quick and powerful, and sharper than any two-edged sword, piercing even to the dividing asunder soul and spirit, and of joints and marrow, and is a discerner of the thoughts and intents of the heart."

- God owns all that is in the earth and is generous. Since God created the heavens and the earth all things under heaven belongs to Him. Genesis 14:22 "And Abram said to the king of Sodom, I have lift up mine hand unto the LORD, the most high God, the possessor of heaven and earth." Deuteronomy 10:14 "Behold, the heaven and the heaven of heavens is the Lord's thy God, also with all that therein is." Psalm 24:1 "The earth is the LORD's, and all its fullness, thereof; the world and all that dwell therein." Psalm 51:11-13 "[11] Cast me not away from thy presence, and take not thy Holy Spirit from me. [12] Restore unto me the joy of Thy salvation, and uphold me by Thy free spirit. [13] Then I will teach transgressors Thy ways, and sinners shall be converted unto Thee." 1 Corinthians 10:26 (NIV) "For, "The earth is the Lord's, and everything in it." Romans 8:32-33 "[32] He that spared not His own Son, but delivered Him up for us all, how shall He not with Him also freely give us all things? [33] Who shall lay any thing to the charge of God's elect? It is God that justifieth."

- God sets His own authority. When Moses saw the burning bush, he asked God what he should tell the Israelites what His Name was, God said in Exodus 3:14 "And God said to Moses, "I AM that I AM." (aka YAHWEH) And He said, "Thus shalt thou say unto the children of Israel, 'I AM hath sent me unto you.'" That declaration then set His authority above all creation, including mankind. His name translates to the English name of Jehovah, our Lord, and Sovereign. Being Sovereign He has complete authority over man and all creation. As Americans in the 21$^{st}$ century, we do not easily relate to the concept of Sovereign and subordinate. The subordinate is reliant on the Sovereign for just about everything regarding sustainability and safety. In today's world of Political Correctness, everybody is equal; therefore, there is no accountability.

- God claims Himself above all other gods and as such, He and He alone is worthy of our loyalty, praise, and love. Exodus 20:1-6 "¹ And God spake all these words, saying, ² I am the LORD thy God, which have brought thee out of the land of Egypt, out of the house of bondage.³ Thou shalt have no other gods before me. ⁴ Thou shalt not make unto thee any graven image, or any likeness of any thing that is in heaven above, or that is in the earth beneath, or that is in the water under the earth. ⁵ Thou shalt not bow down thyself to them, nor serve them: for I the LORD thy God am a jealous God, visiting the iniquity of the fathers upon the children unto the third and fourth generation of them that hate Me; ⁶ And shewing mercy unto thousands of them that love Me, and keep My commandments." Psalm 139:14 "I will praise Thee, for I am fearfully and wonderfully made; Marvelous are Thy works, and that my soul knoweth very well." Remember Isaiah 46:9 "Remember the former things of old, for I am God, and there is no else; I am God, and there is none like Me." Isaiah 44:6-8 "⁶ Thus saith the LORD the King of Israel, and his redeemer the LORD of hosts; I am the first, and I am the last; and beside me there is no God. ⁷ And who, as I, shall call, and shall declare it, and set it in order for me, since I appointed the ancient people? and the things that are coming, and shall come, let them shew unto them. ⁸ Fear ye not, neither be afraid: have not I told thee from that time, and have declared it? ye are even my witnesses. Is there a God beside me? yea, there is no God; I know not any." Psalm 150:1-6 "¹ Praise ye the LORD. Praise God in his sanctuary: praise him in the firmament of his power. ² Praise him for his mighty acts: praise him according to his excellent greatness. ³ Praise him with the sound of the trumpet: praise him with the psaltery and harp. ⁴ Praise him with the timbrel and dance: praise him with stringed instruments and organs. ⁵ Praise him upon the loud cymbals: praise him upon the high sounding cymbals. ⁶ Let every thing that hath breath praise the LORD. Praise ye the LORD." Psalm 113:3 "From the rising of the sun unto the going down of the same the LORD's name is to be praised." God inhabits our praise. Psalm 22:3 "But Thou art holy, O thou that inhabitest the praises of Israel." To be clear, God made us in *His* image including with the traits of free will, intelligence, and expression. Instead of creating automatons, He created a being that has the capacity to assess, appreciate, and freely offer gratitude and praise for His effort. God extends the same prerequisite courtesy to His son Jesus and the Holy Spirit. Revelation 3:20 (NKJV) "Behold, I (Jesus) stand at the door and knock. If anyone hears My voice and opens the door, I will come in to him and dine with him, and he with Me." John 4:22-24 "22 Ye worship ye know not what: we know what we worship: for salvation is of the Jews. 23 But the hour cometh, and now is, when the true worshippers shall worship the Father in spirit and in truth: for the Father seeketh such to worship him. 24 God is a Spirit: and they that worship him must worship him in spirit and in truth." John 14:17 "Even the Spirit of truth, whom the world cannot receive because it seeth Him not; but ye know Him, for He dwelleth with you and will be in you."

- God is constant and does not change. Malachi 3:6 "For I am the LORD, I change not; therefore ye sons of Jacob are not consumed." Job 23:13 (NKJV) "But He is unique, and who can make Him change? And whatever His soul desires, that He does." While we often say God never changes, do we really understand the breadth of time and space that quality embodies? Psalm 90:2 "Before the mountains were brought forth, or ever thou hadst formed the earth and the world, even from everlasting to everlasting, Thou art God." When God gives His word, He does not break it or change it. If He did, how could we trust in His promises like Deuteronomy 31:6 "Be strong and of a good courage, fear not, nor be afraid of them: for the LORD thy God, he it is that doth go with thee; he will not fail thee, nor forsake thee." 1 John 1:9 "If we confess our sins, he is faithful and just to forgive us our sins and to cleanse us from all unrighteousness." They would be meaningless. As the William Marion Runyan hymn, *Great is Thy Faithfulness*, says "Thou changest not, Thy compassions, they fail not, As Thou hast been Thou forever wilt be." Someone once said that if you feel separated from God, it is you that has moved, not Him.

- God gave humankind His highest valued trait, free will. Genesis 1:27 "So God created mankind in His own image; in the image of God He created them; male and female He created them." Genesis 5:1 (NKJV) "This is the book of the genealogy of Adam. In the day that God created man, He made him in the likeness of God." This means that God gave some of his traits to his creation. Paramount among them, is free will. Maybe a better way to define it is to say we have the freedom (and responsibility) of choice. Choose correctly and you get eternal life; however, choose incorrectly, you will be eternally separated from God. Deuteronomy 30:19-20 "¹⁹ I call heaven and earth to record this day against you, that I have set before you life and death, blessing and cursing: therefore choose life, that both thou and thy seed may live: ²⁰ That thou mayest love the LORD thy God, and that thou mayest obey his voice, and that thou mayest cleave unto him: for he is thy life, and the length of thy days: that thou mayest dwell in the land which the LORD swore unto thy fathers, to Abraham, to Isaac, and to Jacob, to give them." God had to give man a free will so that He could experience true love from His creation, so that He will be glorified. He wanted man to love Him willingly. Free will allows man to do that. Not doing so goes against reason, and God is a logical person, which is why He saw it right to give mankind the freedom to choose for himself. He hoped that we'd use it to give Him pleasure and bring glory and honor to Him. Unfortunately, He knew they wouldn't, even when He created them. So even from the beginning, He put into place a way back to Him.

- God is a God of justice. He will reward the faithful with blessings and reprimand the unfaithful. Isaiah 30:18 "And therefore will the Lord wait, that He may be gracious unto you; and therefore, will He be exalted, that He may have mercy upon you. For the Lord is a God of judgment; blessed are all those who wait for Him." Deuteronomy 32:4 (NKJV) "He is the Rock, His work is perfect; for all His ways are justice, A God of truth and without injustice; Righteous and upright is He." Isaiah 59:2 "But your iniquities have separated between you and your God, and your sins have hid His face from you, that He will not hear." Proverbs 10:16(NIV) "The wages of the righteous is life, but the earnings of the wicked are sin and death." Romans 6:23 "For the wages of sin is death, but the gift of God is eternal life in Christ Jesus our Lord." While there may be varying degrees of sin and punishment in this life, they are all equal in that they will keep us from the presence of God in the next. There are many examples of God holding off the sentence that justice demands in the hopes that we would turn away from our selfish ways and look to him. When a sin or offense is committed, the guilty must have a penalty, otherwise, there would be no point or reward for being "good." It is the basis for our system of justice. God offered His own son to pay that debt price with His own blood. He freely subjected Himself to suffering, died and rose again. With that victory, He joined His Father as being worthy to be praised and worshipped. He still would have had to do so if there were only one person on earth. God rejoices when one of His creation accepts His gift. Luke 15:10 (NIV) "In the same way, I tell you, there is rejoicing in the presence of the angels of God over one sinner who repents." Conversely, God takes no pleasure when one of His creation is consigned to hell. Ezekiel 33:11 "Say to them: 'As I live,' saith the Lord GOD, 'I have no pleasure in the death of the wicked, but that the wicked turn from his way and live. Turn ye, turn ye from your evil ways! For why will ye die, O house of Israel?" John 3:17 "For God sent not His Son into the world to condemn the world, but that the world through Him might be saved." I believe that God grieves greatly when He is forced to send a soul to hell because the price of redemption was paid with His Own son's blood.

- God's grace and mercy are limitless and will last forever. Grace is the gift of forgiveness that one does not deserve, while mercy is the removal (pardon) of our guilt for our transgression. God has both in abundance and is longing to give to those who ask. Psalm 86:15 "But thou, O Lord, art a God full of compassion, and gracious, longsuffering and plenteous in mercy and truth." Hebrews 4:16 "Let us then with confidence draw near to the throne of grace, that we may receive mercy and find grace to help in time of need." 2 Corinthians 9:8-9 (NIV) "8 And God is able to bless you abundantly, so that in all things at all times, having all that you need, you will abound in every good work. 9 As it is written: "They have freely scattered their gifts to the poor; their righteousness endures forever." Once He forgives your sins He will separate you from it to remember it no more. Psalm 103:11-12 "11 For as the heavens are high above the earth, so great is His mercy toward them that fear Him; 12 As far as the east is from the west, so hath He removed our transgressions from us." Isaiah 43:25 "I, even I, am He who blots out your transgressions for My own sake; and remembers your sins no more." Micah 7:19 "He will turn again, he will have compassion on us, He will subdue our iniquities, and thou wilt cast all their sins into the depths of the sea." Hebrews 8:12 "For I will be merciful to their unrighteousness, and their sins and their iniquities (past, present and future) will I remember no more." Psalm 32:1-2 (NIV) "1 Blessed is the one whose transgressions are forgiven, whose sins are covered. 2 Blessed is the one whose sin the LORD does not count against them and in whose spirit is no deceit." Psalm 103:2-3 "2 Bless the Lord O my soul and forget not all His benefits; 3 who forgiveth all thine iniquities, who healeth all thy diseases." Romans 4:7-8 "7 Saying, "Blessed are they whose iniquities are forgiven, and whose sins are covered. [8] Blessed is the man to whom the Lord will not impute sin." God wants to forgive our transgressions but it requires us to ask. The Bible also says there is one sin that cannot be absolved, blasphemy against the Holy Spirit. Matthew 12:31-32 "[31] Wherefore I say unto you, all manner of sin and blasphemy shall be forgiven unto men: but the blasphemy against the Holy Ghost shall not be forgiven unto men. [32] And whosoever speaketh a word against the Son of man, it shall be forgiven him: but whosoever speaketh against the Holy Ghost, it shall not be forgiven him, neither in this world, neither in the world to come." Mark 3:28-29 "[28] Verily I say unto you, all sins shall be forgiven unto the sons of men, and blasphemies wherewith soever they shall blaspheme: [29] But he that shall blaspheme against the Holy Ghost hath never forgiveness, but is in danger of eternal damnation." Luke calls those fellow Jews who heard the message but discounted the meaning in favor of following "the law" the same term used by Moses earlier. Acts 7:51-53 "[51] Ye stiff-necked and uncircumcised in heart and ears! Ye do always resist the Holy Ghost; as your fathers did, so do ye. [52] Which of the prophets have not your fathers persecuted? And they have slain them which shewed before of the Just One, of whom ye have been now the betrayers and murderers, [53] who have received the law by the direction of angels and have not kept it."

- He is a covenant or promise keeper. The covenant relationship is the most sacred bond between God Almighty and mankind. It is the basis of reward and curse, justice v injustice, and trustworthiness or untrustworthiness. When God gives His word, He does not break it and it holds forever. There is no other name under heaven to swear to higher than God Himself. Hebrews 6:13 (NKJV) "For when God made a promise to Abraham because he could swear by no greater, He swore by Himself." Isaiah 45:22-23 "[22] Look unto Me, and be ye saved, all the ends of the earth! For I am God, and there is none else. [23] I have sworn by Myself; the word has gone out of My mouth in righteousness, and shall not return, that to Me every knee shall bow, every tongue shall swear." God can do whatever He wants, but will not operate outside these tenants. If He makes an exception for one and not for another, how could we trust Him or His word? 2 Corinthians 1:20 (NIV) "For no matter how many promises God has made, they are "Yes" in Christ. And so through him the "Amen" is spoken by us to the glory of God." If there is one lesson the covenants and prophets will reveal, it is that God always gives warning for people to change their evil ways and turn to Him before judgment is exercised. Proverbs 18:24 "A man that hath friends must shew himself friendly, and there is a friend that sticketh closer than a brother." We may fall away from Him but He will never leave us. We will be referring to God's covenants, both unconditional and conditional, with His chosen people a little later on.

- God is a God of truth, and as such, He does not lie, nor is He deceitful to his children. Psalm 31:5 "Into Thine hand I commit my spirit; thou hast redeemed me, O LORD God of truth." Psalm 119:160 "Thy word is true from the beginning, and every one of Thy righteous judgments endureth forever." John 17:17 "Sanctify them through Thy truth. Thy word is truth." Hebrews 6:18 (NLV) "God gave these two things that cannot be changed and God cannot lie. We who have turned to Him can have great comfort knowing that He will do what He has promised." Titus 1:2 "In hope of eternal life which God, who cannot lie, promised before the world began." Numbers 23:19 "God is not a man, that He should lie, neither the son of man, that He should repent. Hath He said, and shall He not do it? Or has He spoken, and shall He not make it good?" 1 Samuel 15:29 (NIV) "He who is the Glory of Israel does not lie or change his mind; for He is not a human being, that He should change his mind." It is not in His nature to be deceitful. James 1:13 "Let no man say when he is tempted, "I am tempted by God "; for God cannot be tempted by evil, neither tempteth He any man." His ways are also higher than the mind of man can comprehend. Isaiah 55:8-9 "8 For My thoughts are not your thoughts, neither are your ways My ways," saith the LORD."9 For as the heavens are higher than the earth, so are My ways higher than your ways, and My thoughts than your thoughts."

- God does not operate in linear time like we do (omnipresent). He operates out of the boundaries of normal time and space. 2 Peter 3:8 (NIV) "But do not forget this one thing, dear friends: With the Lord a day is like a thousand years, and a thousand years are like a day." Psalm 90:4 "For a thousand years in Thy sight are but as yesterday when it is past, and as a watch in the night." Remember Isaiah 46:10 "Declaring the end from the beginning, and from ancient times the things that are not yet done, saying, My counsel shall stand, and I will do all My pleasure." He designed His plan of salvation even before the worlds were created. 2 Timothy 1:9 "Who hath saved us and called us with a holy calling, not according to our works, but according to His own purpose and grace, which was given us in

Christ Jesus before the world began." Unlike us, who can only see the past and present, God sees the past, present, and future as the same. Revelation 1:8 "I am Alpha and Omega, the beginning and the ending," saith the Lord, "which is and which was, and which is to come, the Almighty." The end HE is bringing us to is eternal life with Him. John 3:16 "For God so loved the world that he gave his only begotten Son, that whosoever believeth in him should not perish, but have everlasting life."

- God sets His own calendar. The Feasts of the LORD are recorded and begin in Leviticus 23:1-2 "¹ And the LORD spake unto Moses, saying, ² Speak unto the children of Israel, and say unto them, concerning the feasts of the LORD, which ye shall proclaim to be holy convocations, even these are My feasts." There are two important words, which we will examine in the original Hebrew. 1) The word for "holy convocations" is Strong's #H4744 "miqra" which means a sacred assembly or dress rehearsal. 2) The word for "Feast" is Strong's #H4150 "mow`ed." It means an "appointed time" like to set a specific day to hold aside. All the festival days were aligned to celebrate the two harvest cycles around the spring rain and fall rain. They were also arranged around the full moon or lunar cycle around which the Hebraic calendar is calculated. God again shows us the example of a pattern (i.e. the yearly cycle). We will know in advance what to expect when Jesus reigns in the Millennium. We will be referring to these Feasts several times throughout this book. They will be relevant and explained further on with Moses, and then with Jesus.

- God works in patterns both, mathematically and in cycles, as the aforementioned Feasts of the Lord. Colossians 2:16-17 (NIV) "¹⁶ Therefore do not let anyone judge you by what you eat or drink, or with regard to a religious festival, a New Moon celebration or a Sabbath day. ¹⁷ These are a shadow of the things that were to come; the reality, however, is found in Christ." The number 7 is known as the number of perfection. There are 7 days in the week, the 7x7 year cycle and its multiple variations (i.e. 490 cycle (7x7x10)), 70 years of exile in Babylon for the Jews, and the 7 churches in the opening of the book of Revelation. There are also patterns of His workings in the past and what to look for in the future. The first example of God working in a pattern will be mentioned when we look at Abraham. We will also be referring back to God's working in patterns when we talk about Moses and his experience at Mount Sinai.

- God knows all (omniscient) and is perfect. 1 John 3:20 "For if our heart condemn us, God is greater than our heart, and knoweth all things." Psalm 147:5 "Great is our Lord, and of great in power; His understanding is infinite." Job 37:16 (NKJV) "Do you know how the clouds are balanced, Those wondrous works of Him who is perfect in knowledge?" Proverbs 1:7 "The fear of the LORD is the beginning of knowledge, but fools despise wisdom and instruction." Knowledge is imparted to the believers and ignorance is the byproduct of the unbeliever. Proverbs 1:28-29 "28 Then shall they call upon Me, but I will not answer; they will seek Me early, but they shall not find Me. 29 For that they hated knowledge and did not choose the fear of the LORD." God formed the plan of prophecy and Jesus' sacrifice before the universe was made. Earlier on, we talked about God as Creator and the progression of the universe's creation. One of the most asked questions is "If God knows everything and He knew that Satan and Adam and Eve would sin, then why did He allow it?" Let's look at this in greater detail. The Bible does not specifically say when the angels and Satan were created, but Bible scholars believe that according to Job 38:6-7 "6 Whereupon are the foundations thereof fastened? Or who laid the corner stone thereof. 7 When the morning stars sang together, and all the sons of God shouted for joy?" they may have been created before He created the universe. It is also believed that the angels were present at earth's creation. Genesis 1:26 "And God said, "Let us make man in our image, after our likeness:" It is believed that the "our" referred to in the above verse are angels. Genesis 2:1 "Thus the heavens and the earth were finished, and all the host of them." The word for "host" Strong's #H6635 is "tsba." It translates as angels and has dual applications to the king of Tyre and Satan. Ezekiel 28:12-16 "12 Son of man, take up a lamentation upon the king of Tyrus, and say unto him, thus saith the Lord GOD; "Thou sealest up the sum, full of wisdom, and perfect in beauty. 13 Thou hast been in Eden the garden of God; every precious stone was thy covering, the sardius, topaz, and the diamond, the beryl, the onyx, and the jasper, the sapphire, the emerald, and the carbuncle, and gold: the workmanship of thy tabrets and of thy pipes was prepared in thee in the day that thou wast created. 14 Thou art the anointed cherub that covereth; and I have set thee so: thou wast upon the holy mountain of God; thou hast walked up and down in the midst of the stones of fire. 15 Thou wast perfect in thy ways from the day that thou wast created, till iniquity was found in thee. 16 By the multitude of thy merchandise they have filled the midst of thee with violence, and thou hast sinned: therefore, I will cast thee as profane out of the mountain of God: and I will destroy thee, O covering cherub, from the midst of the stones of fire." In Psalm 8:5 "For Thou hast made him a little lower than the angels, and hast crowned him with glory and honor." and Hebrews 2:7 (NKJV) "You have made him a little lower than the angels; You have crowned him with glory and honor and set him over the works of Your hands (earthly realm)." Both groups were made at God's command. God placed angels above man by giving angels nonphysical spiritual bodies and man physical spiritual bodies with a soul. Mark 10:6 "But from the beginning of the creation God made them (human) male and female." God created angels to carry out his instruction and deliver messages to His people (i.e. Michael and Gabriel). God did not want Adam to be lonely so He created a wife for him. Genesis 2:18 and 22 (NIV) "18 The LORD God said, "It is not good for the man to be alone. I will make a helper suitable for him." and "22 Then the LORD God made a woman from the rib he had taken out of the man, and he brought her to the man." Sin is not introduced until Genesis chapter 3 when Satan appeared as a snake to deceive Adam and Eve. The Bible does not say when Lucifer/Satan fell from grace, however, I think the iniquity the above verses refers to is the sin of pride. It was pride that caused Satan to think he could pull off a palace coup and dislodge God from His throne. Isaiah 14:12-17 "12 How art thou fallen from heaven, O Lucifer, son of the morning! how art thou cut down to the ground, which didst weaken the nations! 13 For thou hast said in thine heart, I will ascend into heaven, I will exalt my throne above the stars of God: I will sit also upon the mount of the congregation, in the sides of the north: 14 I will ascend above the heights of the clouds; I will be like the most High. 15 Yet thou shalt be brought down to hell, to the sides of the pit. 16 They that see thee shall narrowly look upon thee, and consider thee, saying, "Is this the man that made the earth to tremble, that did shake kingdoms; 17 That made the world as a wilderness, and destroyed the cities thereof; that opened not the house of his prisoners?" Failing that, he tried to deceive God's creation, which consisted of some angels, and subsequently man, into thinking he (Satan) was as powerful as God and his equal. He still has not fully understood how wrong he is. His reward was being unceremoniously kicked out of God's presence. This could have occurred anytime from when God created the angels, including Lucifer, to before the physical world to the beginning of Genesis chapter 3 when Satan first appears. Satan used deception and pride to tempt Adam and Eve to try to make themselves equal with God by eating of the tree of life. Genesis 3:4-5 (NKJV) "4 Then the serpent said to the woman, "You will not surely die. 5 For God knows that in the day you eat of it your eyes will be opened, and you will be like God, knowing good and evil." When God confronted them, instead of owning up and confessing their sin, they tried to deflect the blame, a singularity human reaction, and were expelled. He also knew there would be those who would not follow His laws, either by design, unintentional consequences, or ignorance. Their failure to consider their standing regarding their eternal placement in this life will have devastating results in the next. God allowed Satan and Adam make poor choices so that when Jesus returns to set up His eternal kingdom, as told in the end of the Book of Revelation, His victory will be complete and final.

- God is wise. The definition of wisdom is taking knowledge and applying an action or understanding correctly for the greater good. Along with free will, God imparted wisdom to His creation, or at least a portion of the ability to observe, assess and ascertain whether the source of the situation comes from either God or elsewhere. In short, the ability to discern right from wrong. Proverbs 1:2-3 "2 To know wisdom and instruction, to perceive the words of understanding. 3 To receive the instruction of wisdom, justice, judgment, and equity." Proverbs 9:10 "The fear of the LORD is the beginning of wisdom, and the knowledge of the Holy is understanding." Isaiah 31:2 "Yet He also is wise and will bring evil, and will not call back His words, but will arise against the house of evildoers, and against the help of them that work iniquity." 2 Samuel 14:20 "To fetch about this form of speech hath thy servant Joab done this thing: and My lord is wise, according to the wisdom of an angel of God, to know all things that are in the earth." Romans 11:33 (NKJV) "Oh, how great are God's riches and wisdom and knowledge! How impossible it is for us to understand His decisions and His ways!" 1 Corinthians 1:25 "Because the foolishness of God is wiser than human men, and the weakness of God is stronger than men." 1 Corinthians 12:8 "For to one is given by the Spirit the word of wisdom, to another the word of knowledge by the same Spirit." 1 Timothy 1:17 "Now unto the King eternal, immortal, invisible, the only wise God, be honor and glory forever and ever. Amen." James 1:5 (NIV) "If any of you lacks wisdom, you should ask God, who gives generously to all without finding fault, and it will be given to you." James 3:13-17 (NIV) "13 Who is wise and understanding among you? Let them show it by their good life, by deeds done in the humility that comes from wisdom. 14 But if you harbor bitter envy and selfish ambition in your hearts, do not boast about it or deny the truth. 15 Such "wisdom" does not come down from heaven but is earthly, unspiritual, demonic. ¹⁶ For where you have envy and selfish ambition, there you find disorder and every evil practice. ¹⁷ But the wisdom that comes from heaven is first of all pure; then peace-loving, considerate, submissive, full of mercy and good fruit, impartial and sincere." Jude 25 "To the only wise God our Saviour, be glory and majesty, dominion and power, both now and ever. Amen." As the Irish say, here's the rub, we get ourselves into trouble when we choose poorly.

- God sees all and nothing is hidden from Him. Hebrews 4:13 "Neither is there any creature that is not manifest in His sight: but all things are naked and opened unto the eyes of Him with whom we have to do." Jeremiah 23:24 "Can anyone hide himself in secret places that I shall not see him?" saith the LORD; "Do I not fill heaven and earth?" saith the LORD." Psalm 139:7-8 (NIV) "⁷ Where can I go from Your Spirit? Where can I flee from Your presence? ⁸ If I go up to the heavens, You are there; If I make my bed in the depths, You are there." Psalm 69:5 "O God, Thou knoweth my foolishness; and my sins are not hid from Thee." Matthew 12:36 "But I say to you that every idle word that men shall speak, they shall give account thereof in the day of judgment." One day we will be called into His presence to give an account of our life. It will be at the Great White Throne Judgment for those who failed to make the right choice when they had the opportunity to do so in this life. Isaiah 1:28 "And the destruction of transgressors and of the sinners shall be together, and they that forsake the LORD shall be consumed." Ezekiel 11:5 "And the Spirit of the LORD fell upon me, and said to me, "Speak! 'Thus saith the LORD: "Thus have ye said, O house of Israel; for I know the things that come into your mind, every one of them." Mark 4:22 (NKJV) "For there is nothing hidden which will not be revealed, nor has anything been kept secret but that it should come to light." Matthew 10:26 (NKJV) "Therefore do not fear them. For there is nothing covered that will not be revealed and hidden that will not be known."

- God is a God of patience, long-suffering, and second chances. There is one principle that God respects, obedience brings blessing and disobedience brings judgment. Deuteronomy 5:33 (NIV) "Walk in obedience to all that the LORD your God has commanded you, so that you may live and prosper and prolong your days in the land that you will possess (see the Mosaic Covenant below)." Proverbs 28:13 (NKJV) "Whoever conceals his transgressions will not prosper, but he who confesses and forsakes them will obtain mercy." The Old Testament mentions God being "slow to anger" several times. Exodus 34:6-7 "⁶ And the LORD passed by before him, and proclaimed, The LORD, The LORD God, merciful and gracious, longsuffering, and abundant in goodness and truth, ⁷ Keeping mercy for thousands, forgiving iniquity and transgression and sin, and that will by no means clear the guilty; visiting the iniquity of the fathers upon the children, and upon the children's children, unto the third and to the fourth generation." Psalm 30:5 "For His anger endureth but a moment, His favor is life; weeping may endure for a night, but joy cometh in the morning." Psalm 103:7-9 "⁷ He made known his ways to Moses, His acts to the children of Israel: ⁸ The LORD is merciful and gracious, slow to anger, and plenteous in mercy. ⁹ He will not always chide, neither will he keep his anger forever." 2 Peter 3:9 "The Lord is not slack concerning His promise, as some men count slackness, but is longsuffering to us, not willing that any should perish but that all should come to repentance." Peter stresses that God's will is that we share His gift of life rather than lose it to death forever. In service to God's trait of Justice, this is the only trait that has to have a finite end. God has been and still is patiently waiting for each person, Jew or Gentile, to accept His gift of redemption.

- Jesus is the Son of God AND the Son of Man. The Jewish leadership of the time had a preconceived narrow idea of what the Messiah would be. Defined as an expected king or deliverer of the Jews they were looking for a military leader, they totally missed the point. Jesus came to be the only pathway back to God. Jesus and God are the same. John 10:30 (NKJV) "I and the Father are one." It is at this point that God makes a way and makes a new covenant by graphing those who are uncircumcised (gentiles) unto Himself. John 1:14 "And the Word was made flesh and dwelt among us, (and we beheld his glory, the glory as of the only begotten of Father,) full of grace and truth." When Jesus was born, they did not see Him for who He was. John 1:11 "He came unto his own, and his own received him not." Jesus had the same quality of attributes of God. He is consistent. Hebrews 13:8 "Jesus Christ is the same yesterday, today, and forever." There is power in His voice. Matthew 28:18 "And Jesus came and spake unto them saying, "All power is given unto me in heaven and in earth." When Jesus spoke, He calmed the storm, He healed the sick, made the blind see, the deaf hear, the lame walk and the dead live. He may have performed scores of miracles, if not hundreds. However, there are only 27 recorded miracles Jesus performed where

He healed the sick. John 20:30-31 (NIV) "30 Jesus performed many other signs in the presence of His disciples, which are not recorded in this book. 31 But these are written that you may believe that Jesus is the Messiah, the Son of God, and that by believing you may have life in His name." Finally, Jesus and God both deserve our gratitude and devotion because they are equals. Philippians 2:5-11 "5 Let this mind be in you which was also in Christ Jesus, 6 who, being in the form of God, thought it not robbery to be equal with God, 7 but made Himself of no reputation, and took upon Him the form of a servant, and was made in the likeness of men. 8 And being found in fashion as a man, He humbled Himself, and became obedient unto death, even the death of the cross. 9 Wherefore God also has highly exalted Him, and given Him a name which is above every name. 10 That at the name of Jesus every knee should bow, of things in heaven, and things in on earth, and of those under the earth, 11 and that every tongue should confess that Jesus Christ is Lord, to the glory of God the Father." Hebrews 12:26-28 "26 Whose voice then shook the earth: but now He hath promised, saying, yet once more I shake not the earth only, but also heaven. 27 And this word, yet once more, signifieth the removing of those things that are shaken, as of things that are made, that those things which cannot be shaken may remain. 28 Wherefore we receiving a kingdom which cannot be moved, let us have grace, whereby we may serve God acceptably with reverence and godly fear." Jesus Christ IS God's son.

So, let's begin. We'll try to identify and follow the prophetic thread that runs through the Bible. Since we have first established that God's word is a sure foundation, the second loop when exploring the issue of prophecy is that most people who are confused by it think that it does not start until the Book of Revelation. Actually, the first mention of a prophetic thought is in Genesis 3:14-15 "14 And the LORD God said unto the serpent, Because thou hast done this, thou art cursed above all cattle, and above every beast of the field; upon thy belly shalt thou go, and dust shalt thou eat all the days of thy life: 15 And I will put enmity between thee and the woman, and between thy seed and her seed; it shall bruise thy head, and thou shalt bruise his heel." Enmity, which is defined as a feeling or condition of hostility, hatred, or ill will. Satan hates mankind, and especially the Jewish people, because God chose the Hebrews as his beloved people and to be His conduit for our redemption. Deuteronomy 14:2 (NKJV) "For you (the Hebrews) are a holy (from the Hebrew word root meaning "set apart" or "above') people to the LORD your God, and the LORD has chosen you to be a people for Himself, a special treasure above all the peoples who are on the face of the earth." Through them, we have the Patriarchs, covenants and laws (upon which all Judeo-Christian laws are based), the Holy Scriptures, the major and minor prophets, the apostles, the blood line and pivotal person on whom His plan of forgiveness and final victory hinges, His son Jesus Christ. Furthermore, the Jewish people are the root for blessing or judgments from God to individuals and the nations. Genesis 12:3 (NKJV) "I will bless those who bless you, and him who dishonors you I will curse, and in you, all the families of the earth shall be blessed." It's fair to say that Christianity cannot validate its existence without Judaism but Judaism can validate its existence without Christianity. Even when the early Jewish tribes disappointed Him by worshipping other false Gods, He still gave his word to keep and bring them back to the land He promised their forefathers. Deuteronomy 30:3 (NIV) "Then the LORD your God will restore your fortunes and have compassion on you and gather you again from all the nations where he scattered you."

The third loop is whether or not we can we decipher or unravel God's mysteries. God's word says is the answer is yes. Jesus said in Matthew 13:11 "He answered and said unto them, "Because it is given unto you to know the mysteries of the kingdom of heaven, but to them (unbelievers) it is not given." This seems to indicate that those mysteries can be revealed but only to those who profess Jesus as Lord (Messiah) and seek His face. Deuteronomy 29:29 "The secret things belong unto the LORD our God, but those things which are revealed belong unto us and to our children forever, that we may do all the words of this law." Matthew 6:33 "But seek ye first the kingdom of God, and His righteousness, and all these things shall be added to you." Ephesians 3:1-7 "[1] For this cause I Paul, the prisoner of Jesus Christ for you Gentiles, [2] If ye have heard of the dispensation of the grace of God which is given me to you-ward: [3] How that by revelation He made known unto me the mystery; (as I wrote afore in few words, [4] Whereby, when ye read, ye may understand my knowledge in the mystery of Christ) [5] Which in other ages was not made known unto the sons of men, as it is now revealed unto his holy apostles and prophets by the Spirit; [6] That the Gentiles should be fellow heirs, and of the same body, and partakers of his promise in Christ by the gospel: [7] Whereof I was made a minister, according to the gift of the grace of God given unto me by the effectual working of his power." Paul called God's plan a mystery. However, a mystery is only a mystery until it becomes revealed. Romans 16:25-27 "[25] Now to Him that is of power to establish you according to My gospel, and the preaching of Jesus Christ, according to the revelation of the mystery, which was kept secret since the world began, [26] But now is made manifest, and by the scriptures of the prophets, according to the commandment of the everlasting God, made known to all nations for the obedience of faith: [27] To God only wise, be glory through Jesus Christ forever. Amen." Colossians 1:25-27 "25 Whereof I (Paul) am made a minister, according to the dispensation of God which is given to me for you, to fulfil the word of God; 26 Even the mystery which hath been hid from ages and from generations, but now is made manifest to his saints: 27 To whom God would make known what is the riches of the glory of this mystery among the Gentiles; which is Christ in you, the hope of glory." Paul confirms that God knew in advance and laid the foundation before creation that He would need to provide a way to atone for the sins of men in order for us to be able to be redeemed and find way back to a relationship with Him. Ephesians 1:4 (NIV) "For He chose us in him before the creation of the world to be holy and blameless in His sight." When examining this mystery, it is said Old Testament mysteries are "concealed", and the New Testament mysteries are "revealed." God portioned out only small amounts of information regarding prophecies to many individuals over the centuries. He gave other prophets other pieces of information like a jig saw puzzle. Around 606 BCE, God gave specific instructions to Daniel in regards to end time prophecies. Daniel 12:4 "But thou, O Daniel, shut up the words, and seal the book, even to the time of the end: many shall run to and fro, and knowledge shall be increased." Daniel 12:9 "And he said, "Go thy way, Daniel, for the words are closed up and sealed till the time of the end." These passages suggest there was only so much information God was willing to give Daniel and a limited amount of understanding was given to him. This limit would be in place until God deems it time to share more. God sent messages through the "prophets" of God which were not well appreciated or received. In fact, several of the prophets were killed by the Hebrew authorities because they didn't like the message. 1 Kings 19:10 "And he (Elijah) said, I have been very jealous for the LORD God of hosts: for the children of Israel have forsaken Thy covenant, thrown down Thine altars, and slain Thy prophets with the sword; and I, even I only, am left; and they seek my life, to take it away." Fast forward to 2018 and we have had nearly 3000 years to read, consider, and understand what was previously not understood. Solving this mystery is sort of like looking at a painting. If you were to step back you would be able to take in the whole picture and have a greater appreciation of it than if you were to look up closely, where your field of vision is less. By putting these stories in context, it will help us get the correct perspective on where we are, prophetically speaking. It is crucial to understanding the prophecies of the end times we will need to look at the narrative history in the Bible which brings us to our next thread.

# Chapter 3

# "The Covenants"

The fourth loop is to whom God speaks. Earlier we talked about IF and HOW God made Himself known to the Hebrew people. Now, we will examine WHAT He said. As we already stated, God spoke to the early Hebrew ancestors in the Old Testament as it was written in Ancient Hebrew and a small amount of Aramaic. He inspired the early church in the New Testament written in Greek. There are different, but connected, themes in the two testaments messages that involve prophecy. Why is it important to study to understand that God spoke to the Hebrews and what He said? Because in order to understand what God's plan is, one has to realize that the plan started with and will end with His chosen people. He calls them the apple of His eye. Deuteronomy 32:9-10 "9 For the LORD's portion is His people; Jacob is the lot of His inheritance. 10 He found him in a desert land, and in the waste howling wilderness; He led him about, He instructed him, He kept him as the apple of His eye." The Jewish people are God's chosen people. Once more, when God chooses you, He chooses you forever.

God communicated with the early Hebrew fathers through the practice of Covenants. We teach our children that their actions come with both good and bad consequences. God used covenants to instruct His chosen people. The Old Testament is full of history of God's chosen people and their attempts (some succeeded and some failed) to obey God's law and receive God's mercy, blessing, and forgiveness. It also is full of the assurance of prophecy for the restoration, in the truest sense of the word, of the land and the people of Israel, not gentiles, via the Messiah.

- God spoke directly to Adam and Eve when He put them in the Garden of Eden. Genesis 3:8-9 "8 And they heard the voice of the LORD God walking in the garden in the cool of the day, and Adam and his wife hid themselves from the presence of the LORD God among the trees of the garden. 9 And the LORD God called to Adam and said to him, "Where art thou?" They trembled because they knew they had disobeyed God and now were naked and exposed. They had been given everything they needed. The only rule God gave was that they could not eat from only one tree, but they did. Remember God's "master plan" was prearranged before the worlds began. It was not put into play until Adam and Eve sinned and they were expelled out of the Garden of Eden. To be clear, they were not expelled for the transgression of eating the forbidden fruit, rather, they were expelled because they did not accept responsibility for their sin and seek forgiveness. Instead, Adam and Eve tried to point fingers at each other. For the last 6000 years or so, man continued to fall short just, like the first Adam and Eve. The result was a break from God's grace, for us and for them. However, God wanted to bring them us all back under His covenant protection. With the introduction of sin, man's default setting for his heart and spirit changed from sinless to sinful.

- God, then spoke to Noah. God waited patiently for at least 100 years while Noah preached to the men of that time to accept responsibility while he built an ark, they didn't. No one believed Noah until the doors were shut and it started to rain. They realized they were too late to make the right choice as the waters increased. God made a covenant with Noah. Genesis 9:15-17 (NKJV) "[15] and I will remember my covenant which is between Me and you and every living creature of all flesh; the waters shall never again become a flood to destroy all flesh. [16] The rainbow shall be in the cloud, and I will look at it to remember the everlasting covenant between God and every living creature of all flesh that is on the earth. [17] And God said to Noah, "This is the sign of the covenant which I have established between Me and all flesh that is on the earth."

- God spoke to Abram and entered into an EVERLASTING UNCONDITIONAL COVENANT with Abram and his descendants, the Hebrew people, which stands to this day. Genesis 17:1-13 "[1] And when Abram was ninety years old and nine, the LORD appeared to Abram, and said unto him, I am the Almighty God; walk before me, and be thou perfect. [2] And I will make my covenant between me and thee and will multiply thee exceedingly. [3] And Abram fell on his face: and God talked with him, saying, [4] As for me, behold, my covenant is with thee, and thou shalt be a father of many nations. [5] Neither shall thy name any more be called Abram, but thy name shall be Abraham; for a father of many nations have I made thee. [6] And I will make thee exceeding fruitful, and I will make nations of thee, and kings shall come out of thee. [7] And I will establish my covenant between me and thee and thy seed after thee in their generations for an EVERLASTING COVENANT, to be a God unto thee, and to thy seed after thee. ⁸ And I will give unto thee, and to thy seed after thee, the land wherein thou art a stranger, all the land of Canaan, for an everlasting possession; and I will be their God. ⁹ And God said unto Abraham, "Thou shalt keep my covenant therefore, thou, and thy seed after thee in their generations. ¹⁰ This is my covenant, which ye shall keep, between me and you and thy seed after thee; Every man child among you shall be circumcised. ¹¹ And ye shall circumcise the flesh of your foreskin; and it shall be a token of the covenant betwixt me and you. ¹² And he that is eight days old shall be circumcised among you, every man child in your generations, he that is born in the house, or bought with money of any stranger, which is not of thy seed. ¹³ He that is born in thy house, and he that is bought with thy money, must needs be circumcised: and my covenant shall be in your flesh for an everlasting covenant." When God chooses you, He chooses you forever. So, God's part of the agreement was the land grant and God's eternal blessing and promise to be protector/provider for Abram and that God's promise would be passed to his seed (subsequent generations) forever. Additionally, Abram's name would change to Abraham (father of many nations). Abraham's part was that all male children would be circumcised and He (Yahweh) would be their God. From that point in time, there would be only two types of people, the circumcised (the Hebrews) and the uncircumcised (everyone else aka the Gentiles).

- God reaffirmed Abraham's covenant with Isaac and Jacob. Abraham and his wife Sarah, both now over 100 years old, had a son, Isaac. God tested Abraham's commitment to the covenant by commanding him to offer his son Isaac as an offering. Genesis 22:2 (NKJV) "Then He said, "Take now your son, your only son Isaac, whom you love, and go to the land of Moriah, and offer him there as a burnt offering on one of the mountains of which I shall tell you." The Bible does not say how old Isaac was at the time, but scholars believe him to be between a pre-teenager to a young adult as he would need to travel, by foot, a fair distance to Mt. Moriah and carry a bundle of firewood. This picture of offering a favored son as a sacrifice to atone for sin is a preview of how God will use His Son, Jesus, as a sacrifice to atone for the sin all of mankind. It also demonstrates God's attribute of working in patterns. As a point of significance, before Abraham and Sarah conceived Isaac, Sarah (then around the age of 75) had not yet been able to give Abraham a son to pass his wealth and inheritance aka the birthright. At

Sarah's insistence, she allowed her maid Hagar, to be a surrogate of sorts. Hagar conceived and birthed Ishmael, who would later become known as the Father of the Arabs. After Isaac was born, Hagar became worried that Ishmael would be killed so they fled from the camp. Genesis 21:9-13 "9 And Sarah saw the son of Hagar the Egyptian, which she had born unto Abraham, mocking. 10 Wherefore she said to Abraham, "Cast out this bondwoman and her son; for the son of this bondwoman shall not be heir with my son, even with Isaac." 11 And the thing was very grievous in Abraham's sight because of his son. 12 And God said to Abraham, "Let it not be grievous in thy sight because of the lad and because of your bondwoman. In all that Sarah hath said unto thee, harken unto her voice; for in Isaac thy seed shall be called. 13 And also of the son of the bondwoman will I make a nation because he is thy seed." We will refer back to this when we look at Arabs vs Muslim after we look at the conflict Israel will be involved before the Antichrist can appear. Genesis 26:24 "And the LORD appeared unto him (Isaac) the same night and said, "I am the God of thy father Abraham; fear not, for I am with thee, and will bless thee, and multiply thy seed for My servant Abraham's sake." With Jacob God sealed the deal with a name change. Genesis 35:9-12 "9 And God appeared unto Jacob again, when he came out of Padanaram, and blessed him. 10 And God said unto him, thy name is Jacob: thy name shall not be called any more Jacob, but Israel shall be thy name: and he called his name Israel. 11 And God said unto him, I am God Almighty: be fruitful and multiply; a nation and a company of nations shall be of thee, and kings shall come out of thy loins; 12 And the land which I gave Abraham and Isaac, to thee I will give it, and to thy seed after thee will I give the land." God promised Abraham and his descendants the land of Israel and after many centuries of being out of the land, they returned to possess their promised homeland in 1948. We'll go into the significance of this date later.

- The next thread is the story of Joseph. God plans ahead. The life stories of Joseph and Jesus parallel each other. Genesis 15:13 (NKJV) "Then He said to Abram: "Know certainly that your descendants will be strangers in a land that is not theirs and will serve them, and they will afflict them four hundred years." In order for God to make an escape strategy for Israel from Egypt, they first needed to get there. Out of fear and jealousy, Joseph was sold into slavery to Egypt by his brothers. There, he flourished and became the top advisor to Pharaoh. Pharaoh had a dream and only Joseph could interpret it. Genesis 41:29-30 (NIV) "29 Seven years of great abundance are coming throughout the land of Egypt, 30 but seven years of famine will follow them. Then all the abundance in Egypt will be forgotten, and the famine will ravage the land." When the famine arrived, it affected the whole known world, including the tribe of Israel. Joseph's brothers came to petition Pharaoh for food. They did not recognize their brother until Joseph gave them an audience to grant their request. Joseph emerged and made himself known to the brothers as the instrument of their salvation, as would happen to Jesus. Joseph was put in place by God so he could be when and where he was needed to help Israel survive. Genesis 45:5 "Now therefore be not grieved nor angry with yourselves that ye sold me hither; for God did send me before you to preserve life." Genesis 50:20 (NIV) "You intended to harm me, but God intended it for good to accomplish what is now being done, the saving of many lives." God gave the Jews a picture of what was to come at the end of days. Ultimately, God used something appeared to be horrendous consequences for Joseph, but ended up bringing Him glory.

- After Joseph's death, the Israelites were made slaves; that is until He sent a deliverer by the name of Moses. When the time was right, God heard the Hebrews cries and appointed Moses to liberate and lead the Hebrews out of Eygpt. Exodus 2:23-25 "23 Now it came to pass in the process of time, that the king of Egypt died. And the children of Israel sighed by reason of the bondage, and they cried, and their cry came up to God by reason of the bondage. 24 So God heard their groaning, and God remembered His covenant with Abraham, with Isaac, and with Jacob. 25 And God looked upon the children of Israel, and God acknowledged them." Everybody, including the unchurched, has heard the story of Moses from the movie "The Ten Commandments" with Charlton Heston. The Bible tells the story how Moses negotiated with Pharaoh to free the Israelites from bondage and then bring them the Law from God Almighty Himself. Like most books made into movies, there are some important details missing in this version of the story. Moses' story and the history of the early Hebrews from Adam through Joseph are told in the first five books of the Bible called the Pentateuch. There, we find details of Moses' birth, the reason for his own personal exile, and his finding God in the burning bush on top of Mt. Heron in Midian. From there, he and his brother Aaron approached Pharaoh. After God defeated the Egyptian priests and gods by sending ten plagues. Pharaoh then released the Israelites where Moses led them out across the desert to the Red Sea. There, as Pharaoh's chariots were about to overtake the Israelites, God made a way out by parting the waters. He then guided them into the wilderness where they stopped upon their arrival to Mount Sinai. There, God gave them very specific laws, including the Ten Commandments. For the purpose of our discussion, this is where the story becomes relevant. What is less well known and arguably more important are three key points made with Moses and the fleeing Israelites. They are brought under a new conditional covenant, called the Mosaic Covenant (including the Ten Commandments), the Law of Sabbath Year, and the Feast Days of the Lord. The bargaining session took place when the Israelites were camped at Mount Sinai three months after they left Egypt. Exodus 19:1 (NLV) "In the third month after the people of Israel left Egypt, they came to the Sinai Desert on the same day."

- The Mosaic Covenant. Unlike the unconditional everlasting covenants of Abraham, Isaac and Jacob, God's covenant with Moses and the Israelites is conditional. It is based on the premise that with obedience comes blessing and disobedience comes curses. Deuteronomy 28:1-2 (NKJV) "1 Now it shall come to pass, if you diligently obey the voice of the LORD your God, to observe carefully all His commandments which I command you today, that the LORD your God will set you high above all nations of the earth. 2 And all these blessings shall come upon you and overtake you, because you obey the voice of the LORD your God." Deuteronomy 28:15 (NKJV) "But it shall come to pass, if you do not obey the voice of the LORD your God, to observe carefully all His commandments and His statutes which I command you today, that all these curses will come upon you and overtake you." Deuteronomy 30:1-3 (NIV) "1 When all these blessings and curses I have set before you come on you and you take them to heart wherever the LORD your God disperses you among the nations, 2 and when you and your children return to the LORD your God and obey Him with all your heart and with all your soul according to everything I command you today, 3 then the LORD your God will restore your fortunes and have compassion on you and gather you again from all the nations where He scattered you." Details of the covenant begin in Exodus 19 and continue to the end of the book. Leviticus, Numbers, and Deuteronomy also have elements of the covenant. Exodus 19:4-6 (NKJV) "4 'You have seen what I did to the Egyptians, and how I bore you on eagles' wings and brought you to Myself. 5 Now therefore, IF you will indeed obey My voice and keep My covenant, THEN you shall be a special treasure to Me above all people; for all the earth is Mine. 6 And you shall be to Me a kingdom of priests and a holy nation.' These are the words which you shall speak to the children of Israel.' Moses brought the proposal to the people and they agreed. Exodus 19:7-8 "7 And Moses came and called for the elders of the people, and laid before their faces all these words which the LORD commanded him. 8And all the people answered together and said, "All that the LORD hath spoken we will do." And Moses returned the words of the people unto the Lord." Moses then went back up again to deliver the agreement. In addition to the conditions, God stipulated that only Moses can be allowed in the presence of God. Exodus 19:12 (NKJV) "You shall set bounds for the people all around, saying, 'Take heed to yourselves that you do not go up to the mountain or touch its base. Whoever touches the mountain shall surely be put to death.'" Then God details the terms of the covenant in Exodus chapters 20-24. It started with God giving Moses the Ten Commandments, which focused on the Israelites having no other God before Him or make any carved image (idol) nor worship it. God demands priority over any other God as He is a jealous God. He also explicitly mentioned the importance of keeping the Sabbath, and other details regarding behavior to fellow tribesmen. Moses came down and they reaffirmed their agreement in Exodus 24:7 (NKJV) "Then he took the Book of the Covenant and read in the hearing of the people. And they said, "All that the LORD has said we will do, and be obedient." Keep in mind at this point there were no tablets. Moses made another trip back up and brought the approved agreement to God on top of the mountain. Exodus 24:12 (NKJV) "Then the LORD said to Moses, "Come up to Me on the mountain and be there; and I will give you tablets of stone, and the law and commandments which I have written, that you may teach them." Exodus 24:18 (NKJV) "So Moses went into the midst of the cloud and went up into the mountain. And Moses was on the mountain forty days and forty nights." While on top of the mountain, according to Exodus 25-31, God gives instructions (floor plans) to build a tabernacle to specific construction requirements, including dimensions and materials. The tabernacle was a building that could be moved. Exodus 25:8-9 (NKJV) "8 And let them make Me a sanctuary, that I may dwell among them. 9 According to all that I show you, that is, the pattern of the tabernacle and the pattern of all its furnishings, just so you shall make it." God gives instructions as to where the tabernacle furniture is to be placed, and where the twelve tribes are to camp in relationship to the tabernacle. There are also instructions on priestly garments, the reiteration of God being the only one true God and keeping the Sabbath, dimensions for building an ark for the written word of God, altar and incense, restriction on food, offerings, and sacrifice, instruments, and placement of lamp stands and furniture. All these are relevant because they are precise duplicate measurements of heaven from God. Henceforward, when He came to be among His people there would be a place that was sanctified enough for Him to sit. Exodus 25:22 (NKJV) "And there I will meet with you, and I will speak with you from above the mercy seat, from between the two cherubim which are on the ark of the Testimony, about everything which I will give you in commandment to the children of Israel." These are also the same proportions Solomon uses later to build his temple. Special emphasis on keeping the Sabbath is highlighted in Exodus 31:12-18 (NKJV) "[12] And the LORD spoke to Moses, saying, [13] "Speak also to the children of Israel, saying: 'Surely My Sabbaths you shall keep, for it is a sign between Me and you throughout your generations, that you may know that I am the LORD who sanctifies you. [14] You shall keep the Sabbath, therefore, for it is holy to you. Everyone who profanes it shall surely be put to death; for whoever does any work on it, that person shall be cut off from among his people. [15] Work shall be done for six days, but the seventh is the Sabbath of rest, holy to the LORD. Whoever does any work on the Sabbath day, he shall surely be put to death. [16] Therefore the children of Israel shall keep the Sabbath, to observe the Sabbath throughout their generations as a perpetual covenant. [17] It is a sign between Me and the children of Israel forever; for in six days the LORD made the heavens and the earth, and on the seventh day He rested and was refreshed. [18] And when He had made an end of speaking with him on Mount Sinai, He gave Moses two tablets of the Testimony, tablets of stone, written with the finger of God." Before Moses came back down in Exodus 32, we learn that the people were afraid because they hadn't seen or heard from Moses for some time. They thought he might be dead, causing them to fashion a golden calf to worship, breaking the first commandment they just pledged to obey. This angered God greatly and He almost destroyed them all. Exodus 32:7-10 "[7] And the LORD said unto Moses, Go, get thee down; for thy people, which thou broughtest out of the land of Egypt, have corrupted themselves: [8] They have turned aside quickly out of the way which I commanded them: they have made them a molten calf, and have worshipped it, and have sacrificed thereunto, and said, "These be thy gods, O Israel, which have brought thee up out of the land of Egypt. [9] And the LORD said unto Moses, I have seen this people, and, behold, it is a stiffnecked people: [10] Now therefore let me alone, that my wrath may wax hot against them, and that I may consume them: and I will make of thee a great nation." However, Moses interceded and talked

Him out of it. Moses did not fully appreciate the level of debauchery until he got closer to camp. In a rage, he destroyed the two stone tablets God just gave him. Exodus 32:19 "And it came to pass, as soon as he came near the camp, that he saw the calf and the dancing. And Moses' anger waxed hot, and he cast the tablets out of his hands and brake them beneath the mount." Moses then went down and killed about 3000 people responsible for partaking in this "great sin." Exodus 32:28 "And the children of Levi did according to the word of Moses. And there fell of the people that day about about three thousand men." Moses then negotiated successfully with God for forgiveness. In Exodus 33-40 God then commands them to leave the Mount Sinai camp. Exodus 33:1 (NKJV) "Then the LORD said to Moses, "Depart and go up from here, you and the people whom you have brought out of the land of Egypt, to the land of which I swore to Abraham, Isaac, and Jacob, saying, 'To your descendants I will give it." Demonstrating again when God gives His word, He keeps it. Moses was then instructed to prepare two new tablets of stone so God could rewrite to replace them. Exodus 34:1-4 (NKJV) "[1] And the LORD said to Moses, "Cut two tablets of stone like the first ones, and I will write on these tablets the words that were on the first tablets which you broke. [2] So be ready in the morning, and come up in the morning to Mount Sinai, and present yourself to Me there on the top of the mountain. [3] And no man shall come up with you, and let no man be seen throughout all the mountain; let neither flocks nor herds feed before that mountain." [4] So he cut two tablets of stone like the first ones. Then Moses rose early in the morning and went up Mount Sinai, as the LORD had commanded him; and he took in his hand the two tablets of stone." God then reaffirmed His covenant with His people and gave the Israelites marching orders to leave the Mount Sinai area. Exodus 34:10-11 "[10] And He said: "Behold, I make a covenant. Before all thy people I will do marvels such as have not been done in all the earth, nor in any nation; and all the people among which thou art shall see the work of the LORD. For it is a terrible thing that I will do with thee. [11] Observe thou that which I command thee this day. Behold, I drive out from before thee the Amorite and the Canaanite and the Hittite and the Perizzite and the Hivite and the Jebusite." Exodus 34:27-28 "[27] And the LORD said to Moses, "Write these words, for after the tenor of these words I have made a covenant with thee and with Israel." [28] And he was there with the LORD forty days and forty nights; he did neither eat bread nor drink water. And he wrote on the tablets the words of the covenant, the Ten Commandments." To house these sacred and powerful tablets the dimensions of the Ark of the Covenant are listed in Exodus 37:1-9 "[1]And Bezaleel made the ark of shittim wood: two cubits and a half was the length of it, and a cubit and a half the breadth of it, and a cubit and a half the height of it: [2] And he overlaid it with pure gold within and without, and made a crown of gold to it round about. [3] And he cast for it four rings of gold, to be set by the four corners of it; even two rings upon the one side of it, and two rings upon the other side of it. [4] And he made staves of shittim wood, and overlaid them with gold. [5] And he put the staves into the rings by the sides of the ark, to bear the ark. [6] And he made the mercy seat of pure gold: two cubits and a half was the length thereof, and one cubit and a half the breadth thereof. [7] And he made two cherubims of gold, beaten out of one piece made he them, on the two ends of the mercy seat; [8] One cherub on the end on this side, and another cherub on the other end on that side: out of the mercy seat made he the cherubims on the two ends thereof. [9] And the cherubims spread out their wings on high, and covered with their wings over the mercy seat, with their faces one to another; even to the mercy seatward were the faces of the cherubims." Once completed, they packed their camp and followed God back into the desert. Numbers 10:33 "And they departed from the mount of the LORD three days' journey; and the Ark of the Covenant of the LORD went before them in the three days' journey, to search out a resting place for them."

- We just looked closely at God's Ten Commandments, now we will look at the Law of the Sabbath Year and the seven cycles for seven years (49) followed by the Year of Jubilee (50). Exodus 20, 25 and 31. The Law of Sabbath is not only for one day out of seven, but is also so for one year out of seven. While we are focused in Leviticus, it gives us the detail that God commanded the Israelites to observe a Sabbath year and to let the land rest. Leviticus 25:1-4 "[1] And the LORD spake unto Moses in mount Sinai, saying, [2] Speak unto the children of Israel, and say unto them, "When ye come into the land which I give you, then shall the land keep a sabbath unto the LORD. [3] Six years thou shalt sow thy field, and six years thou shalt prune thy vineyard, and gather in the fruit thereof; [4] But in the seventh year shall be a sabbath of rest unto the land, a sabbath for the LORD: thou shalt neither sow thy field, nor prune thy vineyard." This is known as the Law of Sabbath Year. In addition to letting the land rest, debts are forgiven. Deuteronomy 15:1-2 "[1] At the end of every seven years thou shalt make a release. [2] And this is the manner of the release: Every creditor that lendeth ought unto his neighbour shall release it; he shall not exact it of his neighbour, or of his brother; because it is called the

Lord's release." After seven cycles of seven years (7x7=49), the fiftieth year is called the Year of Jubilee. In addition to the release of debt, ownership of purchased shall revert back to the original owner. It is a Holy Decree. Leviticus 25:8-15 "⁸ And thou shalt number seven sabbaths of years unto thee, seven times seven years; and the space of the seven sabbaths of years shall be unto thee forty and nine years. ⁹ Then shalt thou cause the trumpet of the jubilee to sound on the tenth day of the seventh month, in the day of atonement shall ye make the trumpet sound throughout all your land. ¹⁰ And ye shall hallow the fiftieth year, and proclaim liberty throughout all the land unto all the inhabitants thereof: it shall be a jubilee unto you; and ye shall return every man unto his possession, and ye shall return every man unto his family. ¹¹ A jubilee shall that fiftieth year be unto you: ye shall not sow, neither reap that which groweth of itself in it, nor gather the grapes in it of thy vine undressed. ¹² For it is the jubilee; it shall be holy unto you: ye shall eat the increase thereof out of the field. ¹³ In the year of this jubilee ye shall return every man unto his possession. ¹⁴ And if thou sell ought unto thy neighbour, or buyest ought of thy neighbour's hand, ye shall not oppress one another: ¹⁵ According to the number of years after the jubilee thou shalt buy of thy neighbour, and according unto the number of years of the fruits he shall sell unto thee." We will refer back to this issue later when an issue that Jeremiah and the ten tribes of Judah being sent into exile is discussed.

- The Feast Days of the Lord. We introduced this section at the beginning in chapter 2 when we looked at God setting His own calendar. These days are sometimes referred to as the Jewish Feasts, but that is a misnomer they are God's appointed times or "Feast Days." In Leviticus 23, God set up a schedule when He would come to visit His chosen people, and where He could preside over them and they could come and worship Him. The seven Feast Days are divided into two periods to coincide with the spring rains and the fall rains. The spring period has (in order) Passover, Unleavened Bread, First Fruits, and Pentecost. The fall Feasts have Trumpets, Day of Atonement, and Tabernacles, as recorded in Exodus, Leviticus, Numbers, and Deuteronomy. However, they are presented chronologically, inclusively and concisely in Leviticus 23. The chart below shows how the Feasts shaped the lives of the early Israelites' yearly cycle, which was centered around worship and communion with God Himself.

| | Bible | Month | Feast Day | Origin of Tradition |
|---|---|---|---|---|
| **SPRING FEASTS** | Leviticus 23:5 "In the fourteenth day of the first month at even is the Lord's Passover." | Nisan 14 (Mar/April) | Passover beginning of Orthodox New Year | The night before the Exodus, the tenth plague of Egypt was that the firstborn of each house was to be killed, Jew and Gentile. To avoid the calamity, an unblemished lamb was sacrificed and its blood was spread on the door posts and lintels so that when the Angel of Death came upon it, he would "pass over" that house and spare the first born. |
| | Leviticus 23:6 "And on the fifteenth day of the same month is the Feast of Unleavened Bread to the Lord; seven days ye must eat unleavened bread." | Nisan 15-21 (Mar/April) | Unleavened Bread | The preparation for the flight was so quick that, they did not have time to make bread with yeast, so they made it without. Yeast, or leaven, is a symbol of sin. The bread or matzah was baked flat with stripes and piercings. For seven days, devoted Jews would not eat bread with yeast to symbolize the denial of sin. It was also customary to hide away a portion of the matzah by wrapping it and placing it out of sight. |

| Leviticus 23:10-11 | Nisan 16-17 (Mar/April) | Offering of First Fruits | Before the Spring Harvests of barley and wheat began, a farmer would cut a small portion and bring it to the tabernacle or temple priest to as an offering to God and seek His blessing. This action would sanctify or justify the following crop. In the fall there was a harvest of grapes that also went through this act. |
|---|---|---|---|

Leviticus 23:10-11 "[10] Speak to the children of Israel, and say unto them: 'When ye come into the land which I give unto you, and reap the harvest thereof, then ye shall bring a sheaf of the first fruits of your harvest to the priest. [11] And shall wave the sheaf before the LORD, to be accepted for you; on the morrow after the Sabbath the priest shall wave it."

| Leviticus 23:15-16 "¹⁵ And ye shall count unto you from the morrow after the Sabbath, from the day that ye brought the sheaf of the wave offering: seven Sabbaths shall be complete. ¹⁶ Even unto the morrow after the seventh Sabbath shall ye number fifty days and ye shall offer a new meat offering to the Lord." | Sivan 6 (May) | Feast of Weeks aka Pentecost or Shavuot | The literal translation of Pentecost is "fifty days." It commences fifty days after the Offering of First Fruits. It is also believed to be the day God Himself came down to Mount Sinai in a whirlwind of fire after the Exodus to give Moses the Law. |
|---|---|---|---|

## FALL FEASTS

| | | | | |
|---|---|---|---|---|
| Leviticus 23:24 "Speak unto the children of Israel, saying: 'In the seventh month, in the first day of the month, shall ye have a sabbath, a memorial of blowing of trumpets, an holy convocation." | Tishri 1-10 (Sept/Oct) | Feast of Trumpets aka Yom Teruah (Day of Trumpets) Rosh Hashanah (beginning of Civil New Year) the Wedding Feast of the Messiah | All Feasts except this one transpires during the full moon. The Feast of Trumpets occurs at the new moon, which is "hidden" or not visible. Two men of high reproach keep watch, and when the sliver of the moon is first seen, they go to the priests to announce the beginning of the Feast. At that time a "shofar" is sounded in long, short, and staccato blasts that follow a set sequence totaling 99 blasts. It concludes with a 100th blast, known as the "Last Trump." The subsequent 10 day period is also known as the Days of Awe. It is a period of self-reflection that culminates with repenting of one's sins. |
| Leviticus 23:27 "Also on the tenth day of this seventh month there shall be the Day of Atonement. It shall be an holy convocation unto you; and ye shall afflict your souls, and offer an offering made by fire to the Lord." | Tishri 10 (Sept/Oct) | Day of Atonement aka Yom Kippur | The Highest of Holy Days in Judaism. It is believed to be the day God would physically visit the tabernacle or temple and dwell among men. Only the High Priest was allowed to enter the Holy of Holies to intercede and seek atonement for his people. The "Great Trump" is sounded at this Feast to herald the coming of God. |

| | | | |
|---|---|---|---|
| Leviticus 23:42-43 "⁴² Ye shall dwell in booths seven days. All that are Israelites born shall dwell in booths. ⁴³ That your generations may know that I made the children of Israel dwell in booths when I brought them out of the land of Egypt: I am the Lord your God." | Tishri 15-21 (Sept/Oct) | Feast of Booths aka Tabernacles, Sukkot | Jewish people would construct a "sukkah," a small hut where during the seven-day observance meals were served there. It commemorates the 40-year wilderness journey after the Exodus. It is one of three Feasts (with Passover and Weeks) that require all men to travel to Jerusalem for a pilgrimage. |

Continuing on, just as a point of reference, the title of the Book of Numbers refers to the "numbers" of able-bodied men that could go to battle. They are counted in taking two censuses, one in the beginning and one towards the end of the book. Numbers 1:1-3 "¹ And the LORD spake unto Moses in the Wilderness of Sinai, in the tabernacle of the congregation, on the first day of the second month, in the second year after they were come out of the land of Egypt, saying: ² "Take ye the sum of all the congregation of the children of Israel, after their families, by the houses of their fathers, with the number of their names, every male by their polls, ³ from twenty years old and upward, all that are able to go forth to war in Israel. Thou and Aaron shall number them by their armies."

We will be looking at two examples of God's judgment of the Israelites. Specifically, when they did not trust and obey Him about crossing over Jordan into the land of Canaan, and when Moses' authority as God's chosen leader was challenged. The first example in Numbers is about the nation being called to gather and leave the area for Canaan. In

Numbers, we are given a little more detail of the first two years of the Sinai wilderness. Numbers 10:12-13 "¹² And the children of Israel took their journeys out of the wilderness of Sinai; and the cloud rested in the wilderness of Paran. ¹³ And they first took their journey according to the commandment of the LORD by the hand of Moses." God was looking to fulfill one of His promises He made to Moses at the burning bush encounter. Namely Exodus 3:8 (NIV) "So I have come down to rescue them from the hand of the Egyptians, and to bring them up out of that land to a good and spacious land, a land flowing with milk and honey, the home of the Canaanites, Hittites, Amorites, Perizzites, Hivites and Jebusites." God ordered Moses to move the people away from Mount Sinai to head toward Canaan. In preparation for the Canaan campaign, God commanded Moses to send spies before they attacked Canaan. Numbers 13:1-2 (NKJV) "¹ And the LORD spoke to Moses, saying, ² "Send men to spy out the land of Canaan, which I am giving to the children of Israel; from each tribe of their fathers you shall send a man, everyone a leader among them." The majority of the returning spies said the Israelites could not defeat the giants. Only Joshua and Caleb said if God was on their side, they could defeat the Canaanites. Numbers 14:6-8 (NKJV) "⁶ But Joshua the son of Nun and Caleb the son of Jephunneh, who were among those who had spied out the land, tore their clothes; ⁷ and they spoke to all the congregation of the children of Israel, saying: "The land we passed through to spy out is an exceedingly good land. ⁸ If the LORD delights in us, then He will bring us into this land and give it to us, 'a land which flows with milk and honey." The heads of the tribes were scared and did not believe God (even after seeing Pharaoh's army drown in the Red Sea) and turned to leave. God became angry at them and wanted to destroy them. Again, Moses interceded and God spared them, but they did have a penalty to pay. Numbers 14:22-23 (NKJV) "²² Because all these men who have seen My glory and the signs which I did in Egypt and in the wilderness, and have put Me to the test now these ten times, and have not heeded My voice, ²³ they certainly shall not see the land of which I swore to their fathers, nor shall any of those who rejected Me see it." For their disobedience, they were forced to wander the wilderness for the next 38 years until that generation passed.

The second example gives details of a revolt that tried to overthrow Moses, who was God's choice to be the leader. There was a revolt led by Korah, Abiram, and Dathan (played by Edward G. Robinson in the movie) against Moses. Because Moses was God's emissary, the revolt was put down by God, who opened the earth and swallowed the three leaders and their followers. Numbers 16:28-33 (NIV) "²⁸ Then Moses said, "This is how you will know that the LORD has sent me to do all these things and that it was not my idea: ²⁹ If these men die a natural death and suffer the fate of all mankind, then the LORD has not sent me.

³⁰ But if the LORD brings about something totally new, and the earth opens its mouth and swallows them, with everything that belongs to them, and they go down alive into the realm of the dead, then you will know that these men have treated the LORD with contempt." ³¹ As soon as he finished saying all this, the ground under them split apart ³² and the earth opened its mouth and swallowed them and their households, and all those associated with Korah, together with their possessions. ³³ They went down alive into the realm of the dead, with everything they owned; the earth closed over them, and they perished and were gone from the community." These transgressions of not listening and following God's direction angered Him. Numbers 32:13 "And the LORD's anger was kindled against Israel, and He made them wander in the wilderness forty years until all the generation that had done evil in the sight of the LORD was consumed." However, even in His anger, God provides for His children. Exodus 16:35 "And the children of Israel did eat manna forty years until they came to a land inhabited; they did eat manna until they came unto the border of the land of Canaan."

Deuteronomy covers the last two years in the wildness. Moses' covenant was restated in Deuteronomy 11:26-28 "²⁶ Behold, I set before you this day a blessing and a curse; ²⁷ A blessing, if ye obey the commandments of the LORD your God, which I command you this day: ²⁸ And a curse, if ye will not obey the commandments of the LORD your God, but turn aside out of the way which I command you this day, to go after other gods, which ye have not known." It also tells us of the changing of the guard with Joshua. Deuteronomy 34:5-6 (NKJV) "⁵ So Moses the servant of the LORD died there in the land of Moab, according to the word of the LORD. ⁶ And He buried him in a valley in the land of Moab, opposite Beth Peor; but no one knows his grave to this day."

After Moses leadership was passed to Joshua. Deuteronomy 34:9 "And Joshua the son of Nun was full of the spirit of wisdom, for Moses had laid his hands on him; and the children of Israel harkened unto him and did as the LORD had commanded Moses." Joshua received his commission from God. Joshua 1:1-3 "¹ Now after the death of Moses the servant of the LORD it came to pass, that the LORD spake unto Joshua the son of Nun, Moses' minister, saying, ² Moses My servant is dead; now therefore arise, go over this Jordan, thou, and all this people, unto the land which I do give to them, even to the children of Israel. ³ Every place that the sole of your foot shall tread upon, that have I given unto you, as I said unto Moses." Joshua 1:5 (NIV) "Just as I was with Moses, so I will be with you. I will not leave you or forsake you." Joshua 5:6 "For the children of Israel walked forty years in the wilderness, till all the people that were men of war, which came out of Egypt, were consumed, because they obeyed not the voice of the LORD: unto whom the LORD swore that he would not shew them the land, which the LORD swore unto their fathers that he would give us, a land that floweth with milk and honey." After the forty years, God led the Israelites into Canaan and began conquering various cities. This included the city of Jericho where the walls fell at the sound of the trumpets. Under Joshua's leadership and obedience to God's word they entered the land and destroyed their opponents in a string of battles and received the blessing of people and land.

This was a long way to prove and demonstrate God's lynch pin principle with His chosen people that obedience brings blessing and disobedience brings judgment. God chose Moses and the Jewish people to demonstrate as the prime example of this conditional covenant relationship. It is also critical in understanding God's desire to have a beneficial relationship with all people. A little later we will be looking at how this affects "the church" when we are talking about Peter and Paul. This connection, which is still in place, continued for some generations under the era of the Judges until the era of Kings began with Saul, David, and Solomon. God blessed the land and leaders because of their adherences to God's word. Under King Saul, the first United Kingdom of Israel was birthed. God restated His covenant with David, who founded Jerusalem. God put His name on the city. The literal translation of Jerusalem is "City of God" or "City of Peace." It is also sometimes referred to as the City of David. God also made a special covenant with King David which predetermined the blood line lineage of Jesus. 2 Samuel 7:12-13 (NKJV) "[12] When your days are fulfilled and you rest with your fathers, I will set up your seed after you, who will come from your body, and I will establish His (Jesus) kingdom. [13] He shall build a house for My name, and I will establish the throne of His kingdom forever." Solomon was commissioned by God to build His temple. He used the same proportions of the tabernacle layout to permanently re-create what was used in the wilderness. Solomon's Temple was also built to house the Ark of the Covenant. 1 Kings 8:6 (NKJV) "Then the priests brought in the ark of the covenant of the LORD to its place, into the inner sanctuary of the temple, to the Most Holy Place, under the wings of the cherubim." God reiterated Moses' covenant to Solomon in 2 Chronicles 7:14 "If My people who are called by My name will humble themselves, and pray and seek My face, and turn from their wicked ways, then I will hear from heaven and will forgive their sin and will heal their land." Psalm 33:12 "Blessed is the nation whose God is the Lord, and the people whom He hath chosen for His own inheritance."

# Chapter 4

## "The Prophets"

Sadly, over the course of the next several generations, the Israelites went back to their old ways of worshipping other gods. God pleaded and warned the Israelites through the prophets, (i.e. Daniel, Ezekiel, Isaiah, Jeremiah, and others), to turn from their ways and seek repentance. Some did, but most didn't. The prophet's words of warning fell on deaf ears. Ezekiel 36:22-29 (NKJV) "22 Therefore, say to the house of Israel, 'Thus says the Lord God: "I do not do this for your sake, O house of Israel, but for My holy name's sake, which you have profaned among the nations wherever you went. 23 And I will sanctify My great name, which has been profaned among the nations, which you have profaned in their midst; and the nations shall know that I am the Lord," says the Lord God, "when I am hallowed in you before their eyes. 24 For I will take you from among the nations, gather you out of all countries, and bring you into your own land. 25 Then I will sprinkle clean water on you, and you shall be clean; I will cleanse you from all your filthiness and from all your idols. 26 I will give you a new heart and put a new spirit within you; I will take the heart of stone out of your flesh and give you a heart of flesh. 27 I will put My Spirit within you and cause you to walk in My statutes, and you will keep My judgments and do them. 28 Then you shall dwell in the land that I gave to your fathers; you shall be My people, and I will be your God. 29 I will deliver you from all your uncleanness." Out of their continual and flagrant disobedience, they provoked God's anger toward them. 2 Chronicles 36:15-16 "15 And the Lord God of their fathers sent to them by His messengers, rising up betimes, and sending; because He had compassion on his people, and on His dwelling place: 16 But they mocked the messengers of God, and despised His words, and misused His prophets, until the wrath of the Lord arose against His people, till there was no remedy." As Moses did earlier, Jeremiah called the Hebrews stiff-necked. Jeremiah 7:23-26 "23 But this thing commanded I them, saying, "Obey My voice, and I will be your God, and ye shall be My people: and walk ye in all the ways that I have commanded you, that it may be well unto you. 24 But they hearkened not, nor inclined their ear, but walked in the counsels and in the imagination of their evil heart, and went backward, and not forward. 25 Since the day that your fathers came forth out of the land of Egypt unto this day I have even sent unto you all My servants the prophets, daily rising up early and sending them: 26 Yet they hearkened not unto me, nor inclined their ear, but hardened their neck: they did worse than their fathers." Jeremiah 17:23 (NIV) "Yet they did not listen or pay attention; they were stiff-necked and would not listen or respond to discipline."

Due to their stubbornness and refusal to worship only God and follow His commandments, they were subjected to punishment that again included being put into bondage and slavery in other countries. Their punishment decreed that the United Kingdom be split into two sections as a result of a civil war. The Bible tells us they were divided into the northern ten tribes called Israel and the southern two tribes of Judah and Benjamin called Judah (from where we get the term, Jew). In 2 Kings 17, God allowed the Assyrians to capture the northern ten tribes in 722 BCE, who were never to return, and fell from its place in history. Or wound they? These became known as the "Lost Ten Tribes." By contrast, in 2 Kings chapters 24-25, God allowed the Babylonians to conquer the southern two tribes in 606 BCE and put them into exile, but only for a period of 70 years because they did not keep the Law of the Sabbath Year, as told to Moses above in Leviticus 25. The Jews did not keep the Sabbath Year for 490 years. If we take the 490 years divided by 7, this equals 70 years owed to God. He always collects what is owed to Him. Jeremiah 25:11 "And this whole land shall be a desolation, and an astonishment; and these nations shall serve the king of Babylon seventy years." Additionally, Solomon's temple was destroyed the first time along with its temple furniture and treasures within, including the Ark of the Covenant, which was taken back to Babylon as a prize. 2 Chronicles 36:18-21(NIV) "18 He carried to Babylon all the articles from the temple of God, both large and small, and the treasures of the LORD's temple and the treasures of the king and his officials. 19 They set fire to God's temple and broke down the wall of Jerusalem; they burned all the palaces and destroyed everything of value there. 20 He carried into exile to Babylon the remnant, who escaped from the sword, and they became servants to him and his successors until the kingdom of Persia came to power. 21 The land enjoyed its sabbath rests; all the time of its desolation it rested, until the seventy years were completed in fulfillment of the word of the LORD spoken by Jeremiah." Their exile also served a purpose for keeping a remnant of the Israelites so David's lineage and so that the related prophecies could stay intact. Ezra 9:7-8 "7 Since the days of our fathers have we been in a great trespass unto this day; and for our iniquities have we, our kings, and our priests, been delivered into the hand of the kings of the lands, to the sword, to captivity, and to a spoil, and to confusion of face, as it is this day. 8 And now for a little space grace hath been shewed from the LORD our God, to leave us a remnant to escape, and to give us a nail in His holy place, that our God may lighten our eyes, and give us a little reviving in our bondage." Jeremiah 31:7 "For thus saith the LORD: "Sing with gladness for Jacob, and shout among the chief of the nations; publish ye, praise ye, and say, 'O LORD, save Thy people, the remnant of Israel!" History confirms again what is written in the Bible. Ezra 1:1-3 "¹ Now in the first year of Cyrus king of Persia, that the word of the LORD by the mouth of Jeremiah might be fulfilled, the LORD stirred up the spirit of Cyrus king of Persia, that he made a proclamation throughout all his kingdom, and put it also in writing, saying, ² Thus saith Cyrus king of Persia, The LORD God of heaven hath given me all the kingdoms of the earth; and He hath charged me to build Him an house at Jerusalem, which is in Judah. ³ Who is there among you of all his people? his God be with him, and let him go up to Jerusalem, which is in Judah, and build the house of the LORD God of Israel, (He is the God,) which is in Jerusalem." Jeremiah and Daniel were relatively contemporaries and ministered unto the southern two tribes of Judah. They also shared similar prophesies in that they revolve around the 70-year figure. This must be significant considering that Jeremiah's prophecy was completed for the full 70 years, but Daniel's prophecy has yet to be completed. We will examine "Daniel's 70-week prophecy" in detail as it relates to the end of days later in chapter 6.

Before we look at our next loop, let's step out of this narrative while we look at Daniel and the crucial role he played in relating to Israel and the end times. Daniel's story is important to the continuation of God's blessing to the Israelites. Through Daniel, God revealed his plan for the world. In chapter 2, he interprets a dream for King Nebuchadnezzar. First, the dream. Daniel 2:31-35 (NKJV) "³¹ You, O king, were watching; and behold a great image! This great image, whose splendor was excellent, stood before you; and its form was awesome. ³² This image's head was of fine gold, its chest and arms of silver, its belly, and thighs of bronze, ³³ its legs of iron, its feet partly of iron and partly of clay. ³⁴ You watched while a stone was cut out without hands, which struck the image on its feet of iron and clay, and broke them in pieces. ³⁵ Then the iron, the clay, the bronze, the silver, and the gold were crushed together, and became like chaff from the summer threshing floors; the wind carried them away so that no trace of them was found. And the stone that struck the image became a great mountain and filled the whole earth." Now, the interpretation. Daniel 2:36-42 (NKJV) "³⁶ This is the dream. Now we will tell the interpretation of it before the king. ³⁷ You, O king, are a king of kings. For the God of heaven has given you a kingdom, power, strength, and glory; ³⁸ and wherever the children of men dwell, or the beasts of the field and the birds of the heaven, He has given them into your hand, and has made you ruler over them all—you are this head of gold. 39 But after you shall arise another kingdom inferior to yours; then another, a third kingdom of bronze, which shall rule over all the earth. 40 And the fourth kingdom shall be as strong as iron, inasmuch as iron breaks in pieces and shatters everything; and like iron that crushes, that kingdom will break in pieces and crush all the others. 41 Whereas you saw the feet and toes, partly of potter's clay and partly of iron, the kingdom shall be divided; yet the strength of the iron shall be in it, just as you saw the iron mixed with ceramic clay. 42 And as the toes of the feet were partly of iron and partly of clay, so the kingdom shall be partly strong and partly fragile." The Great Statue has been studied by many scholars and historians. The most common conclusion suggests that the head of gold, chest and arms of silver, thighs of bronze, and legs of iron have all been played out in history, though the feet of iron and clay and 10 toes have yet to come. The premise of the coming one world leader is repeated to Daniel in chapter 7 under when Daniel was living under King Belshazzar. Daniel 7:23-25 (NKJV) "23 Thus he said: 'The fourth Beast shall be the fourth kingdom on earth, which shall be different from all other kingdoms, and shall devour the whole earth, trample it and break it in pieces. 24 The ten horns are ten kings who shall arise from this kingdom. And another shall rise after them; He shall be different from the first ones and shall subdue three kings. 25 He shall speak pompous words against the Most High, shall persecute the saints of the Most High, and shall intend to change times and law. Then the saints shall be given into his hand for a time and times and half a time." Finally, God brings Daniel's mission purpose to an end. Daniel 12:8-9 "8 And I heard, but I understood not: then said I, O my Lord, what shall be the end of these things? 9 And he said, "Go thy way, Daniel: for the words are closed up and sealed till the time of the end." Notice that God only gave Daniel so much information. A promise of more information being revealed will come at the time of the end. We will expound on this when we unpack the Tribulation towards the end of this book.

Let's get back to our storyline. God gave Isaiah specific prophecies of the coming Messiah. However, God also allowed the Jews to be blinded to the coming Messiah. Isaiah 6:9-10 "9 And he said, Go, and tell this people, "Hear ye indeed, but understand not; and see ye indeed, but perceive not. 10 Make the heart of this people fat, and make their ears heavy, and shut their eyes; lest they see with their eyes, and hear with their ears, and understand with their heart, and convert, and be healed." Each time the Hebrews/Jews failed God, He extended Himself to get them to seek God, repent, and be redeemed. However, for the most part, they didn't, which was to their detriment. History says that after Babylon (the head of gold in Nebuchadnezzar's dream that Daniel interpreted in chapter 2) fell to Persia (as envisioned as the chest and arms of silver) in 539 BCE. In 536 BCE, under Cyrus, the King of Persia, the Jews were allowed to return and rebuild Solomon's temple. This completed the 70 years owed to God as prophesied by Jeremiah. 2 Chronicles 36:22-23 "22 Now in the first year of Cyrus king of Persia, that the word of the LORD spoken by the mouth of Jeremiah might be accomplished, the LORD stirred up the spirit of Cyrus king of Persia, that he made a proclamation throughout all his kingdom, and put it also in writing, saying, 23 Thus Cyrus king of Persia, "All the kingdoms of the earth hath the LORD God of heaven given me; and He hath charged me to build Him an house in Jerusalem, which is in Judah. Who is there among you of all his people? The LORD his God be with him, and let him go up."

In 470 BCE Persia was under a new king, Xerxes, who married a Jewish maiden, Esther. Esther 2:17 "And the king loved Esther above all the women, and she obtained grace and favour in his sight more than all the virgins; so that he set the royal crown upon her head, and made her queen instead of Vashti." The King's Viceroy, Haman, plotted against Esther's uncle, Mordechai and the Jews, to have them hanged from the gallows because they would not worship him as God. When Esther exposed this plot to King Xerxes, he became enraged and had Haman hung on the same gallows. Esther 7:9-10 (NKJV) "9 Now Harbonah, one of the eunuchs, said to the king, "Look! The gallows, fifty cubits high, which Haman made for Mordecai, who spoke good on the king's behalf, is standing at the house of Haman." Then the king said, "Hang him on it!" 10 So they hanged Haman on the gallows that he had prepared for Mordecai. Then the king's wrath subsided." This victory over genocide became known as the Festival of Purim, which is still observed today. The Old Testament closes out with 16 books of the Prophets. There are approximately 400 years of silence between the end of the Old Testament and the beginning of the New Testament. We will address the two legs of iron from Daniel's statue when we look at church history.

Before we proceed further, we need to remember the timeline and dates that are mentioned throughout. We have used dates in terms of BCE or AD as these dates are used on our Gentile civil calendar. The Jewish calendar is based on a lunar cycle with a 360-day year and a leap month every so often. It is sometimes referred to as a prophetic calendar. Our gentile civic calendar is based on a solar cycle with a 365-day year. For Jewish folks, the current year is 5778 (not 2018) and will change to 5779 in September at Rosh Hashanah. Without going into too many details, our calendar is based off a calendar reworked in the middle of the 3rd century called the Julian Calendar after Pope Julius I. It was based on the civil Roman calendar which was reworked by Pope Julius I. He calculated and decreed Jesus' birth on December 25, and issued by edict to declare the year (AD 342). In 1582, Pope Gregory XIII amended it to the form we use now, which was named after him, the Gregorian calendar. Most historians, both biblical and secular, agree the calculations were flawed. Jesus was actually born in September between 2 to 4 BCE. The Bible does not tell us how old He was when He began His three-year ministry, nor when He made His sacrifice, though this is guesstimated to be sometime between 27-33 AD. This difference in marking time will become more relevant as we progress.

# Chapter 5

## "The Bridge"

History again supplies some information in that the Roman Empire invaded and conquered the repatriated Israelites and Jerusalem in 63 BCE. The Romans set up an authoritative governmental administration's occupation over the Jews, who were allowed to keep their civil and ritualistic practices. Israel would then remain in the Promised Land under the Roman Empire for over 130 years until 70 AD.

The New Testament opens, with a completely different tone as compared to the Old Testament: however, it continues in thought, which is God reaching out to the Jewish people to bring them back to Him. Right from the beginning, Matthew bridges the two Testaments with his opening evidence. Matthew 1:1 "The book of the genealogy of Jesus Christ, the Son of David, and the Son of Abraham." The following 17 verses of Matthew 1 recount Jesus' genealogy to include Jesse, King David, and Abraham. The Gospel texts focus less on law and more grace. John 1:17 "For the law was given by Moses, but grace and truth came through Jesus Christ." Before we continue, a point needs to be made here. The main focus of Jesus' ministry was the Jews, not "the Gentile church," of which we are a part. His disciples were Jewish, His family was Jewish, and He was Jewish. He often preached and taught in the local Jewish temples. The teachings and parables of Jesus were directed to His immediate audience, the Jews of the day, although I am sure there were gentiles in some of those open-air sermons. However, His sacrifice was for all, Jew and Gentile alike. John 3:16-17 "$^{16}$ For God so loved the world that He gave His only begotten Son, that whoever believeth in Him should not perish but have everlasting life. $^{17}$ For God sent not His Son into the world to condemn the world, but that the world through Him might be saved." Notice the previous verses say "whoever" and "world." It is inclusive of every soul ever born. The four gospels and beginning of Acts are first person eyewitness accounts by the apostles of the life, teachings, ministry, death, resurrection, and ascension of Jesus. When one contemplates the vast divide between God and man, the only bridge that can span the gap is the blood stained cross. We will look more closely at the roles that Jesus Christ, Peter, Paul, and the church plays in God's master plan later also in this book.

Our next loop's focus is directed to the Hebrews and what has happened specifically to them in regards to prophecies listed in the Bible. Daniel 10:14 "Now I am come to make thee understand what shall befall thy people in the latter days: for yet the vision is for many days." The partial list below are the fulfilled prophecies centered around Israel's return to the land promised to them. After the destruction of Solomon's temple, the Jews were subsequently expelled out of the promised land, but because of God's covenant with Abraham, they would not be out forever. The Jewish people were put into slavery and shipped like cattle to Rome to build the Coliseum and other public works. Those who did not go were dispersed into the four corners of the known world known as the Diaspora. This is the beginning of the Gentiles control and occupation of Israel and Jerusalem, which continued until 1948 when the state of Israel was reestablished and put under self-control. Before they could come back, the Bible does state that there will be a "times of the Gentiles." Luke 21:24 "And they shall fall by the edge of the sword, and shall be led away captive into all nations: and Jerusalem shall be trodden down of the Gentiles, until the times of the Gentiles be fulfilled." When we get to the questions later in Matthew 24 this will be better explained. The short version of this phrase means that control of the land of Israel and the city of Jerusalem (and occupation of the Temple) will not be self-ruled, but rather ruled by outsiders. It also means that there is a predetermined end date. We will also look at this more closely after we talk about Jesus as Messiah and Prophet. For now, though we are concentrating on the Jews. As we just mentioned, Roman Legions occupied Israel and Jerusalem at the time of Christ's birth. As time moved on, different gentile empires wrestled control from each other. These included the Byzantines, a succession of Arab dynasties, the Crusaders, the Mamelukes, the Ottoman Empire, and finally, the British Empire, who controlled it throughout both world wars. As a compensation of sorts for the Holocaust, in 1948, the modern day State of Israel was reborn as foretold where Isaiah spoke of Israel being reborn in one day Isaiah 66:7-8 (NKJV) "7 Before she was in labor, she gave birth; Before her pain came, She delivered a male child. 8 Who has heard such a thing? Who has seen such things? Shall the earth be made to give birth in one day? Or shall a nation be born at once? For as soon as Zion was in labor, she gave birth to her children." Isaiah 10:20-22 "20 And it shall come to pass in that day, that the remnant of Israel, and such as are escaped of the house of Jacob, shall no more again stay upon him that smote them; but shall stay upon the LORD, the Holy One of Israel, in truth. 21 The remnant shall return, even the remnant of Jacob, unto the mighty God. 22 For though thy people Israel be as the sand of the sea, yet a remnant of them shall return: the consumption decreed shall overflow with righteousness." Most, if not all, prophecy scholars agree that Christ's second coming could not happen until the Israelites were physically back in their promised homeland which happened in 1948.

The following are several important, and relevant prophecies given to Israel concerning the actual return to the land during the end times that have been fulfilled in our lifetime. These highlighted passages are only some and are by no means a complete list.

- The Hebrew language will be revived in Israel. Jeremiah 31:23 "Thus saith the LORD of hosts, the God of Israel: "As yet they shall use this speech in the land of Judah and in its cities thereof, when I shall bring again their captivity: 'The LORD bless you, O habitation of justice, and mountain of holiness." Zephaniah 3:9 (NKJV) "For then I will restore to the peoples a pure language, that they all may call on the name of the LORD, to serve Him with one accord." This was revitalized in the late 1800's and completed in 1921 by Eliezer Yitzhak Perlman.

- The Dry Bones Live Ezekiel 37:1-14 "¹ The hand of the LORD was upon me, and carried me out in the spirit of the LORD, and set me down in the midst of the valley which was full of bones, ² And caused me to pass by them round about: and, behold, there were very many in the open valley; and, lo, they were very dry. ³ And He said unto me, Son of man, can these bones live? And I answered, O Lord GOD, Thou knowest. ⁴ Again He said unto me, Prophesy upon these bones, and say unto them, O ye dry bones, hear the word of the LORD. ⁵ Thus saith the Lord GOD unto these bones; Behold, I will cause breath to enter into you, and ye shall live: ⁶ And I will lay sinews upon you, and will bring up flesh upon you, and cover you with skin, and put breath in you, and ye shall live; and ye shall know that I am the LORD. ⁷ So I prophesied as I was commanded: and as I prophesied, there was a noise, and behold a shaking, and the bones came together, bone to his bone. ⁸ And when I beheld, lo, the sinews and the flesh came up upon them, and the skin covered them above: but there was no breath in them. ⁹ Then said He unto me, Prophesy unto the wind, prophesy, son of man, and say to the wind, thus saith the Lord GOD; Come from the four winds, O breath, and breathe upon these slain, that they may live. ¹⁰ So I prophesied as He commanded me, and the breath came into them, and they lived, and stood up upon their feet, an exceeding great army. ¹¹ Then He said unto me, Son of man, these bones are the whole house of Israel: behold, they say, our bones are dried, and our hope is lost: we are cut off for our parts. [12] Therefore prophesy and say unto them, thus saith the Lord GOD; Behold, O my people, I will open your graves, and cause you to come up out of your graves, and bring you into the land of Israel. [13] And ye shall know that I am the LORD, when I have opened your graves, O my people, and brought you up out of your graves, [14] And shall put My spirit in you, and ye shall live, and I shall place you in your own land: then shall ye know that I the LORD have spoken it, and performed it, saith the LORD." Many believe that this passage was fulfilled in the Holocaust during 1933-36 in Hitler's final solution.

- ✼ A remnant of Israel will be re-established as a nation. Isaiah 11:11-12 "[11] And it shall come to pass in that day, that the Lord shall set his hand again the second time to recover the remnant of His people, which shall be left, from Assyria, and from Egypt, and from Pathros, and from Cush, and from Elam, and from Shinar, and from Hamath, and from the islands of the sea. [12] And he shall set up an ensign for the nations, and shall assemble the outcasts of Israel, and gather together the dispersed of Judah from the four corners of the earth."

- ✼ The people of Israel would return to "their own land" and be the vessel from where 144,000 missionaries would come. Ezekiel 34:13 "And I will bring them out from the people, and gather them from the countries, and will bring them to their own land, and feed them upon the mountains of Israel by the rivers, and in all the inhabited places of the country." Jeremiah 31:10 "Hear the word of the LORD, O ye nations, and declare it in the isles afar off, and say, 'He that scattered Israel will gather him, and keep him, as a shepherd doth His flock.'" As we learned earlier, there were two tribes who survived to maintain a continual thread for the nation of Israel, while the other 10 tribes were captured and removed to the far off country of Assyria. From there, they seemed to simply disappear from history, but not from God's view. When Israel is reborn and her peoples repatriated (Aliyah), there would be representatives from ALL twelve tribes. God, the designer of DNA genetic coding, will know from which tribe they belong. Representatives from all twelve tribes must be present in order so that the 144,000 missionaries of Revelation can be recruited. Revelation 7:4-8 (NKJV) "[4] And I heard the number of those who were sealed. One hundred and forty-four thousand of all the tribes of the children of Israel were sealed:

⁵ of the tribe of Judah twelve thousand were sealed;
of the tribe of Reuben twelve thousand were sealed;
of the tribe of Gad twelve thousand were sealed;
⁶ of the tribe of Asher twelve thousand were sealed;
of the tribe of Naphtali twelve thousand were sealed;
of the tribe of Manasseh twelve thousand were sealed;
⁷ of the tribe of Simeon twelve thousand were sealed;
of the tribe of Levi twelve thousand were sealed;
of the tribe of Issachar twelve thousand were sealed;
⁸ of the tribe of Zebulun twelve thousand were sealed;
of the tribe of Joseph twelve thousand were sealed;
of the tribe of Benjamin twelve thousand were sealed."

✡ Jacob's descendants would regain control of Israel and would never again be removed from it. Amos 9:14-15 "¹⁴ And I will bring again the captivity of My people of Israel, and they shall build the waste cities, and inhabit them; and they shall plant vineyards, and drink the wine thereof; they shall also make gardens, and eat the fruit of them. ¹⁵ And I will plant them upon their land, and they shall no more be pulled up out of their land which I have given them, saith the LORD thy God." Jeremiah 30:1-3 "¹ The word that came to Jeremiah from the LORD, saying, ² Thus speaketh the LORD God of Israel, saying, "Write thee all the words that I have spoken unto thee in a book. ³ For, lo, the days come, saith the LORD, that I will bring again the captivity of My people Israel and Judah, saith the LORD: and I will cause them to return to the land that I gave to their fathers, and they shall possess it."

✡ Israel will come back as one nation, not two. Hosea 1:11 "Then shall the children of Judah and the children of Israel be gathered together, and appoint for themselves one head; and they shall come up out of the land, for great will be the day of Jezreel!" Ezekiel 37:21-22 "²¹ And say unto them, Thus saith the Lord GOD; Behold, I will take the children of Israel from among the heathen, whither they be gone, and will gather them on every side, and bring them into their own land: ²² And I will make them one nation in the land upon the mountains of Israel; and one king shall be king to them all: and they shall be no more two nations, neither shall they be divided into two kingdoms any more at all."

- ✡ The Star of David will be on the Israeli flag. Isaiah 11:10 (NIV) "In that day the Root of Jesse will stand as a banner for the peoples; the nations will rally to him, and his resting place will be glorious."

- ✡ The Desert will bloom and blossom. Isaiah 35:1 (NIV) "The desert and the parched land will be glad; the wilderness will rejoice and blossom. Like the crocus."

- ✡ Jerusalem will be reclaimed as the capital of Israel. In 1967, the Jews recaptured Jerusalem from the Gentiles in the Six Day War. We will develop this topic when we talk about Jerusalem being a burdensome stone and the time of the Gentile occupation ending when we talk about the political condition of the Jews between the Rapture and the beginning of the Tribulation.

# Chapter 6

# "The End of Days"

To close out this section, which focuses on the Jews, let's explore the idea of the "end of days" or "end times." Soon, a time will come when God will bring about a conclusion of His pre-arranged plan for His chosen people and the rest of the people of the earth, believers and unbelievers alike. What do we mean by "end times?" Earlier, we talked about God's ability to see the beginning and the end as the same. That idea is represented in Genesis 1:1 and John 1:1, which both open with "In the beginning." If there is a beginning, there must be an end. The Old Testament mentions this seven-year time period as the "days of wrath." Job 21:30 "That the wicked are reserved for the day of destruction. They shall be brought forth to the Day of Wrath." Isaiah 13:9 "Behold, the day of the Lord cometh, cruel both with wrath and fierce anger, to lay the land desolate; and He shall destroy the sinners thereof out of it." Isaiah 26:20-21 (NKJV) "[20] Come, my people, enter your chambers, and shut your doors behind you; Hide yourself, as it were, for a little moment, Until the indignation is past. [21] For behold, the Lord comes out of His place to punish the inhabitants of the earth for their iniquity; the earth will also disclose her blood, and will no more cover her slain." Ezekiel 20:34 (NIV) "I will bring you from the nations and gather you from the countries where you have been scattered with a mighty hand and an outstretched arm and with outpoured wrath." Romans 2:5-12 (NIV) "[25] But because of your stubbornness and your unrepentant heart, you are storing up wrath against yourself for the day of God's wrath, when His righteous judgment will be revealed. [6] God "will repay each person according to what they have done." [7] To those who by persistence in doing good seek glory, honor, and immortality, He will give eternal life. [8] But for those who are self-seeking and who reject the truth and follow evil, there will be wrath and anger. [9] There will be trouble and distress for every human being who does evil: first for the Jew, then for the Gentile; [10] but glory, honor, and peace for everyone who does good: first for the Jew, then for the Gentile. [11] For God does not show favoritism. [12] All who sin apart from the law will also perish apart from the law, and all who sin under the law will be judged by the law." That day is also known by other expressions such as "in that day," "the day of the Lord," "latter days," "the wrath to come," "judgment day," "the end times," "the last days," "Tribulation (first half)," and "the great Tribulation (second half)," which is also known as "Jacob's trouble." In Jeremiah 30:7 "Alas! For that day is great, so that none is like it; it is even the time of Jacob's trouble, but he shall be saved out of it." This concept of end times is recorded as early as Jacob's Last Words to his Sons in Genesis 49:1 "And Jacob called unto his sons, and said, "Gather yourselves together, that I may tell you which shall befall you in the last days." Numbers 24:14 (NKJV) "And now, indeed, I am going to My people. Come, I will advise you what these people will do to your people in the latter days." This seems to endorse the writer's belief that there would be a time when time as we perceive it would come to an end. We Gentiles may be more familiar with the term "Tribulation." Matthew 24:21 "For then shall be great Tribulation, such as was not since the beginning of the world to this time, no, nor ever shall be."

Arguably the most important passage about the Jews and a seven-year period of judgment to come is found in Daniel 9 and is known as the "70-week prophecy." In this prophecy, emphasis is placed on the Jews as what we call the "church" was not yet established when God spoke to Daniel. Daniel 9:24-27 (NASB) "24 Seventy weeks have been decreed for your people and your holy city, to finish the transgression, to make an end of sin, to make atonement for iniquity, to bring in everlasting righteousness, to seal up vision and prophecy and to anoint the holiest place. 25 So you are to know and discern that from the issuing of a decree to restore and rebuild Jerusalem until Messiah the Prince there will be seven weeks and sixty-two weeks (a total of 69, 1 week is to come); it will be built again, with plaza and moat, even in times of distress. 26 Then after the sixty-two weeks the Messiah will be cut off (Jesus' crucifixion) and have nothing, and the people of the prince who is to come will destroy the city and the sanctuary. And its end will come with a flood; even to the end there will be war; desolations are determined. 27 Then he shall confirm a covenant with many for one week; But in the middle of the week He shall bring an end to sacrifice and offering. And on the wing of abominations shall be one who makes desolate, even until the consummation, which is determined, is poured out on the desolate."

There are several points that need to be explained.

- Bible and Prophecy scholars teach that the word "week" referred to in vs 24 is a period of "years," not a seven-day week as we understand it. Strong's #H7620 lists the word for "week" is "*shabuwa* `,.*"* which better translates to "year." There are other phrases or idioms primarily for the second 3 ½ years. Daniel 7:25 (NIV) "He will speak against the Most High and oppress his holy people and try to change the set times and the laws. The holy people will be delivered into his hands for a time, times and half a time." The word for "time" is Strong's #H5732 "iddan" which translates to "year." So, a time (1 year), times (2 years) and a half time (1/2 year). It is also referred to as 42 months and 1,260 days. A prophetic year is 360 days so if you work out the math they all confirm the length of 3 ½ years.

- Vs. 25 and 26 mentions the beginning of this time period as "the issuing of a decree" or an edict. The natural question is "which decree?" Cyrus is credited with issuing a handful of decrees. There are more a than few who support the edict from Cyrus in 536 BCE, which allowed the Jews to return to their homeland, as the edict to which the text refers. Ezra 1:1-2 "[1] Now in the first year of Cyrus king of Persia, that the word of the LORD by the mouth of Jeremiah might be fulfilled, the LORD stirred up the spirit of Cyrus king of Persia, that he made a proclamation throughout all his kingdom, and put it also in writing, saying, [2] Thus saith Cyrus king of Persia, "The LORD God of heaven hath given me all the kingdoms of the earth; and he hath charged me to build him an house at Jerusalem, which is in Judah." The other common edict is the edict given to Ezra by Artaxerxes in 457 BCE that allowed worship in the temple. Ezra 7:11-13 [11] Now this is the copy of the letter that the king Artaxerxes gave unto Ezra the priest, the scribe, even a scribe of the words of the commandments of the LORD, and of his statutes to Israel. [12] Artaxerxes, king of kings, unto Ezra the priest, a scribe of the law of the God of heaven, perfect peace, and at such a time. [13] I make a decree, that all they of the people of Israel, and of his priests and Levites, in my realm, which are minded of their own freewill to go up to Jerusalem, go with thee."

- Additionally, vs 26 also clearly states that there are a total of 69 weeks/years. So, the math suggests 69x7=483. If you work back from the date of 30-33 AD when Christ was crucified fulfilling the "Messiah being cut off," the previous decree dates above are too early. However, according to Sir Robert Anderson who published his book "The Coming Prince" in 1894, where he painstakingly converted the Jewish calendar to the Gregorian calendar. He calculated that the decree given to Nehemiah from Artaxerxes to rebuild Jerusalem's walls corroborates with secular historians of 445 BCE. Not just from timing but also from the mention of "building with plaza and moat." Nehemiah 2:7-8 "⁷ Moreover I (Nehemiah) said unto the king (Artaxerxes), "If it please the king, let letters be given me to the governors beyond the river, that they may convey me over till I come into Judah; ⁸ and a letter unto Asaph the keeper of the king's forest, that he may give me timber to make beams for the gates of the palace which appertained to the house, and for the wall of the city (Jerusalem), and for the house that I shall enter into. And the king granted me, according to the good hand of my God upon me."

- For particular note, this ties in with the 490 years Sabbath Year cycle. Remember, the Jews did not observe the Sabbath Year law and were exiled to Babylon for 70 years. The Jews must be in possession of the land, Jerusalem must be its capital, and the temple must be in operation for God's clock to tick. That clock stopped when Jesus was crucified, leaving a balance of 7 years to take place. Two conditions happened, one in 1948 with the rebirth of the State of Israel reclaiming the land, and two Jerusalem was reclaimed is in the hands of the Jews in 1967. However, the clock could not start because the Jews were not in possession of the temple mount; it was in Arab control, and still is. The clock will not restart until the Antichrist confirms his covenant at the beginning of the Tribulation. Daniel 9:27a "Then he (the Antichrist) shall confirm a covenant with many for one week." We will explore this in detail when we look at the Tribulation after we look at Jesus and the ministries of Peter and Paul to the Gentiles.

The purpose of this period of 7 weeks/years has two objectives. One is that the children of Israel will have their eyes opened to accepting Jesus as the Messiah. As we mentioned before, the religious leaders of the Jews at Jesus' time had a preconceived idea of what the Messiah would be. They were looking for a military leader who would lead them to overthrow their occupiers, the Roman Empire. They were blinded to Jesus' mission to change hearts and souls as described by Ezekiel 36:26-27 "²⁶ A new heart also will I give you, and a new spirit will I put within you: and I will take away the stony heart out of your flesh, and I will give you an heart of flesh. ²⁷ And I will put my spirit within you, and cause you to walk in my statutes, and ye shall keep my judgments, and do them." His mission was to renew the original spirit of relationship by changing the hearts and minds of men from the inside rather than by force, which is what the leadership of the Jews was looking for. Jesus further explained the Jewish leadership's blindness to Him as Messiah in

Matthew 13:13-15 (NIV) "¹³ This is why I speak to them in parables: "Though seeing, they do not see; though hearing, they do not hear or understand. ¹⁴ In them is fulfilled the prophecy of Isaiah (found in Isaiah 6:9-10). "You will be ever hearing but never understanding; you will be ever seeing but never perceiving." ¹⁵ For this people's heart has become calloused; they hardly hear with their ears, and they have closed their eyes. Otherwise, they might see with their eyes, hear with their ears, understand with their hearts and turn, and I would heal them." Isaiah 29:18 "And in that day the deaf shall hear the words of the book, and the eyes of the blind shall see out of obscurity, and out of darkness." Jeremiah 9:7 "Therefore thus says the LORD of hosts: "Behold, I will melt them and try them; for how shall I do for the daughter of My people?" Jeremiah 30:11 (NIV) "I am with you and will save you,' declares the LORD. 'Though I completely destroy all the nations among which I scatter you, I will not completely destroy you. I will discipline you but only in due measure; I will not let you go entirely unpunished." Luke 21:9-19 "⁹ But when ye shall hear of wars and commotions, be not terrified: for these things must first come to pass; but the end is not by and by. ¹⁰ Then said He unto them, Nation shall rise against nation, and kingdom against kingdom: ¹¹ And great earthquakes shall be in divers places, and famines, and pestilences; and fearful sights and great signs shall there be from heaven. ¹² But before all these, they shall lay their hands on you, and persecute you, delivering you up to the synagogues, and into prisons, being brought before kings and rulers for my name's sake. ¹³ And it shall turn to you for a testimony. ¹⁴ Settle it therefore in your hearts, not to meditate before what ye shall answer: ¹⁵ For I will give you a mouth and wisdom, which all your adversaries shall not be able to gainsay nor resist. ¹⁶ And ye shall be betrayed both by parents, and brethren, and kinsfolks, and friends; and some of you shall they cause to be put to death. ¹⁷ And ye shall be hated of all men for My name's sake. ¹⁸ But there shall not an hair of your head perish. ¹⁹ In your patience possess ye your souls." All this is so the Jews will finally see, acknowledge, and accept Jesus as Messiah. Ironically though, there were times when Jesus interacted with demons and they had no trouble acknowledging Him as Messiah. The following passages and stories clearly show that the demons of hell know God is King above all. Luke 4:41 (NKJV) "And demons also came out of many, crying out and saying, "You are the Christ, the Son of God!" And He, rebuking them, did not allow them to speak, for they knew that He was the Christ." James 2:19 (NKJV) "You believe that there is one God. You do well. Even the demons believe and tremble!" Mark 1:23-27 "²³ Now there was a man in their synagogue with an unclean spirit. And he cried out, ²⁴ saying, "Let *us* alone! What have we to do with You, Jesus of Nazareth? Did You come to destroy us? I know who You are—the Holy One of God!" ²⁵ But Jesus rebuked him, saying, "Be quiet, and come out of him!" ²⁶ And when the unclean spirit had convulsed him and cried out with a loud voice, he came out of him. ²⁷ Then they were all amazed, so that they questioned among themselves, saying, "What is this? What new doctrine *is* this? For with authority He commands even the unclean spirits, and they obey Him."

Two, God must execute His righteous wrath and judgment on all rebellious nonbelievers, Jew and Gentile. In the beginning of this session, we acknowledged God's trait of patience and that it has a self-imposed limit. At some point, God will say enough is enough. Psalm 110:5 (NKJV) "The Lord is at Your right hand; He shall execute kings in the day of His wrath." Isaiah 13:9 "Behold, the day of the LORD cometh, cruel both with wrath and fierce anger, to lay the land desolate; and He shall destroy the sinners thereof out of it." Isaiah 34:1-5 "¹ Come near, ye nations, to hear; and hearken, ye people: let the earth hear, and all that is therein; the world, and all things that come forth of it. ² For the indignation of the LORD is upon all nations, and His fury upon all their armies: He hath utterly destroyed them, He hath delivered them to the slaughter. ³ Their slain also shall be cast out, and their stink shall come up out of their carcases, and the mountains shall be melted with their blood. ⁴ And all the host of heaven shall be dissolved, and the heavens shall be rolled together as a scroll: and all their host shall fall down, as the leaf falleth off from the vine, and as a falling fig from the fig tree. ⁵ For My sword shall be bathed in heaven: behold, it shall come down upon Idumea, and upon the people of My curse, to judgment." Jeremiah 23:20 (NKJV) "The anger of the LORD will not turn back until He has executed and performed the thoughts of His heart. In the latter days, you will understand it perfectly." Jeremiah 30:24 "The fierce anger of the LORD shall not return, until He hath done it, and until He have performed the intents of His heart. In the latter days ye shall consider it." Joel 3:1-2 "¹For, behold, in those days, and in that time, when I shall bring again the captivity of Judah and Jerusalem, ² I will also gather all nations, and will bring them down into the valley of Jehoshaphat, and will plead with them there for My people and for My heritage Israel, whom they have scattered among the nations, and parted My land." Nahum 1:2-3 (NIV) "² The LORD is a jealous and avenging God; the LORD takes vengeance and is filled with wrath. The LORD takes vengeance on His foes and vents His wrath against His enemies. ³ The LORD is slow to anger but great in power; His way is in the whirlwind and the storm, and clouds are the dust of His feet." Daniel 11:35-36 (NKJV) "³⁵ And some of those of understanding shall fall, to refine them, purify them, and make white, until the time of the end; because it is still for the appointed time. ³⁶ Then the King shall do according to His own will: He shall exalt and magnify himself above every god, shall speak blasphemies against the God of gods, and shall prosper till the wrath has been accomplished; for what has been determined shall be done." John 3:36 "He that believeth on the Son hath everlasting life: and he that believeth not the Son shall not see life; but the wrath of God abideth on him." 1 John 5:11-12 (NIV) "[11] And this is the testimony: God has given us eternal life, and this life is in His Son. [12] Whoever has the Son has life; whoever does not have the Son of God does not have life." God's promise of living a righteous life that leads to eternal life would be meaningless if there were no alternative punishment to counterbalance it. Jude verses 14-15 "[14] And Enoch also, the seventh from Adam, prophesied of these, saying, Behold, the Lord cometh with ten thousands of His saints, [15] To execute judgment upon all, and to convince all that are ungodly among them of all their ungodly deeds which they have ungodly committed, and of all their hard speeches which ungodly sinners have spoken against Him." 2 Peter 3:7 "But the heavens and the earth, which are now, by the same word, are kept in store, reserved unto fire against the day of judgment and perdition of ungodly men." The result will be that all people Jews and Gentiles alike will know that Jesus Christ is Lord. Revelation 1:7 "Behold, He is cometh with clouds, and every eye shall see Him, even they also which pierced Him. And all kindreds of the earth shall wail because of Him. Even so, Amen." We will go into more detail about how this will affect the Jews and those still alive and what this time will look like after we explore Peter and Paul's missions to the Gentiles.

There is one final sign to look for before the return of the King. Specifcally, that the Spirit of the Lord will be poured out, as is mentioned by the prophet Joel and Peter in Acts. Joel 2:28-29 (NIV) "[28] And afterward, I will pour out My Spirit on all people. Your sons and daughters will prophesy, your old men will dream dreams, your young men will see visions. [29] Even on My servants, both men and women, I will pour out my Spirit in those (last) days." Acts 2:16-18 "[16] But this is that which was spoken by the prophet Joel; [17] And it shall come to pass in the last days, saith God, I will pour out of My Spirit upon all flesh: and your sons and your daughters shall prophesy, and your young men shall see visions, and your old men shall dream dreams: [18] And on My servants and on My hand maidens I will pour out in those days of my Spirit; and they shall prophesy." Even though there is data saying church attendance in traditional mainline America is on decline, there is also data confirming the spirit of the Lord rising worldwide as more and more people accept Christ.

# Chapter 7

# "I Am the Vine"

This is a good place to interject what Jesus actually said about becoming a follower or disciple of Him. We touched upon Jesus, equipping His disciples with the power and ability to heal the sick, in Jesus' name, when we looked at Jesus as the Son of God and the Son of Man. Jesus commissioned His disciples to do the same. Matthew 10:1 "And when He had called unto Him His twelve disciples, He gave them power against unclean spirits, to cast them out, and to heal all manner of sickness and all manner of disease." Jesus was speaking to His twelve handpicked disciples or apostles. Jesus had many followers, but He chose only twelve to take under His wing. Mark 3:14-19 "14 And He ordained twelve, that they should be with Him, and that He might send them forth to preach, 15 and to have power to heal sicknesses, and to cast out devils: 16 And Simon He surnamed Peter; 17 And James the son of Zebedee, and John the brother of James; and He surnamed them Boanerges, which is, The sons of thunder: 18 And Andrew, and Philip, and Bartholomew, and Matthew, and Thomas, and James the son of Alphaeus, and Thaddaeus, and Simon the Canaanite, 19 And Judas Iscariot, which also betrayed him: and they went into an house." Jesus left them with new commandments and in turn to following generastions. Matthew 22:37-40 "37 Jesus said unto him, "Thou shalt love the Lord thy God with all thy heart, and with all thy soul, and with all thy mind." 38 This is the first and great commandment. 39 And the second is like unto it, "Thou shalt love thy neighbour as thyself." 40 On these two commandments hang all the law and the prophets." John 14:15 "If you love Me, keep My commandments." John 14:19-21 "19 Yet a little while, and the world seeth Me no more; but ye see Me: because I live, ye shall live also. 20 At that day ye shall know that I am in My Father, and ye in Me, and I in you. 21 He that hath My commandments, and keepeth them, he it is that loveth Me: and he that loveth Me shall be loved of my Father, and I will love him, and will manifest myself to him." John 15:12-17 (NKJV) "12 This is My commandment, that you love one another as I have loved you. 13 Greater love has no one than this, than to lay down one's life for his friends. 14 You are My friends if you do whatever I command you. 15 No longer do I call you servants, for a servant does not know what his master is doing; but I have called you friends, for all things that I heard from My Father I have made known to you. [16] You did not choose Me, but I chose you and appointed you that you should go and bear fruit and that your fruit should remain, that whatever you ask the Father in My name He may give you. [17] These things I command you, that you love one another." Matthew 28:16-20 (NIV) "[16] Then the eleven disciples went to Galilee, to the mountain where Jesus had told them to go. [17] When they saw him, they worshiped him; but some doubted. [18] Then Jesus came to them and said, "All authority in heaven and on earth has been given to Me. [19] Therefore go and make disciples of all nations, baptizing them in the name of the Father and of the Son and of the Holy Spirit, [20] and teaching them to obey everything I have commanded you. And surely I am with you always, to the very end of the age." Theologians label this passage as the Great Commission. Jesus also warned His disciples that following Him would not be easy, but that it would also be worthwhile and rewarding. In fact, it would be treacherous and potentially life threatening. Jesus plainly said to them that the world would hate them (us) because they (we) chose to follow Christ. John 15:18-19 (NKJV) "[18] If the world hates you, ye know that it hated Me before it hated you. [19] If ye were of the world, the world would love his own: but because ye are not of the world, but I have chosen you out of the world, therefore the world hates you." John 16:33 "These things I have spoken unto you, that in Me you might have peace. In the world ye shall have tribulation, but be of good cheer, I have overcome the world." Luke 6:37-38 "[37] Judge not, and ye shall not be judged: condemn not, and ye shall not be condemned: forgive, and ye shall be forgiven: [38] Give, and it shall be given unto you; good measure, pressed down, and shaken together, and running over, shall men give into your bosom. For with the same measure that ye mete withal it shall be measured to you again." Paul and John also reinforce the importance of loving one another. Romans 8:28-29 "[28] And we know that all things work together for good to them that love God, to those who are the called according to His purpose. [29] For whom He did foreknew, He also did predestine to be conformed to the image of His Son, that He might be the firstborn among many brethren." 1 Corinthians 13:13 (NIV) "[13] And now these three remain: faith, hope and love. But the greatest of these is love." In its simplest terms, the cost is great but the benefits and rewards are far greater. 1 John 4:7-10 (NIV) "[7] Dear friends, let us love one another, for love comes from God. Everyone who loves has been born of God and knows God. [8] Whoever does not love does not know God, because God is love. [9] This is how God showed his love among us: He sent his one and only Son into the world that we might live through him. [10] This is love: not that we loved God, but that he loved us and sent his Son as an atoning sacrifice for our sins." We will come back to Peter and Paul and their missions to the Jews and Gentiles after we look at Jesus and His mission.

We'll now put a bookmark in this narrative about Israel and look at how Jesus influenced the Gentile world, or more specifically, what became known as "the church" regarding God's plan. I think the first question is that, as a community of Gentile believers, do we have the right to claim Jesus' promises to us? Both Jesus and Paul use the gardening metaphor of grafting a "new vine" to "the root" as a way to demonstrate how the gentiles can acquire direct access to Yahweh. Jesus said in John 15:1-8 (NKJV) "[1] I am the true vine, and My Father is the vinedresser. [2] Every branch in Me that does not bear fruit He takes away, and every branch that bears fruit He prunes, that it may bear more fruit. [3] You are already clean because of the word which I have spoken to you. [4] Abide in Me, and I in you. As the branch cannot bear fruit of itself, unless it abides in the vine, neither can you, unless you abide in Me. [5] "I am the vine, you are the branches. He who abides in Me, and I in him, bears much fruit; for without Me you can do nothing. [6] If anyone does not abide in Me, he is cast out as a branch and is withered; and they gather them and throw them into the fire, and they are burned. [7] If you abide in Me, and My words abide in you, you will ask what you desire, and it shall be done for you. [8] By this My Father is glorified, that you bear much fruit; so you will be My disciples." Paul said in Romans 11:16-18 (NIV) "[16] If the part of the dough offered as first fruits is holy, then the whole batch is holy; if the root is holy, so are the branches. [17] If some of the branches have been broken off, and you, though a wild olive shoot, have been grafted in among the others and now share in the nourishing sap from the olive root, [18] do not consider yourself to be superior to those other branches. If you do, consider this: You do not support the root, but the root supports you." Paul also uses the analogy of adoption for us gentiles to be considered part of the family of God. Ephesians 1:4-6 "[4] According as he hath chosen us in him before the foundation of the world, that we should be holy and without blame before Him in love: [5] Having predestinated us unto the adoption of children by Jesus Christ to Himself, according to the good pleasure of his will, [6] To the praise of the glory of His grace, wherein He hath made us accepted in the beloved." Paul also called us gentiles "heirs," which solidifies our inclusion into the family of God Almighty. Ephesians 3:6 "That the Gentiles should be fellow heirs, of the same body, and partakers of His promise in Christ by the gospel." Galatians 3:26-29 (NIV) "[26] So in Christ Jesus you are all children of God through faith, [27] for all of you who were baptized into Christ have clothed yourselves with Christ. [28] There is neither Jew nor Gentile, neither slave nor free, nor is there male and female, for you are all one in Christ Jesus. [29] If you belong to Christ, then you are Abraham's seed, and heirs according to the promise." Romans 8:14-17 "¹⁴ For as many as are led by the Spirit of God, they are the sons of God. ¹⁵ For ye have not received the spirit of bondage again to fear; but ye have received the Spirit of adoption, whereby we cry, Abba, Father. ¹⁶ The Spirit itself beareth witness with our spirit, that we are the children of God: ¹⁷ And if children, then heirs; heirs of God, and joint-heirs with Christ; if so be that we suffer with him, that we may be also glorified together." This, along with Jesus' mission to bring a new covenant to those who receive His gift confirms our right to do so. Just to be clear, redemption or salvation is available to us not by anything we have done or deserve, but by His grace to extend His forgiveness and mercy towards us. As He said to Martha at the death of Lazarus, John 11:25-26 "²⁵ Jesus said unto her, I am the resurrection, and the life: he that believeth in me, though he were dead, yet shall he live: ²⁶ And whosoever liveth and believeth in me shall never die. Believest thou this?" Jesus also reached out directly to gentiles. There is a well-known story of Jesus reaching out to the Gentile Samaritan woman at the well. John 4:7-14 "⁷ There cometh a woman of Samaria to draw water: Jesus saith unto her, Give Me to drink. ⁸ (For his disciples were gone away unto the city to buy meat.) ⁹ Then saith the woman of Samaria unto him, "How is it that thou, being a Jew, askest drink of me, which am a woman of Samaria? for the Jews have no dealings with the Samaritans. ¹⁰ Jesus answered and said unto her, "If thou knewest the gift of God, and who it is that saith to thee, give me to drink; thou wouldest have asked of him, and he would have given thee living water. ¹¹ The woman saith unto him, Sir, thou hast nothing to draw with, and the well is deep: from whence then hast thou that living water? ¹² Art thou greater than our father Jacob, which gave us the well, and drank thereof himself, and his children, and his cattle? ¹³ Jesus answered and said unto her, "Whosoever drinketh of this water shall thirst again: ¹⁴ But whosoever drinketh of the water that I shall give him shall never thirst; but the water that I shall give him shall be in him a well of water springing up into everlasting life."

# Chapter 8

# "The Messiah: First Advent"

Now we will segue to Jesus' role as the instrument of redemption to restore the Jews, and by extension, bring all mankind back into fellowship. God's master plan hangs on this one premise, God's plan begins and ends with His son, Jesus. Without the authentication of Jesus' validation as the Messiah, all of God's promises would be worthless. Jesus is the cornerstone. Psalm 118:22 "The stone which the builders rejected has become the chief cornerstone." It's confirmed in Luke 20:17 "Then He looked at them and said, "What then is this that is written: 'The stone which the builders rejected has become the chief cornerstone'?" He is seen as the Lion and the Lamb. A Lion is a symbol of authority and strength. He is called the Lion of the tribe of Judah. Revelation 5:5 (NKJV) "But one of the elders said to me, "Do not weep. Behold, the Lion of the tribe of Judah, the Root of David, has prevailed to open the scroll and to loose its seven seals." A lamb symbolizes humility and purity. Isaiah 53:7 "He was oppressed and He was afflicted, Yet He opened not His mouth; He was led as a lamb to the slaughter, and as a sheep, before its shearers is silent, So He opened not His mouth." Jesus is the Messiah, the Paschal Lamb of God, a prophet, and a covenant/promise keeper. John 13:19 "Now I tell you before it comes, that when it does come to pass, you may believe that I am He."

- First and foremost, He was to be Messiah. Messiah is from the Hebrew for "anointed one" or "chosen one." In the Greek, the language of the New Testament, the word used is "Christos," which then translates to English, as "Christ." So, Jesus Christ means Jesus is the chosen one. The obvious question is what was He chosen to do? He was chosen to be the conduit as Redeemer and Savior to both Jew and Gentile. Remember Isaiah 6:9-10 said "the Jews eyes were blinded and did not recognize Jesus as the Messiah." To be clear, Orthodox Jews did not then and do not now acknowledge Jesus as Messiah. To them, the coming of the Messiah has still not happened. For them, when the Messiah does come, He will be making a First Appearance. The Gentile church does recognize Jesus as Son of God, and therefore, the Messiah as do some Jewish converts known as Messianic Jews. We acknowledge his birth, death, and resurrection as the fulfillment of the Messianic prophecies. Paul addresses this in Romans 11:7-8 "7 What then? Israel has not obtained what it seeks, but the elect have obtained it, and the rest were blinded. 8 Just as it is written: "God has given them a spirit of stupor, Eyes that they should not see and ears that they should not hear, to this very day." The day of the Lord will remove the blindness of which Isaiah spoke. The following prophecies and their fulfillment support the belief that God intervened supernaturally into our world. As we said in the beginning, there are at least over 400 prophecies concerning the Messiah and Jesus fulfilling them, but this list we only have 21 that cover both His birth and time at the cross.

| | Prophecies About Jesus as the Messiah | Old Testament Scripture NIV | New Testament Fulfillment NIV |
|---|---|---|---|
| 1 | The Messiah would be born in Bethlehem. | Micah 5:2 "But you, Bethlehem Ephrathah, though you are small among the clans of Judah, out of you will come for me one who will be ruler over Israel, whose origins are from of old, from ancient times." | Matthew 2:1 "After Jesus was born in Bethlehem in Judea, during the time of King Herod, Magi from the east came to Jerusalem." |
| 2 | The Messiah would be born of a virgin. And call His name Immanuel. | Isaiah 7:14 "Therefore the Lord himself will give you a sign: The virgin will conceive and give birth to a son, and will call him Immanuel." | Matthew 1:22-23 "22 All this took place to fulfill what the Lord had said through the prophet: 23 "The virgin will conceive and give birth to a son, and they will call him Immanuel (which means "God with us")." |

| | | | |
|---|---|---|---|
| 3 | The Messiah would come from the line of Abraham. | Genesis 22:18 "And through your offspring, all nations on earth will be blessed, because you have obeyed me." | Matthew 1:1 "This is the genealogy of Jesus the Messiah, the son of David, and the son of Abraham." |
| 4 | The Messiah would come from the tribe of Judah. | Genesis 49:10 "The scepter will not depart from Judah, nor the ruler's staff from between his feet, until He to whom it belongs shall come and the obedience of the nations shall be His." | Hebrews 7:14 "For it is clear that our Lord descended from Judah, and in regard to that tribe Moses said nothing about priests." |
| 5 | The Messiah's throne will be anointed and eternal. | Daniel 2:44 "In the time of those kings, the God of heaven will set up a kingdom that will never be destroyed, nor will it be left to another people. It will crush all those kingdoms and bring them to an end, but it will itself endure forever." | Luke 1:33 "And He will reign over Jacob's descendants forever; His kingdom will never end." |

| | | | |
|---|---|---|---|
| 6 | A massacre of children would happen in the Messiah's birthplace. | Jeremiah 31:15 "This is what the Lord says: "A voice is heard in Ramah, mourning and great weeping, Rachel weeping for her children and refusing to be comforted because they are no more." | Matthew 2:16-18 "[16] When Herod realized that he had been outwitted by the Magi, he was furious, and he gave orders to kill all the boys in Bethlehem and its vicinity who were two years old and under, in accordance with the time he had learned from the Magi. [17] Then what was said through the prophet Jeremiah was fulfilled: [18] "A voice is heard in Ramah, weeping and great mourning, Rachel weeping for her children and refusing to be comforted, because they are no more." |
| 7 | The Messiah would spend a season in Egypt. | Hosea 11:1 "When Israel was a child, I loved him, and out of Egypt I called my son." | Matthew 2:14-15 "[14] So he got up, took the child and his mother during the night and left for Egypt, [15] where he stayed until the death of Herod. And so was fulfilled what the Lord had said through the prophet: "Out of Egypt I called my son." |

| | | | |
|---|---|---|---|
| 8 | A messenger would prepare the way for the Messiah. | Isaiah 40:3-5 "³ A voice of one calling: "In the wilderness prepare the way of the Lord; make straight in the desert a highway for our God. ⁴ Every valley shall be raised up, every mountain and hill made low; the rough ground shall become level, the rugged places a plain. ⁵ And the glory of the Lord will be revealed, and all people will see it together. For the mouth of the Lord has spoken." | Luke 3:3-6 "³ He went into all the country around the Jordan, preaching a baptism of repentance for the forgiveness of sins. ⁴ As it is written in the book of the words of Isaiah the prophet: "A voice of one calling in the wilderness, 'Prepare the way of the Lord, make straight paths for him. ⁵ Every valley shall be filled in, every mountain and hill made low. The crooked roads shall become straight, the rough ways smooth. ⁶ And all people will see God's salvation.' " |
| 9 | The Messiah would be rejected by His own people. | Isaiah 53:3 "He was despised and rejected by mankind, a man of suffering, and familiar with pain. Like one from whom people hide their faces he was despised, and we held him in low esteem." | John 1:11 "He came to that which was His own, but His own did not receive Him." |

| 10 | The Messiah would be a prophet. | Deuteronomy 18:15 "The Lord your God will raise up for you a prophet like me from among you, from your fellow Israelites. You must listen to him." | Acts 3:20-22 "[20] And that He may send the Messiah, who has been appointed for you, even Jesus. [21] Heaven must receive him until the time comes for God to restore everything, as He promised long ago through His holy prophets. [22] For Moses said, 'The Lord your God will raise up for you a prophet like me from among your own people; you must listen to everything he tells you.'" |
|---|---|---|---|
| 11 | The Messiah would be declared the Son of God. | Psalm 2:7 "I will proclaim the Lord's decree: He said to me, "You are My son; today I have become your father." | Matthew 3:16-17 "[16] As soon as Jesus was baptized, He went up out of the water. At that moment heaven was opened, and He saw the Spirit of God descending like a dove and alighting on Him. [17] And a voice from heaven said, "This is my Son, whom I love; with Him, I am well pleased." |
| 12 | The Messiah would speak in parables. | Psalm 78:2-4 "[2] I will open my mouth with a parable; I will utter hidden things, things from of old [3] things we have heard and known, things our ancestors have told us. [4] We will not hide them from their descendants; | Matthew 13:34-35 "[34] Jesus spoke all these things to the crowd in parables; He did not say anything to them without using a parable. [35] So was fulfilled what was spoken through the prophet: "I will open my mouth in parables, I will utter things hidden since the creation of the world." |

| | | | |
|---|---|---|---|
| | | | we will tell the next generation the praiseworthy deeds of the Lord, His power, and the wonders He has done." |
| 13 | The Messiah would be called King. | Zechariah 9:9 "Rejoice greatly, Daughter Zion! Shout, Daughter Jerusalem! See, your king comes to you, righteous and victorious, lowly and riding on a donkey, on a colt, the foal of a donkey." | Mark 11:7-11 "7 When they brought the colt to Jesus and threw their cloaks over it, He sat on it. 8 Many people spread their cloaks on the road, while others spread branches they had cut in the fields. 9 Those who went ahead and those who followed shouted, "Hosanna!" "Blessed is He who comes in the name of the Lord!" 10 "Blessed is the coming kingdom of our father David!" "Hosanna in the highest heaven!" 11 Jesus entered Jerusalem and went into the temple courts. He looked around at everything, but since it was already late, He went out to Bethany with the Twelve." |

| | | | |
|---|---|---|---|
| 14 | The Messiah's hands and feet would be pierced. | Zechariah 12:10 "And I will pour out on the house of David and the inhabitants of Jerusalem a spirit of grace and supplication. They will look on Me, the one they have pierced, and they will mourn for Him as one mourns for an only child, and grieve bitterly for Him as one grieves for a firstborn son." | Luke 24:39 "Look at my hands and my feet. It is I myself! Touch me and see; a ghost does not have flesh and bones, as you see I have."<br><br>John 19:37 "And again another Scripture says, "They shall look on Him whom they pierced." |
| 15 | The soldiers would gamble for Messiah's garments. | Psalm 22:18 "They divide my clothes among them and cast lots for my garment." | Luke 23:34 "Jesus said, "Father, forgive them, for they do not know what they are doing." And they divided up his clothes by casting lots." |

| | | | |
|---|---|---|---|
| 16 | The Messiah's bones would not be broken. | Psalm 34:20 "He protects all his bones, not one of them will be broken." | John 19:33-36 "33 But when they came to Jesus and found that He was already dead, they did not break His legs. 34 Instead, one of the soldiers pierced Jesus' side with a spear, bringing a sudden flow of blood and water. 35 The man who saw it has given testimony, and his testimony is true. He knows that he tells the truth, and he testifies so that you also may believe. 36 These things happened so that the scripture would be fulfilled: "Not one of His bones will be broken." |
| 17 | The Messiah would be buried with the rich. | Isaiah 53:9 "He was assigned a grave with the wicked, and with the rich in his death, though He had done no violence, nor was any deceit in His mouth." | Matthew 27:57-60 "57 As evening approached, there came a rich man from Arimathea, named Joseph, who had himself become a disciple of Jesus. 58 Going to Pilate, he asked for Jesus' body, and Pilate ordered that it be given to him. 59 Joseph took the body, wrapped it in a clean linen cloth, 60 and placed it in his own new tomb that he had cut out of the rock. He rolled a big stone in front of the entrance to the tomb and went away." |
| 18 | The Messiah would resurrect from the dead. | Psalm 16:10 "Because you will not abandon me to the realm of the dead, nor will you | Matthew 28:5-6 "5 The angel said to the women, "Do not be afraid, for I know that you are looking for Jesus, who was crucified. 6 He is not here; He has risen, just as He |

| | | | |
|---|---|---|---|
| | | let your faithful one see decay." | said. Come and see the place where He lay." |
| 19 | The Messiah would ascend to heaven. | Psalm 24:9-10 "⁹ Lift up your heads, your gates; lift them up, you ancient doors, that the King of glory may come in. ¹⁰ Who is he, this King of glory? The Lord Almighty, He is the King of Glory." | Luke 24:51 "While He was blessing them, He left them and was taken up into heaven." |
| 20 | The Messiah would be seated at God's right hand. | Psalm 110:1 "The Lord says to my Lord: "Sit at my right hand until I make your enemies a footstool for your feet." | Mark 16:19 "After the Lord Jesus had spoken to them, He was taken up into heaven and He sat at the right hand of God." |
| 21 | The Messiah would be a sacrifice for sin. | Isaiah 53:10 "Yet it was the Lord's will to crush Him and cause him to suffer, and though the Lord makes His life an offering for sin, He will see His offspring and prolong His days, and the will of the Lord will prosper in His hand." | Romans 5:6-8 "⁶ You see, at just the right time, when we were still powerless, Christ died for the ungodly. ⁷ Very rarely will anyone die for a righteous person, though for a good person someone might possibly dare to die. ⁸ But God demonstrates his own love for us in this: While we were still sinners, Christ died for us." |

Remember at the outset of our exploration, we looked at why we should study prophecy, we mentioned there were 400 prophecies that were fulfilled by Christ's first coming when He came as a baby, which we call the Advent, and at His crucifixion and resurrection, at the time we call Easter. We also mentioned that there are over 1,400 prophecies yet to be fulfilled and will do so at Christ's second coming as the Conquering King Messiah. Jesus knew He needed to return to heaven, so He would be able to make a second appearance. Again, John 14:1-3 "[1] Let not your heart be troubled; you believe in God, believe also in Me. [2] In My Father's house are many mansions; if it were not so, I would have told you. I go to prepare a place for you. [3] And if I go and prepare a place for you, I will come again and receive you to Myself; that where I am, there you may be also." The next appearance is called His Second Coming or Second Advent. However, there appears to be conflicting accounts of this arrival. This will be better explained after we finish exploring Jesus' role as a prophet, and covenant/promise keeper sections, where we look at the Rapture vs. the Second Coming. For now, though, remember when we looked at Jesus being the Son of God and the Son of man, the Jewish leadership of the time had a preconceived narrow idea of what the Messiah would be. Below is a partial list of Old Testament prophecies that will reinforce and herald the arrival of the Messiah as the Conquering King. That event will be unmistakable and seen by the whole earth.

Isaiah 66:15-16 (NKJV) "[15] For behold, the LORD will come with fire and with His chariots, like a whirlwind, to render His anger with fury, and His rebuke with flames of fire. [16] For by fire and by His sword. The LORD will judge all flesh, and the slain of the LORD shall be many."

Jeremiah 25:30-31 "[30] Therefore, prophesy against them all these words, and say to them: 'The LORD will roar from on high, and utter His voice from His holy habitation; He will roar mightily against His fold. He will give a shout, as those who tread the grapes, against all the inhabitants of the earth. [31] A noise will come to the ends of the earth for the LORD has a controversy with the nations; He will plead His case with all flesh. He will give those who are wicked to the sword,' says the LORD."

Daniel 7:13-14 "[13] I was watching in the night visions, and, behold, one like the Son of Man, Coming with the clouds of heaven! He came to the Ancient of Days, and they brought Him near before Him. [14] Then to Him was given dominion and glory and a kingdom, that all peoples, nations, and languages should serve Him. His dominion is an everlasting dominion, which shall not pass away, And His kingdom the one Which shall not be destroyed."

Jeremiah 3:17 "At that time Jerusalem shall be called the Throne of the LORD, and all the nations shall be gathered to it, to the name of the LORD, to Jerusalem. No more shall they follow the dictates of their evil hearts."

Isaiah 24:19-20 "19 The earth is violently broken, the earth is split open, the earth is shaken exceedingly. 20 The earth shall reel to and fro like a drunkard, and shall totter like a hut; its transgression shall be heavy upon it, and it will fall, and not rise again."

- Jesus is The Lamb of God. Isaiah 53:7-8 "7 He was oppressed and He was afflicted, yet He opened not His mouth; He was led as a lamb to the slaughter, and as a sheep before its shearers is silent, so He opened not His mouth. 8 He was taken from prison and from judgment, and who will declare His generation? For He was cut off from the land of the living; for the transgressions of My people He was stricken." John 1:29 "The next day John (the Baptist) saw Jesus coming toward him, and said, "Behold! The Lamb of God who takes away the sin of the world!" He was chosen and sent by God His Father, as planned at the beginning of creation, to be the substitute sacrifice or spotless lamb to bring man back into relationship with Him. 1 Peter 1:20 "He indeed was foreordained before the foundation of the world, but was manifest in these last times for you." Jesus is sometimes called the Paschal Lamb referring to the lamb which was selected to be sacrificed at Passover. Like the lamb that the Jewish priests sought out, Jesus was without sin, spot, or blemish. 1 Peter 1:19 "But with the precious blood of Christ, as of a lamb without blemish and without spot." 2 Corinthians 5:21 "For He made Him who knew no sin to be sin for us, that we might become the righteousness of God in Him." 1 Peter 2:21-23 (NKJV) "21 For to this you were called, because Christ also suffered for us, leaving us an example, that you should follow His steps: 22 "Who committed no sin, nor was deceit found in His mouth; 23 who, when He was reviled, did not revile in return; when He suffered, He did not threaten, but committed Himself to Him who judges righteously;" Hebrews 9:28 "So Christ was offered once to bear the sins of many. To those who eagerly wait for Him He will appear a second time, apart from sin, for salvation." He allowed Himself to be sacrificed and become the actual Paschal Lamb. John 10:18 (NKJV) "No one takes it from Me, but I lay it down of Myself. I have the power to lay it down, and I have the power to take it again. This command I have received from My Father." Each Easter is an opportunity to pause and reflect at just how deep God's love for us is that He sent His Son to provide a pathway back to restoration with God the Father. John 15:13 "Greater love has no one than this than to lay down one's life for his friends." Jesus could have chosen not to go through the humility and intense unspeakable persecution. Luke 22:42-44 (NIV) "42 Father, if you are willing, take this cup from me; yet not My will, but yours be done." 43 An angel from heaven appeared to Him and strengthened Him. 44 And being in anguish, He prayed more earnestly, and His sweat was like drops of blood falling to the ground." Mark 14:32-36 "32 Then they came to a place which was named Gethsemane; and He said to His disciples, "Sit here while I pray." 33 And He took Peter, James, and John with Him, and He began to be troubled and deeply distressed. 34 Then He said to them, "My soul is exceedingly sorrowful, even to death. Stay here and watch." 35 He went a little farther, and fell on the ground, and prayed that if it were possible, the hour might pass from Him. 36 And He said, "Abba, Father, all things are possible for You. Take this cup away from Me; nevertheless, not what I will, but what You will." He was searching for any other way for God to redeem mankind, but there was none. Hebrews 9:22 "And according to the law almost all things are purified with blood, and without shedding of blood there is no remission (of sins)." It is crucial to understand that the basis for God's whole plan to be effective, that without Jesus willingly choosing to go through the agony, death, and resurrection, Jesus' gesture would have been futile. This is the lamb the 24 elders in heaven refer to when they exclaim Worthy is the Lamb. Revelation 5:9-12 "9 And they sang a new song, saying: "You are worthy to take the scroll, And to open its seals; For You were slain, And have redeemed us to God by Your blood Out of every tribe and tongue and people and nation, 10 And have made us kings and priests to our God; And we shall reign on the earth." 11 Then I looked, and I heard the voice of many angels around the throne, the living creatures, and the elders; and the number of them was ten thousand times ten thousand, and thousands of thousands, 12 saying with a loud voice: "Worthy is the Lamb who was slain To receive power and riches and wisdom, And strength and honor and glory and blessing!"

- Jesus as a prophet. Let's put some chronological context in this story. Up until this time, His disciples thought Jesus was a great rabbi or prophet. John 11:8 "The disciples said to Him, "Rabbi, lately the Jews sought to stone You, and are You going there again?" Jesus rode into Jerusalem on a donkey or colt at the beginning of the week under the shouts of Hosanna! Up to this point, He had overturned the tables in the temple courtyard and evaded the Pharisees attempt to trick Him regarding paying taxes as told in Matthew and Mark. Matthew 22:21 "They said to Him, "Caesar's." And He said to them, "Render therefore to Caesar the things that are Caesar's, and to God the things that are God's." Mark 12:17 "And Jesus answered and said to them, "Render to Caesar the things that are Caesar's, and to God the things that are God's." And they marveled at Him." Jesus' popularity grew daily and was considered a threat by the Pharisees. The following interaction with His disciples occurred after a day of teaching to the public in parables and two days before they would retire for the day to eat the meal before Passover. Although we, as Christians, accept His words by faith, a historical fact proves Jesus's ability to precisely declare prophecy in Matthew 24:1-2 (NKJV) "¹ Then Jesus went out and departed from the temple, and His disciples came up to show Him the buildings of the temple. ² And Jesus said to them, "Do you not see all these things? Assuredly, I say to you, not one stone shall be left here upon another, that shall not be thrown down." The disciples were puzzled at this so they asked Him three more questions Matthew 24:3 (NKJV) "Now as He sat on the Mount of Olives, the disciples came to Him privately, saying, 1) "Tell us, when will these things be? 2) And what will be the sign of Your coming, 3) and of the end of the age?" His answer is recorded in Matthew 24, Mark 13, and Luke 21, and which church theologians labeled the Olivet Discourse. Just a word to keep in mind, Jesus was speaking pointedly to His Jewish brethren, the disciples, as the "Church" at this time was not yet in existence. Earlier, we spoke about Daniel's 70th week prophecy, Jesus is speaking specifically about that time period here.

    A. The answer to the first question, "when will these things be?" is found only in the Luke account. Luke 21:20-24 "²⁰ But when you see Jerusalem surrounded by armies, then know that its desolation is near. ²¹ Then let those who are in Judea flee to the mountains, let those who are in the midst of her depart, and let not those who are in the country enter her. ²² For these are the days of vengeance, that all things which are written may be fulfilled. ²³ But woe to those who are pregnant and to those who are nursing babies in those days! For there will be great distress in the land and wrath upon this people. ²⁴ And they will fall by the edge of the sword, and be led away captive into all nations. And Jerusalem will be trampled by Gentiles until the times of the Gentiles are fulfilled." Just as predicted in Ezekiel 30:3 (NKJV) "For the day is near, Even the day of the LORD is near; it will be a day of clouds, the time of the Gentiles prophecy." In 70 AD, the Roman Emperor Titus sacked Jerusalem and destroyed Solomon's temple, a second time, thereby fulfilling Jesus' prediction. Furthermore, the "Gentiles" will have control over Jerusalem until their time is concluded. In 1967, Jerusalem was reacquired and controlled by Israel thereby bringing "the times of the Gentiles" to a close as it relates to God's Holy City.

B. To answer the second question, "what will be the signs of Your coming?" Jesus gave the below signs of what to look for before He returns. For your convenience, you will see the corresponding passages from the Book of Revelation and the Four Horseman of the Apocalypse. These points illustrate that Jesus certainly had a knowledge of future events, though God limited the extent of that knowledge. Mark 13:32 "But of that day and hour no one knows, not even the angels in heaven, nor the Son, but only the Father." The phrase is repeated in Matthew 24:36 and omitted in the Luke 21 account.

| theme | biblical quote | foreshadow | companion reference |
|---|---|---|---|
| deception | Matthew 24:4-5, 11, and 23-26 (NKJV) "4 And Jesus answered and said to them: "Take heed that no one deceives you. 5 For many will come in My name, saying, 'I am the Christ,' and will deceive many. 11 Then many false prophets will rise up and deceive many. "23 Then if anyone says to | False Christs, ritualistic religion, new age practices, nonbiblical doctrine, Jonestown, Branch Davidians, LGBTQ agenda | Revelation 6:1-2 "1 Now I saw when the Lamb opened one of the seals; and I heard one of the four living creatures saying with a voice like thunder, "Come and see." 2 And I looked, and behold, a white horse. He who sat on it had a bow, and a crown was given to Him, and He went out conquering and to conquer." |

you, 'Look, here is the Christ!' or 'There!' do not believe it. 24 For false Christ's and false prophets will rise and show great signs and wonders to deceive, if possible, even the elect. 25 See, I have told you beforehand. 26 "Therefore if they say to you, 'Look, He is in the desert!' do not go out; or 'Look, He is in the inner rooms!' do not believe it."

| war | Matthew 24:6-7a (NKJV) "6 And you will hear of wars and rumors of wars. See that you are not troubled; for all these things must come to pass, but the end is not yet. 7a For nation* will rise against nation, and kingdom against kingdom." | Nuclear war is coming to Israel. The "Iranian Deal" ultimately allows Iran to develop a nuclear program while supplying Hamas and Hezbollah with conventional | Revelation 6:3-4 "3 When He opened the second seal, I heard the second living creature saying, "Come and see." 4 Another horse, fiery red, went out. And it was granted to the one who sat on it to take peace from the earth, and that people should kill one another, and there was given to him a great sword." |

Zechariah 14:12 "And this shall be the plague with which the Lord will strike all the people who fought against Jerusalem: Their flesh shall dissolve while they stand on their feet, their eyes shall dissolve in their sockets, and their tongues shall dissolve in their mouths." This is a description of a nuclear blast."

weaponry, including a vast array of rockets. Russia, Iran, and several other radical Islamic countries will conspire to attack Israel. Radical Islam is looking to totally destroy Israel and Russia wants to make a deal for oil so it can once again be a super power. The Gog/Magog war of Ezekiel 38 and 39 is detailed below. News of Iran's nuclear production is at the top of the world's biggest watch list items. Their goal is to "wipe Israel off the map."

| | | | |
|---|---|---|---|
| famines, pestilences, earthquakes | Matthew 24:7b-8 (NKJV) "7b And there will be famines, pestilences, and earthquakes in various places. 8 All these are the beginning of sorrows." ** | There are several African nations, as well as Southeast Asia and parts of South America (Venezuela) that have existing famines. Pestilence such as Aids, Ebola virus, avian flu, and zika have the WHO worried. Earthquakes Katrina, Japan, Hurricane Sandy, dramatic measurable increases in the ring of fire, Cascadia Fault Zones, San Andreas zone, Yellowstone caldera. All three areas are overdue for an eruption. | Revelation 6:5-8 "5 When He opened the third seal, I heard the third living creature say, "Come and see." So, I looked, and behold, a black horse, and he who sat on it had a pair of scales in his hand. 6 And I heard a voice in the midst of the four living creatures saying, "A quart of wheat for a denarius, and three quarts of barley for a denarius; and do not harm the oil and the wine." 7 When He opened the fourth seal, I heard the voice of the fourth living creature saying, "Come and see." 8 So I looked, and behold, a pale horse. And the name of him who sat on it was Death, and Hades followed with him. And power was given to them over a fourth of the earth, to kill with sword, with hunger, with death, and by the beasts of the earth." |

| | | | |
|---|---|---|---|
| anti-Semitism | Matthew 24:9-10 (NKJV) "⁹ Then they will deliver you up to tribulation and kill you, and you will be hated by all nations for My name's sake. ¹⁰ And then many will be offended, will betray one another, and will hate one another." | Holocaust, increase of antisemitism in the US and Europe. Jewish cemeteries are vandalized by kicking over headstones or spray painting swastikas on them or synagogue walls, BDS movement, UN resolution, the Pittsburgh Temple Massacre. | Revelation 6:12-14 "¹² I looked when He opened the sixth seal, and behold, there was a great earthquake; and the sun became black as sackcloth of hair, and the moon became like blood. ¹³ And the stars of heaven fell to the earth, as a fig tree drops its late figs when it is shaken by a mighty wind. ¹⁴ Then the sky receded as a scroll when it is rolled up, and every mountain and island was moved out of its place." |
| breakdown of social values and tribulation saints | Matthew 24:12-13 (NKJV) "¹² And because lawlessness will abound, the love of many will grow cold. ¹³ But he who endures to the end shall be saved (tribulation saints)." | Law enforcements officers under attack, increase in hate crimes, domestic and international terrorism. 9/11, Boston marathon. | Revelation 6:9-11 "⁹ When He opened the fifth seal, I saw under the altar the souls of those who had been slain for the word of God and for the testimony which they held. ¹⁰ And they cried with a loud voice, saying, "How long, O Lord, holy and true, until You judge and avenge our blood on those who dwell on the earth?" ¹¹ Then a white robe was given to each of them; and it was said to them that they should rest a little while longer, until both the |

| | | | |
|---|---|---|---|
| | | | number of their fellow servants and their brethren, who would be killed as they were, was completed." |
| preach to all the world | Matthew 24:14 (NKJV) "And this gospel of the kingdom will be preached in the whole world as a testimony to all nations, and then the end will come." | Technology, global positioning satellites for communication including television. The increase of knowledge. Computers, GPS, the internet, genetic manipulation, medical advancements, cashless transactions | Daniel 12:4 "But thou, O Daniel shut up the words, and seal the book, even to the time of the end: many shall run to and fro, and knowledge shall be increased." |
| Abomination of desolation | Matthew 24:15-20 (NKJV) "15 Therefore when you see the 'abomination of desolation,' spoken of by Daniel the prophet, standing in the holy place " (whoever reads, let him understand), 16 "then let those who | The Third Temple must be in place for the abomination of the AC being worship as god. Architectural plans with reconstructed | Daniel 9:27 "Then he shall confirm a covenant with many for one week; but in the middle of the week, he shall bring an end to sacrifice and offering. And on the wing of abominations shall be one who makes desolate, even until the consummation, which is determined, is poured out on the desolate." |

are in Judea flee to the mountains. ¹⁷ Let him who is on the housetop not go down to take anything out of his house. ¹⁸ And let him who is in the field not go back to get his clothes. ¹⁹ But woe to those who are pregnant and to those who are nursing babies in those days! ²⁰ And pray that your flight may not be in winter or on the Sabbath."

furniture and implements. Temple priests are currently in training for the sacrifices. The ground work for a one world religion is being laid as people are starting to say God and Allah are the same, albeit with different names.

\* The word for "nations" in vs 7 according to the Strong's #G1484 in the original Greek is "ethos." This is where we get our word for ethnic. A better translation is ethnic group vs ethnic group, such as Sunni vs Shiites, Saudis vs Yemenis, Arabs or Muslims vs Jews, the Sudan, the Civil war in Syria, Iraqis vs Kurds, Iran/Hezbollah, Hamas, PLO vs Israelis, N. Korea vs USA, refugees vs Europeans, and so on.

\*\* The word for "sorrows" in vs 8 according to Strong's #G5604, this original Greek word was "odin." The word means the "pain of child birth." Matthew 24:8 (NKJV) "All these are the beginning of sorrows." Matthew 24:8 (NIV) "All these are the beginning of birth pains." This an example of an idiom. The Old English referred to childbirth as "sorrows" and the contemporary versions translates to "birth pains." It is believed that Jesus wanted to express the idea that just before He returns, the calamities listed would occur more frequently and with greater intensity, just like a woman experiences when she goes into labor and is about to deliver.

Jesus ends His answer for this second question when He says in Matthew 24:21-22 (NKJV) "²¹ For then there will be great Tribulation, such as has not been since the beginning of the world until this time, no, nor ever shall be. 22 And unless those days were shortened, no flesh would be saved; but for the elect's sake those days will be shortened." The above events will be very horrific and will snowball from the beginning of the Tribulation until His triumphant return. The Tribulation will be studied at the close of this section. The verses Mathew 24:23-26 are part of the above outline.

C. To answer the final question, "what of the end of the age?" He says in Matthew 24:27-31 (NKJV) "27 For as the lightning comes from the east and flashes to the west, so also will the coming of the Son of Man be. 28 For wherever the carcass is, there the eagles will be gathered together. 29 "Immediately after the Tribulation of those days the sun will be darkened, and the moon will not give its light; the stars will fall from heaven, and the powers of the heavens will be shaken. 30 Then the sign of the Son of Man will appear in heaven, and then all the tribes of the earth will mourn, and they will see the Son of Man coming on the clouds of heaven with power and great glory. 31 And He will send his angels with a loud trumpet call, and they will gather His elect from the four winds, from one end of the heavens to the other." This coming will be loud, vivid, unmistakable, and predictable. The first sentence of Daniel 9:27 (NKJV) says "Then he (the Antichrist) shall confirm a covenant with many for one week (7 years);" has two important elements. First, it confirms the length of time for the coming seven years, and second, that the beginning will start when he delivers the confirmation of a peace treaty between Israel and her enemies. So, if we know the length and the beginning, we can count the seven years of Daniel's 70th week to the expected second coming. Luke gives an additional point. Luke 21:27-28 "27 Then they will see the Son of Man coming in a cloud with power and great glory. 28 Now when these things begin (verses 4-20) to happen, look up and lift up your heads, because your redemption draws near." To emphasize, when these things (vs 4-20) BEGIN (not the middle or end) to happen our redemption, Christ's return, is close at hand. Jesus then switches back to teaching in parables. Usually, when he wanted to give His disciples a deeper or meaningful lesson, He would take them off privately and speak with them. Mark 4:33-34 "33 And with many such parables He spoke the word to them as they were able to hear it. 34 But without a parable, He did not speak to them. And when they were alone, He explained all things to His disciples."

Matthew 13:10-11 "¹⁰ The disciples came to him and asked, "Why do you speak to the people in parables?" ¹¹ He replied, "Because the knowledge of the secrets of the kingdom of heaven has been given to you, but not to them." However, when He wanted to speak to the general public, He used His tried and true teaching method, parables. Jesus gives His disciples a lesson by telling them a few of parables.

1. The Fig Tree Parable. Matthew 24:32-35 (NKJV) "³² Now learn this lesson from the fig tree: As soon as its twigs get tender and its leaves come out, you know that summer is near. ³³ Even so, when you see all these things, you know that it is near, right at the door. ³⁴ Truly I tell you, this generation will certainly not pass away until all these things have happened. ³⁵ Heaven and earth will pass away, but my words will never pass away." Luke 21:28 "Now when these things begin to happen, look up and lift up your heads, because your redemption draws near." There are four short but important points in this parable.

   i. The lesson of this parable is portrayed in that we know the coming of summer is relatively soon when we see the clues of the spring's budding leaves. We may not know the day, but we can be aware of the season.

   ii. The generation that sees all these happening together at the same time will be THE generation that will see Christ come. All the signs must happen at the same time for the end to begin. If there are only 1 or 2 signs the start date cannot happen. This generation is sometimes called the Terminal generation

   iii. He reaffirms His character trait He shares with His Father God that He never changes His word after HE has given it.

   iv. Some also suggest the "fig tree" is a symbol for Israel, so that when we see Israel reassert itself, as they did in 1948, it heralds that the return of the King is near.

2. The Days of Noah. Matthew 24:36-39 (NKJV) "³⁶ But of that day and hour no one knows, not even the angels of heaven, but My Father only. ³⁷ But as the days of Noah were, so also will the coming of the Son of Man be. ³⁸ For as in the days before the flood, they were eating and drinking, marrying and giving in marriage, until the day that Noah entered the ark, ³⁹ and did not know until the flood came and took them all away, so also will the coming of the Son of Man be." There are three important points in this lesson.

   i. The first part of the sentence of vs 36 was a common Jewish idiom in Jesus' day. It is believed to have referred to either of two contexts. One was from an ancient Jewish wedding custom. After the groom and prospective bride were officially promised to each other, (think Joseph and Mary), the groom would return to his father's house where he would create a new living space for him and his new bride. He could not go get her to bring her to her new home until the father told him it was time to go. While the groom was waiting for someone to ask him when he could go, his answer was, "no one knows the day or the hour." This correlates to John 14:1-3 again about going to His Father's house to prepare a room and if He goes, He will return." The second was associated with the Feast of Trumpets, or Rosh Hashanah (Jewish New Year), or the Wedding Feast of the Messiah. Because this Feast day does not begin until the new crescent moon is seen by two Jewish men and then reported to the Sanhedrin (high court), the beginning of the month was unknown. Unlike the other Feasts, which were scheduled to fall on full moons, if someone asked when the beginning of the month was, the phrase "no one knows the day" is said to have referred to this Feast.

   ii. The next point "the days of Noah." is covered in vs 37-39. Luke also weighs in. Luke 17:22-27 "²² Then He said to the disciples, "The days will come when you will desire to see one of the days of the Son of Man, and you will not see it. 23 And they will say to you, 'Look here!' or 'Look there!' Do not go after them or follow them. 24 For as the lightning that flashes out of one part under heaven shines to the other part under heaven, so also the Son of Man will be in His day. 25 But first He must suffer many things and be rejected by this generation. 26 And as it was in the days of Noah, so it will be also in the days of the Son of Man. 27 They ate, they drank, they married wives, they were given in marriage, until the day that Noah entered the ark, and the flood came and destroyed them all." As the texts suggest, during Noah's time, people were going about living their lives, without any thought or consideration of God. There must have been some deep level of rebellion or debauchery that would cause God to wipe the slate clean and start over in Genesis 6:5, 11 and 12 "5 And God saw that the wickedness of man was great in the earth and that every imagination of the thoughts of his heart was only evil continually. 11 The earth also was corrupt before God, and the earth was filled with violence. 12 So God looked upon the earth, and, behold, it was corrupt; for all flesh had corrupted his way upon the earth." If we take a look at the moral indicators of today, I think a case can be made that we are close to those times before the flood. The divorce rate is 1 out of 2, in both the church and secular world, an increase of unmarried people living together and producing children, grandparents raising the 2$^{nd}$ generation because either or both parents are absentee, in jail or hooked on drugs, gay marriage is now as the law of the land. In America, in the first six months of 2016, alone the leading cause of death is abortion with over 500,000 cases reported. The Bible clearly states that God views anyone, and He will hold him or her accountable, who is involved with the killing of the innocents is an abomination. Proverbs 6:16-19 "16 These six things the

LORD hates, yes, seven are an abomination to Him: 17 a proud look, a lying tongue, hands that shed innocent blood, 18 a heart that devises wicked plans, feet that are swift in running to evil, 19 a false witness who speaks lies, and one who sows discord among brethren." Jeremiah 1:5 "Before I formed you in the womb I knew you; before you were born I sanctified you; I ordained you a prophet to the nations." Psalm 139:13-14 "13 For You formed my inward parts; You covered me in my mother's womb. 14 I will praise You, for I am fearfully and wonderfully made; Marvelous are Your works, and that my soul knows very well." As in Noah's day, no one is looking or listening for God, let alone believing that one day God will sit in judgment of us. In this illustration, the storm clouds have gathered, the sky is growing dark, and the first few drops have just started to fall. The flood took them by surprise because they did not heed Noah and his message from God. When Jesus returns, it will take those who are not watching by complete surprise. Those who do not follow Christ's teachings, and prophecy is one of them, will not have the fore knowledge of what signs to watch for. Paul highlights that believers, as sons of light, will have the ability to know the general time of Christ's return and that it will not surprise those who are keeping watch. 1 Thessalonians 5:1-5 "1 But concerning the times and the seasons, brethren, you have no need that I should write to you. 2 For you yourselves know perfectly that the day of the Lord so comes as a thief in the night. 3 For when they say, "Peace and safety!" then sudden destruction comes upon them, as labor pains upon a pregnant woman. And they shall not escape. 4 But you, brethren, are not in darkness, so that this Day should overtake you as a thief. 5 You are all sons of light and sons of the day. We are not of the night nor of darkness." Conversely, the sons of darkness will sew and reap condemnation. John 3:19-21 "19 And this is the condemnation, that the light has come into the world, and men loved darkness rather than light because their deeds were evil. [20] For everyone practicing evil hates the light and does not come to the light, lest his deeds should be exposed. [21] But he who does the truth comes to the light, that his deeds may be clearly seen, that they have been done in God." The only surprise for Christians will experience when we are called into Jesus' presence is who is and who is not there. As a point of interest, there is a movie produced by www.livingwaters.com in Bellflower, CA on YouTube titled "Noah Movie HD Official Full Version." It has been viewed over 2.7 million times. Ray Comfort interviews several people in southern CA. It is shockingly eye opening about the seemingly total blissful ignorance or unbelief of the people who were interviewed. This random slice cross-section of people will leave you shaking your head.

iii. One will be taken. Matthew 24:40-44 (NKJV) "[40] Then two men will be in the field: one will be taken and the other left. [41] Two women will be grinding at the mill: one will be taken and the other left. [42] Watch, therefore, for you do not know what hour your Lord is coming. [43] But know this, that if the master of the house had known what hour the thief would come, he would have watched and not allowed his house to be broken into. [44] Therefore you also be ready, for the Son of Man is coming at an hour you do not expect." The taking away of one of two people in vs 40-43 and the master of the house being caught unaware suggests this coming is in secret and without warning. In vs 44, it states that one should be ready for Christ's return because the time could come at any moment. It is unpredictable. This causes a logistical question, "How can this be when we just learned in vs 27-31 His coming will be loud and predictable?" Luke 12:40 (NKJV) "Therefore you also be ready, for the Son of Man is coming at an hour you do not expect." This apparent inconsistency can only be explained in that the Second Coming must have two phases. Peter and Paul both have insight on this aspect so we will address this when we get to them shortly.

3. The Faithful and Wise Servant Matthew 24:45-51 (NKJV) "⁴⁵ Who then is a faithful and wise servant, whom his master made ruler over his household, to give them food in due season? ⁴⁶ Blessed is that servant whom his master when he comes, will find so doing. ⁴⁷ Assuredly, I say to you that he will make him ruler over all his goods. ⁴⁸ But if that evil servant says in his heart, 'My master is delaying his coming,' ⁴⁹ and begins to beat his fellow servants, and to eat and drink with the drunkards, ⁵⁰ the master of that servant will come on a day when he is not looking for him and at an hour that he is not aware of, ⁵¹ and will cut him in two and appoint him his portion with the hypocrites. There shall be weeping and gnashing of teeth." Simply put Jesus is reinforcing the concept of being prepared so you are not caught unaware of the master's return. Luke and Mark say it better and strongly emphasizes the command to watch. Luke 21:34-36 "³⁴ But take heed to yourselves, lest your hearts be weighed down with carousing, drunkenness, and cares of this life, and that Day (will) come on you unexpectedly. ³⁵ For it will come as a snare on all those who dwell on the face of the whole earth. ³⁶ Watch, therefore, and pray always that you may be counted worthy to escape all these things that will come to pass, and to stand before the Son of Man." Mark 13:35-37 "³⁵ Watch, therefore, for you do not know when the master of the house is coming in the evening, at midnight, at the crowing of the rooster, or in the morning ³⁶ lest, coming suddenly, he find you sleeping. ³⁷ And what I say to you, I say to all: Watch!" Jesus admonished us to be ready and keep alert. Luke's and Mark's narrative ends here whereas Matthew continues with parables in chapter 25. The theme of keeping watch and ready for His return is reinforced with these parables.

4. The Parable of the Wise and Foolish Virgins. Matthew 25:1-13 "¹ Then the kingdom of heaven shall be likened to ten virgins who took their lamps and went out to meet the bridegroom. ² Now five of them

were wise, and five were foolish. 3 Those who were foolish took their lamps and took no oil with them, 4 but the wise took oil in their vessels with their lamps. 5 But while the bridegroom was delayed, they all slumbered and slept. 6 "And at midnight a cry was heard: 'Behold, the bridegroom is coming; go out to meet him!' 7 Then all those virgins arose and trimmed their lamps. 8 And the foolish said to the wise, 'Give us some of your oil, for our lamps, are going out.' 9 But the wise answered, saying, 'No, lest there should not be enough for us and you; but go rather to those who sell, and buy for yourselves.' 10 And while they went to buy, the bridegroom came, and those who were ready went in with him to the wedding, and the door was shut. 11 "Afterward the other virgins came also, saying, 'Lord, Lord, open to us!' 12 But he answered and said, 'Assuredly, I say to you, I do not know you.' 13 "Watch, therefore, for you know neither the day nor the hour in which the Son of Man is coming." The lesson here is that all ten virgins were initially looking for the return of their beloved. However, after a time, five of them were distracted and lost sight of his return. The remaining faithful five stayed the course and remained faithful, so when the beloved did arrive they were ready and were taken to His home.

5. The Parable of the Talents. This parable is well known. The short version is. It deals with the master giving one servant, 5 talents, one servant 2 talents and one servant 1 talent and what they did with the money as good stewards. Matthew 25:14-29 "14 For the kingdom of heaven is like a man traveling to a far country, who called his own servants and delivered his goods to them. 15 And to one he gave five talents, to another two, and to another one, to each according to his own ability; and immediately he went on a journey. 16 Then he who had received the five talents went and traded with them, and made another five talents. 17 And likewise, he who had received two gained two more also. 18 But he who had received one went and dug in the ground, and hid his lord's money. 19 After a long time, the lord of those servants came and settled accounts with them. 20 "So he who had received five talents came and brought five other talents, saying, 'Lord, you delivered to me five talents; look, I have gained five more

talents besides them.' ²¹ His lord said to him, 'Well done, good and faithful servant; you were faithful over a few things, I will make you ruler over many things. Enter into the joy of your lord.' ²² He also who had received two talents came and said, 'Lord, you delivered to me two talents; look, I have gained two more talents besides them.' ²³ His lord said to him, 'Well done, good and faithful servant; you have been faithful over a few things, I will make you ruler over many things. Enter into the joy of your lord.' ²⁴ "Then he who had received the one talent came and said, 'Lord, I knew you to be a hard man, reaping where you have not sown, and gathering where you have not scattered seed. ²⁵ And I was afraid, and went and hid your talent in the ground. Look, there you have what is yours.' ²⁶ "But his lord answered and said to him, 'You wicked and lazy servant, you knew that I reap where I have not sown, and gather where I have not scattered seed. ²⁷ So you ought to have deposited my money with the bankers, and at my coming, I would have received back my own with interest. ²⁸ Therefore take the talent from him, and give it to him who has ten talents. ²⁹ 'For to everyone who has, more will be given, and he will have abundance; but from him who does not have, even what he has will be taken away."

6. The Son of Man will judge the Nations. Matthew 25:31-46 "³¹ When the Son of Man comes in His glory, and all the holy angels with Him, then He will sit on the throne of His glory. ³² All the nations will be gathered before Him, and He will separate them one from another, as a shepherd divides his sheep from the goats. ³³ And He will set the sheep on His right hand, but the goats on the left. ³⁴ Then the King will say to those on His right hand, 'Come, you blessed of My Father, inherit the kingdom prepared for you from the foundation of the world; ³⁵ for I was hungry and you gave Me food; I was thirsty and you gave Me drink; I was a stranger and you took Me in; ³⁶ I was naked and you clothed Me; I was sick and you visited Me; I was in prison and you came to Me.' ³⁷ "Then the righteous will answer Him, saying, 'Lord, when did we see You hungry and feed You, or thirsty and give You drink? ³⁸ When did we see You a stranger and take You in, or naked and clothe You? ³⁹ Or when did we see You sick, or in

prison, and come to You?' ⁴⁰ And the King will answer and say to them, 'Assuredly, I say to you, inasmuch as you did it to one of the least of these My brethren, you did it to Me.' ⁴¹ "Then He will also say to those on the left hand, 'Depart from Me, you cursed, into the everlasting fire prepared for the devil and his angels: ⁴² for I was hungry and you gave Me no food; I was thirsty and you gave Me no drink; ⁴³ I was a stranger and you did not take Me in, naked and you did not clothe Me, sick and in prison and you did not visit Me.' ⁴⁴ "Then they also will answer Him, saying, 'Lord, when did we see You hungry or thirsty or a stranger or naked or sick or in prison, and did not minister to You?' ⁴⁵ Then He will answer them, saying, 'Assuredly, I say to you, inasmuch as you did not do it to one of the least of these, you did not do it to Me.' ⁴⁶ And these will go away into everlasting punishment, but the righteous into eternal life." The chief prophetic point here is in vs 32 where God will sit in judgment over the nations after He returns at the end of the Tribulation.

- Jesus is a covenant/promise keeper. In the first opening topic, why we should study prophecy, Jesus promised He would return. To be able to fulfill that promise of Jesus' birthright to being legitimate, a lawful conduit for God's plan was established by presenting Jesus within a NEW COVENANT. Jeremiah 31:31-33 "³¹ Behold, the days are coming, says the LORD, when I will make a NEW COVENANT with the house of Israel and with the house of Judah ³² not according to the covenant that I made with their fathers in the day that I took them by the hand to lead them out of the land of Egypt, My covenant which they broke, though I was a husband to them, says the LORD. ³³ But this is the covenant that I will make with the house of Israel after those days, says the LORD: I will put My law in their minds, and write it on their hearts, and I will be their God, and they shall be My people." At the evening meal the night before Passover, Jesus prophesied about His betrayal. Matthew 26:20-21 "²⁰ When evening had come, He sat down with the twelve. ²¹ Now as they were eating, He said, "Assuredly, I say to you, one of you will betray Me." He then instituted His NEW COVENANT sacrament, The Lord's Supper. Matthew 26:28 "For this is My blood of the new covenant, which is shed for many for the remission of sins." Luke 22:20 (NKJV) "Likewise He also took the cup after supper, saying, "This cup is the new covenant in My blood, which is shed for you." We traditionally remember His sacrifice and commandment when we celebrate this covenant the first Sunday of each month when we take the communion sacrament. 1 Corinthians 11:25 "In the same manner, He also took the cup after supper, saying, "This cup is the new covenant in My blood. This do, as often as you drink it, in remembrance of Me." This is the one covenant that believers can point to assure the plan of salvation for the forgiveness of sins. Ephesians 1:7 "In Him, we have redemption through His blood, the forgiveness of sins, according to the riches of His grace." Without this covenant, God is not obligated to uphold His word about anything. The symbolism of the wine in the cup is that this covenant is sealed in blood. A blood oath is the most sacred rite that lasts for life, in God's case forever. It comes out of the traditions of Judaism. The ritual mingles the essence of the two participating entities into one. The Bible also mentions a warning about a prerequisite for and judgment against abusing the sacredness of this sacrament. 1 Corinthians 11:27-29 "²⁷ Therefore whoever eats this bread or drinks this cup of the Lord in an unworthy manner will be guilty of the body and blood of the Lord. ²⁸ But let a man examine himself, and so let him eat of the bread and drink of the cup. ²⁹ For he who eats and drinks in an unworthy manner eats and drinks judgment to himself, not discerning the Lord's body." In essence, this means any person who is out of a relationship with Him is not allowed to take communion. The major differences between God's previous covenants and this covenant are;

- A. That it is not exclusive to the Jewish people it is free to all (Jew or Gentile) who ask. Matthew 10:40 (NKJV) "He who receives you receives Me, and he who receives Me receives Him who sent Me." Matthew 11:28 "Come unto me, all ye that labor and are heavy laden, and I will give you rest." It cannot be earned as it is a gift that can only be accepted. Luke 2:10 "Then the angel said to them, "Do not be afraid, for behold, I bring you good tidings of great joy which will be to ALL people." John 8:32 "And you shall know the truth, and the truth shall make you free." John 8:36 "Therefore if the Son makes you free, you shall be free indeed." Jesus bridges the Hebrew world with the gentile world.

- B. Paul reinforces and explains that one cannot acquire the gift of salvation by working for it or by being good enough. Romans 10:13 "For whosoever shall call upon the name of the LORD shall be saved."

Ephesians 2:1-5 (NIV) "¹ As for you, you were dead in your transgressions and sins, ² in which you used to live when you followed the ways of this world and of the ruler of the kingdom of the air, the spirit who is now at work in those who are disobedient. ³ All of us also lived among them at one time, gratifying the cravings of our flesh and following its desires and thoughts. Like the rest, we were by nature deserving of wrath. ⁴ But because of his great love for us, God, who is rich in mercy, ⁵ made us alive with Christ even when we were dead in transgressions—it is by grace you have been saved." Ephesians 2:8-9 "⁸ For by grace are ye saved through faith; and that not of yourselves: it is the gift of God: ⁹ Not of works, lest any man should boast." Galatians 2:15-16 "¹⁵ We who are Jews by nature, and not sinners of the Gentiles, ¹⁶ knowing that a man is not justified by the works of the law but by faith in Jesus Christ, even we have believed in Christ Jesus, that we might be justified by faith in Christ and not by the works of the law; for by the works of the law no flesh shall be justified." The attraction of Jesus' message was radically different in that it can only be acquired by acceptance and not adherence to the law. Jesus lived by example. He came to elevate and move beyond the original purpose of the Law. In other words, He wanted to remove the shackles of slavery by the misunderstanding the Law had become. A prime example is when the Pharisees plotted to trip Jesus up by His ministering to a sick man on the Sabbath. Mark 3:1-6 "¹ And He entered again into the synagogue; and there was a man there which had a withered hand. ² And they watched Him, whether He would heal him on the sabbath day; that they might accuse Him. ³ And he saith unto the man which had the withered hand, Stand forth. ⁴ And He saith unto them, "Is it lawful to do good on the sabbath days, or to do evil? to save life, or to kill?" But they held their peace. ⁵ And when He had looked round about on them with anger, being grieved for the hardness of their hearts, He saith unto the man, Stretch forth thine hand. And he stretched it out: and his hand was restored whole as the other. ⁶ And the Pharisees went forth, and straightway took counsel with the Herodians against him, how they might destroy Him."

C. It reaffirms and specifies the promise of life in heaven with God for eternity to Jew and non-Jew alike. John 3:16-17 "¹⁶ For God so loved the world that He gave His only begotten Son, that whosoever believeth in Him should not perish but have everlasting life. ¹⁷ For God sent not His Son into the world to condemn the world, but that the world through Him might be saved." John 5:24 "Most assuredly, I say to you, he who hears My word and believes in Him who sent Me has everlasting life, and shall not come into judgment, but has passed from death into life." John 10:28 (NKJV) "And I give them eternal life, and they shall never perish; neither shall anyone snatch them out of My hand." John 17:3-4 (NIV) "³ Now this is eternal life: that they know you, the only true God, and Jesus Christ, whom you have sent. ⁴ I have brought you glory on earth by finishing the work you gave me to do." He came to bring life. John 10:10 (NKJV) "The thief does not come except to steal, and to kill, and to destroy. I came that they may have life and have it abundantly."

D. Jesus declared He was the only avenue by which one can connect to God His Father. John 6:44 "No man can come to Me, except the Father which hath sent Me draw him: and I will raise him up at the last day." John 14:6 (NIV) "Jesus answered, "I am the way and the truth and the life. No one comes to the Father except through me." As we mentioned earlier Jesus' initial audience was primarily Jewish. As He gained notoriety He moved from teaching in temples to evangelizing in open air amphitheaters or fields. The Gospels also show that His message of love and grace resonated with not only the average Jew but also with the Gentiles. Luke 21:37-38 "³⁷ And in the day time He was teaching (to the Jews) in the temple, and at night He went out and abode in the mount of Olives. ³⁸ And all the people (Jew and Gentile) came early in the morning to Him in the temple to hear Him."

It should be noted here that there is a prophetic correlation between Jesus, the Feasts of the Lord, and what is to come. As we established earlier, God works in patterns and sets His own calendar. The logical understanding is if God revealed His plan by having Jesus fulfill the Messianic Lamb prophecies in the Spring Feasts, why wouldn't He do so again for the Fall Feasts? These fulfillments are sequential, in a specific order, and grouped together. The fulfillment of the Spring Feasts all happened in a three day period of the same week. Not one Feast on one year and another Feast in a second year. We must keep three things in mind as well look at the Feasts below. 1) As we discovered in the opening of the New Testament and Matthew, Jesus' ministry was to His fellow countrymen. The Feasts of the Lord were established for the Ancient Hebrews as a rehearsal for the rituals of worshipping God. All believers, Jews and Gentiles alike, will need to know them in the Millennium. This will be explained when we look at the four categories in the Millennium later on. 2) If indeed God truly wants us to know His plan, and He does, would He not make it so that we would be able to understand His plan in His word? 3) To truly grasp the progression, one must first understand that the Jewish orthodox day is from sundown to sundown. Events that transpire from dusk through the early morning and into the daylight hours are considered one day. The second day begins at sundown and repeats. God says what He means and means what He says. All that we need to know about His plan is in the Bible. We have had thousands of years to study, discern, and recognize God's word. Only until relatively recent times can we actually see the prophecies coming together. Daniel 12:4 "But thou, O Daniel, shut up the words, and seal the book, even to the time of the end: many shall run to and fro, and knowledge shall be increased." We will look at the signs more closely when we unpacked the Book of Revelation.

<u>Spring Feasts</u>

    🕎 Passover. Jesus was sacrificed on the cross as the Paschal Lamb on Passover. John 19:17-18 "¹⁷ And He bearing His cross went out to a place called the Place of a Skull, which is called in Hebrew, Golgotha. ¹⁸ Where they crucified Him, and two others with Him, one on either side and Jesus in the midst." Jesus and the Disciples were in Jerusalem for Passover because all men were required to come to Jerusalem as listed in the Spring Feast Days when we looked at them with Moses in Leviticus.

    🕎 Unleavened Bread. Jesus was wrapped and hidden away in the tomb. John 19:40 "Then they took the body of Jesus, and wound it in linen clothes with the spices, as the manner of the Jews is to bury." 1 Corinthians 5:7 "Purge out therefore the old leaven, that ye may be a new lump, as ye are unleavened. For even Christ our passover is sacrificed for us."

🕎 Offering of First Fruits. Jesus rose from the dead being the first fruits of blessing to all subsequent believers that die in the Lord. Matthew 28:5-6 (NIV) "5 The angel said to the women, "Do not be afraid, for I know that you are looking for Jesus, who was crucified. 6 He is not here; he has risen, just as he said. Come and see the place where he lay.""

🕎 Feast of Weeks /Pentecost. Like the God Himself coming down to earth after the Exodus, He reinforces the pattern by having the Holy Spirit arrive in a whirlwind of fire. Acts 2:1-3 "1 And when the day of Pentecost was fully come, they were all with one accord in one place. 2 And suddenly there came a sound from heaven as of a rushing mighty wind, and it filled all the house where they were sitting. 3 And there appeared unto them cloven tongues like as of fire, and it sat upon each of them."

Fall Feasts

🕎 Feast of Trumpets/Rosh Hashanah This Feast could have two purposes prophetically. The first could be either the Rapture of the church or the beginning of the Tribulation. 1 Corinthians 15:51-52 "51 Behold, I shew you a mystery; We shall not all sleep, but we shall all be changed, 52 In a moment, in the twinkling of an eye, at the last trump: for the trumpet shall sound, and the dead shall be raised incorruptible, and we shall be changed." 1 Thessalonians 4:16-17 "16 For the Lord Himself shall descend from heaven with a shout, with the voice of an archangel, and with the trump of God. And the dead in Christ will rise first. 17 Then we which are alive and remain shall be caught up together with them in the clouds to meet the Lord in the air. And so shall we ever be with the Lord." The text states that this coming will only be as far as the clouds and be quick. Faster than the blink of an eye or space of time between two heartbeats. The second appearing will require some time to have His angels announce and gather every eye. Matthew 24:31 "And He will send His angels with a great sound of a trumpet, and they will gather together His elect from the four winds, from one end of heaven to the other." Joel 2:1 "Blow ye the trumpet in Zion, and sound an alarm in My holy mountain! Let all the inhabitants of the land tremble; for the day of the LORD is coming, for it is nigh at hand." Bear in mind that this is the only Feast that puts an emphasis on the blowing of the shofar in a specific pattern as we learned earlier when we examined the Feasts of the Lord with Moses. The second could be when Christ arrives with His saints and angels at the end of the Tribulation, but does not actually touch the earth until the Day of Atonement. This would fit in the thought that all three Fall Feasts have to happen sequentially and together like the Spring Feasts. We will put the main differences side by side between the Rapture and the Second Coming further on in chapter 12 when we look at what's on the horizon for the church or the bride of Christ.

Day of Atonement/Yom Kippur. God established the pattern of His physically visiting the Hebrews in the Tabernacle and Temple. Furthermore, High Priests made petitions of Atonement on behalf of the people. The prophetic relevance the Second Coming is that when the Messiah does return He will actually place His foot on terra firma. Zechariah 14:4 "And His feet shall stand in that day upon the mount of Olives, which is before Jerusalem on the east, and the mount of Olives shall cleave in the midst thereof toward the east and toward the west, and there shall be a very great valley; and half of the mountain shall remove toward the north, and half of it toward the south." Jesus will intercede for us as High Priest. Hebrews 2:17 "Wherefore in all things it behoved Him to be made like unto His brethren, that He might be a merciful and faithful high priest in things pertaining to God, to make reconciliation for the sins of the people." We will explore Jesus' role as High Priest when we look at the millennium. This is also the day that the nations will be brought before God to be judged for their treatment of Israel. Joel 3:1-2 (NKJV) "¹ For behold, in those days and at that time, when I bring back the captives of Judah and Jerusalem, ² I will also gather all nations, and bring them down to the Valley of Jehoshaphat; and I will enter into judgment with them there on account of My people,

My heritage Israel, whom they have scattered among the nations; they have also divided up My land." God will place Jesus in the position of authority from where He will judge all humanity. Hebrews 10:12 "But this Man, after He had offered one sacrifice for sins forever, sat down at the right hand of God." Isaiah 11:4 "But with righteousness He shall judge the poor, and reprove with equity for the meek of the earth; and He shall strike the earth with the rod of His mouth, and with the breath of His lips He shall slay the wicked." Psalm 72:7 "In His days shall the righteous flourish, and the abundance of peace so long as the moon endureth."

🕎 Feast of Booths/Tabernacles. This is the beginning of the Millennium, which we will explore in detail later in chapter 21. Revelation 20:4 "And I saw thrones, and they sat upon them, and judgment was given unto them: and I saw the souls of them that were beheaded for the witness of Jesus, and for the word of God, and which had not worshipped the beast, neither his image, neither had received his mark upon their foreheads, or in their hands; and they lived and reigned with Christ a thousand years."

# Chapter 9

# "The Church"

We will now change the prophetic thread as we switch the focus of our discussion to the Gentiles and the specific missions of Peter and Paul. You may have noticed that a good portion of the Bible references used so far regarding the Jews have come from the Old Testament. It is a treasure trove of details about what is to come for the Jews if we take the time to investigate. Deuteronomy 4:29-30 "29 But if from thence thou shalt seek the LORD thy God, thou shalt find Him, if thou seek Him with all thy heart and with all thy soul. 30 When thou art in tribulation, and all these things are come upon thee, even in the latter days, if thou turn to the LORD thy God, and shalt be obedient unto His voice." However, the New Testament was written to encourage both the new Jewish and Gentile converts, which will become known as the "church." The Gospels and first chapter of Acts detail first hand witness accounts of Jesus and His mission. Jesus came to seek and save the lost, regardless of heritage. Luke 19:9-10 "9 And Jesus said unto him, "This day is salvation come to this house, forsomuch, as he also is a son of Abraham. 10 For the Son of Man is come to seek and to save that which was lost." He came to fulfill the scriptures of the Old Testament as Messiah while at the same time launching His mission to the world. Matthew 5:17 (NIV) "Do not think that I have come to abolish the Law or the Prophets; I have not come to abolish them but to fulfill them." Mark 1:14-15 "14 Now after that John (the Baptist) was put in prison, Jesus came into Galilee, preaching the gospel of the kingdom of God, 15 and saying, "the time is fulfilled, and the kingdom of God is at hand. Repent ye, and believe in the gospel."

At the beginning of this narrative, we mentioned how Christianity's existence was dependent on Judaism. The question here is, "Is there a connection between the Jews and the church?" The answer, according to Paul, is yes. Paul said that God has not and will not go back on His word with the Hebrews. The Israelites were not cut out of God's promise of ownership of the land. Abraham's Covenant still stands. Romans 11:1-2a (NIV) "1I ask then: Did God reject his people? By no means! I am an Israelite myself, a descendant of

Abraham, from the tribe of Benjamin. ² God did not reject his people, whom he foreknew." Furthermore, in Romans 11:25 (NIV) "I do not want you to be ignorant of this mystery, brothers and sisters, so that you may not be conceited: Israel has experienced a hardening in part until the full number of the Gentiles has come in," clearly implies that when "the fullness of the Gentiles" is fulfilled, the eyes of His chosen people will be opened and they will see Him as their Messiah. Therefore, we Gentiles should not expect God to replace or substitute the church as His chosen people in His plan. God does have a separate purpose and relationship planned for us (the church) which leads us to the second part of the answer. The gentiles are to provoke the Jews to jealousy so they will ignite a loving one on one relationship attitude toward God, which God has desired all along, not just a ritualistic exchange or rule of law constricting relationship. Romans 11:11-14 (NIV) "¹¹ Again I ask: Did they stumble so as to fall beyond recovery? Not at all! Rather, because of their transgression, salvation has come to the Gentiles to make Israel envious. ¹² But if their transgression means riches for the world, and their loss means riches for the Gentiles, how much greater riches will their full inclusion bring! ¹³ I am talking to you Gentiles. Inasmuch as I am the apostle to the Gentiles, I take pride in my ministry ¹⁴ in the hope that I may somehow arouse my own people to envy and save some of them."

To properly understand where we are going, it is imperative we understand from where we started. The New Testament is replete with stories of men spreading the Gospel of Jesus, even though they occasionally stumbled along the way. Peter and Paul are at the top of the list. God still used them, flawed as they were, to bring glory to Himself and spread His message.

He charged Peter to minister to his fellow Jews. Matthew 10:5-6 "⁵ These twelve Jesus sent forth, and commanded them, saying, "Go not into the way of the Gentiles, and into any city of the Samaritans enter ye not: ⁶ But go rather to the lost sheep of the house of Israel." Peter was a simple fisherman, and he was the first disciple Jesus called. Matthew 4:18-20 (NKJV) "¹⁸ And Jesus, walking by the Sea of Galilee, saw two brothers, Simon called Peter, and Andrew his brother, casting a net into the sea; for they were fishermen. ¹⁹ Then He said to them, "Follow Me, and I will make you fishers of men." ²⁰ They immediately left their nets and followed Him." Peter also had a special, unique relationship with Jesus. Peter was one of Jesus' inner circle made up of Peter, James, and John. Mark 9:2 "And after six days Jesus taketh with him Peter, and James, and John, and leadeth them up into an high mountain apart by themselves: and he was transfigured before them." Peter showed his tendency to be impulsive when he jumped out of the boat the disciples were in during a storm. As we all know, Peter began to sink when he took his focus off Jesus and looked at his surroundings. Matthew 14:28-31 (NIV) 28 "Lord, if it's you," Peter replied, "tell me to come to you on the water." 29 "Come," he said. Then Peter got down out of the boat, walked on the water and came toward Jesus. 30 But when he saw the wind, he was afraid and, beginning to sink, cried out, "Lord, save me!" 31 Immediately Jesus reached out his hand and caught him. "You of little faith," he said, "why did you doubt?"

Peter was first to recognize Jesus as Messiah through anointing from God directly. Because of this, Peter was the first pastor or missionary to the first church or body of believers. Jesus ordained Peter to build His church. Matthew 16:13-18 (NKJV) "13 When Jesus came into the region of Caesarea Philippi, He asked His disciples, saying, "Who do men say that I, the Son of Man, am ?" 14 So they said, "Some say John the Baptist, some Elijah, and others Jeremiah or one of the prophets." 15 He said to them, "But who do you say that I am?" 16 Simon Peter answered and said, "You are the Christ, the Son of the living God." 17 Jesus answered and said to him, "Blessed are you, Simon Bar-Jonah, for flesh and blood has not revealed this to you, but My Father who is in heaven. 18 And I also say to you that you are Peter, and on this rock, I will build My church, and the gates of Hades shall not prevail against it."

As a precursor to the next point about the specific commission for Peter, Jesus refers to Himself as the Good Shepherd. John 10:11 (NKJV) "I am the good shepherd. The good shepherd gives His life for the sheep." Jesus also says His sheep, referring to believers and in Matthew 10:6 above, will know His voice. John 10:27 (NKJV) "My sheep hear My voice, and I know them, and they follow Me." 1 Peter 2:25 "For ye were as sheep going astray; but are now returned unto the Shepherd and Bishop of your souls." Isaiah 53:5-6 "5 But He was wounded for our transgressions, He was bruised for our iniquities; the chastisement for our peace was upon Him, and by His stripes, we are healed. 6 All we like sheep have gone astray; we have turned, every one, to his own way. And the LORD hath laid on Him the iniquity of us all." Peter's equipping for his mission call is complete by the following interaction. John 21:15-17 (NIV) "15 When they had finished eating, Jesus said to Simon Peter, "Simon son of John, do you love me more than these?" "Yes, Lord," he said, "you know that I love you." Jesus said, "Feed my lambs." 16 Again Jesus said, "Simon son of John, do you love me?" He answered, "Yes, Lord, you know that I love you." Jesus said, "Take care of my sheep." 17 The third time he said to him, "Simon son of John, do you love me?" Peter was annoyed because Jesus asked him the third time, "Do you love me?" He said, "Lord, you know all things; you know that I love you." Jesus said, "Feed my sheep."

After Peter's declaration, Jesus asked the twelve to keep His identity to themselves. Matthew 16:20 (NIV) "Then He ordered his disciples not to tell anyone that He was the Messiah."

Peter failed Jesus. Mark 14:66-72 (NIV) "⁶⁶ While Peter was below in the courtyard, one of the servant girls of the high priest came by. ⁶⁷ When she saw Peter warming himself, she looked closely at him. "You also were with that Nazarene, Jesus," she said. ⁶⁸ But he denied it. "I don't know or understand what you're talking about," he said, and went out into the entryway. ⁶⁹ When the servant girl saw him there, she said again to those standing around, "This fellow is one of them." ⁷⁰ Again he denied it. After a little while, those standing near said to Peter, "Surely you are one of them, for you are a Galilean." ⁷¹ He began to call down curses, and he swore to them, "I don't know this man you're talking about." ⁷² Immediately the rooster crowed the second time. Then Peter remembered the word Jesus had spoken to him: "Before the rooster crows twice you will disown me three times." And he broke down and wept." As a gesture of redemption, Peter was the only disciple called by name after Jesus' resurrection even after Peter's failure the night of Jesus' trial. Mark 16:7 (NLT) "Now go and tell his disciples, including Peter, that Jesus is going ahead of you to Galilee. You will see him there, just as he told you before he died."

Peter was present at the beginning of the church. Acts 2:1-4 "¹And when the day of Pentecost was fully come, they were all with one accord in one place. ² And suddenly there came a sound from heaven as of a rushing mighty wind, and it filled all the house where they were sitting. ³ And there appeared unto them cloven tongues like as of fire, and it sat upon each of them. ⁴ And they were all filled with the Holy Ghost, and began to speak with other tongues, as the Spirit gave them utterance." Peter also had the first large scale baptismal service after Jesus ascended to heaven after His resurrection where he preached and over three thousand souls were saved. Acts 2:41 (NIV) "Those who accepted his message were baptized, and about three thousand were added to their number that day."

To be clear, Peter's primary listeners were his fellow Jews but they were not exclusively. 1 Peter 2:9-10 "⁹But ye are a chosen generation, a royal priesthood, an holy nation, a peculiar people; that ye should shew forth the praises of him who hath called you out of darkness into his marvellous light; ¹⁰ Which in time past were not a people, but are now the people of God: which had not obtained mercy, but now have obtained mercy." Peter also preached to the uncircumcised Gentiles. It caused a little friction with Peter's supporters. Peter admonished them to put their dispute aside. 1 Peter 3:8 (NKJV) "Finally, all of you be of one mind, having compassion for one another; love as brothers, be tenderhearted, be courteous." Acts 10:44-48 (NIV) "44 While Peter was still speaking these words, the Holy Spirit came on all who heard the message. 45 The circumcised believers who had come with Peter were astonished that the gift of the Holy Spirit had been poured out even on Gentiles. 46 For they heard them speaking in tongues and praising God. Then Peter said, 47 "Surely no one can stand in the way of their being baptized with water. They have received the Holy Spirit just as we have." 48 So he ordered that they be baptized in the name of Jesus Christ. Then they asked Peter to stay with them for a few days." The Holy Spirit was poured out on those, Jew or Gentile, who claimed Jesus as Lord and quickly spread throughout the known world for the next several hundred years. Peter can be considered one of the first, if not the first, "Christian" even though that term was not coined until Barnabas and Paul did so later. Acts 11:26 "And when he had found him, he brought him unto Antioch. And it came to pass, that a whole year they assembled themselves with the church, and taught much people. And the disciples were called Christians first in Antioch."

Paul was recruited to reach out to the Gentiles. Galatians 2:8 (NIV) "For God, who was at work in Peter as an apostle to the circumcised, was also at work in me as an apostle to the Gentiles." He was well educated as he was part of the religious ruling class known as the Pharisees. Acts 23:6 "But when Paul perceived that one part were Sadducees and the other Pharisees, he cried out in the council, "Men and brethren, I am a Pharisee, the son of a Pharisee; of the hope and resurrection of the dead I am called in question." According to the author of Acts, Luke, Paul acknowledged himself as a zealot. Acts 22:3-5 (NKJV) "3 I am indeed a Jew, born in Tarsus of Cilicia, but brought up in this city at the feet of Gamaliel, taught according to the strictness of our fathers' law, and was zealous toward God as you all are today. 4 I persecuted this way to the death, binding and delivering into prisons both men and women. 5 As also the high priest bears me witness, and all the council of the elders, from whom I also received letters to the brethren, and went to Damascus to bring in chains even those who were there to Jerusalem to be punished." The conversion of Saul the persecutor to Paul the Apostle to the Gentiles is introduced in Acts 9:3-5 (NIV) "3 As he neared Damascus on his journey, suddenly a light from heaven flashed around him. 4 He fell to the ground and heard a voice say to him, "Saul, Saul, why do you persecute me?" 5 "Who are you, Lord?" Saul asked. "I am Jesus, whom you are persecuting," he replied." God specifically sought Saul out. Acts 26:15-18 (NKJV) "15 So I (Paul) said, 'Who are You, Lord?' And He said, 'I am Jesus, whom you are persecuting. 16 But rise and stand on your feet; for I have appeared to you for this purpose, to make you a minister and a witness both of the things which you have seen and of the things which I will yet reveal to you. ¹⁷ I will deliver you from the Jewish people, as well as from the Gentiles, to whom I now send you, ¹⁸ to open their eyes, in order to turn them from darkness to light, and from the power of Satan to God, that they may receive forgiveness of sins and an inheritance among those who are sanctified by faith in Me.' Acts 26:22-23 "²² Having therefore obtained help of God, I continue unto this day, witnessing both to small and great, saying none other things than those which the prophets and Moses did say should come: ²³ That Christ should suffer, and that He should be the first that should rise from the dead, and should shew light unto the people, and to the Gentiles." After Saul's conversion, he referred to himself as Paul and in several letters as an apostle like in Romans 1:1-2 (NIV) "¹Paul, a servant of Christ Jesus, called to be an apostle and set apart for the gospel of God ² the gospel he promised beforehand through his prophets in the Holy Scriptures." 1 Timothy 1:1 "Paul, an apostle of Jesus Christ, by the commandment of God our Savior and the Lord Jesus Christ which is our hope." 1 Timothy 2:7 (CEB) "I was appointed to be a preacher and apostle of this testimony—I'm telling the truth and I'm not lying! I'm a teacher of the Gentiles in faith and truth." The "Holy Scriptures" Paul (as all Jews in his time did) refers to in Romans 1:2 are the Torah, Psalm and Proverbs, and writings of the prophets. We now refer to them as the Old Testament. At this point in time the New Testament had not yet been written. Paul penned most of the New Testament as personal letters of encouragement to the early churches which were in Asia Minor either on one of his four missionary journeys or in prison. There are a few short letters by James, Peter, and John before the Book of Revelation closes out the end of the Bible.

As we saw above with Peter, from time to time he had to struggle with his Jewish supporters questioning the uncircumcised gentiles converting to their new faith system. Paul did not have that issue. As a converted Jewish believer himself, he understood that Christ's message was open to everyone. Romans 1:16-17 "¹⁶ For I am not ashamed of the gospel of Christ, for it is the power of God unto salvation for everyone that believeth, to the Jew first and also to the Greek. ¹⁷ For therein is the righteousness of God revealed from faith to faith; as it is written, "The just shall live by faith." Paul understood that his own salvation was a result of God's grace extended toward him and not as a result of anything he could have done or deserved. 1 Timothy 1:14-15 (NIV) "¹⁴ The grace of our Lord was poured out on me abundantly, along with the faith and love that are in Christ Jesus. ¹⁵ Here is a trustworthy saying that deserves full acceptance: Christ Jesus came into the world to save sinners of whom I am the worst." We also addressed the topic of the Gentiles provoking the Jews to jealousy when we spoke of Christianity's existence being dependent on Judaism. Both Peter's and Paul's missions dovetailed and laid the foundation for the formation of the "church." This melding was the genesis of the body of believers that would become known as the church. The non-Jewish converts grew under Paul and they soon outpaced the Jewish converts because the Holy Spirit ignited a fire in them. It didn't help that the Jewish state was broken apart and sent into exile.

Peter and Paul are the Founding Fathers of the "One Holy Catholic (universal) and Apostolic (of the Apostles) Church." Remember that the New Testament was written in the common language of the day, Koine Greek. The noun the "church" is Strong's #G1577 "ekklēsia." In Greek, nouns, like in some other languages, are designated by gender. In this case, it is classified in the feminine. English does not classify its parts of speech as it is gender neutral. This classification reinforces the supposition that church is referred to as the Bride of Christ. In addition, Paul writes in 2 Corinthians 11:2 "For I am jealous over you with godly jealousy. For I have espoused you to one husband, that I may present you as a chaste virgin (as a bride) to Christ." Ephesians 5:23-24 "23 For the husband is head of the wife, even as Christ is head of the church; and He is the Savior of the body. 24 Therefore, as the church is subject unto Christ, so let the wives be to their own husbands in everything." Revelation 21:9 "And there came unto me one of the seven angels which had the seven vials full of the seven last plagues, and talked with me, saying, "Come hither, I will shew thee the bride, the Lamb's wife."

Here is an abridged version of church history. After the initial ministries of Peter, Paul, and the other Apostles the new religion "Christianity" struggled to survive as they were persecuted and treated violently from the beginning. All of the disciples, except for John the Apostle or as he was also known as John the Revelator, were martyred. John was exiled to Patmos where it is believed to be when he wrote the Book of Revelation about 90-95 AD. The church consisted of converted Jews and Gentiles including Greeks. In 313 AD, the Roman Emperor Constantine ceased the open persecution of Christianity and eventually embraced it as the state religion. This decree opened the door for the flourishing of the new religion, which now ws spoken and written in Latin. However, there was still much in fighting for internal politics for leadership, doctrinal questions, and other liturgical issues. From 325-787 AD, the Seven Ecumenical Councils convened to debate a great many theological issues, rites, canons, and sacraments, and, as we explored in Bible history earlier, which specific writings were to be placed in the Bible. Over time, many other councils convened with the last one in 1962-1965. In 1054, a split happened where the Roman Catholic sect became known as the western church and the Greek Orthodox sect retained the name of the Eastern Church (as envisioned as the legs of iron in Daniel chapter 2). In 1517, Martin Luther nailed his 95 theses which launched the Reformation.

Shortly after that, The Anglican Protestant church (where from a great many denominations were derived including Baptists) was created under Henry VIII in 1532. Over the next few centuries, different Protestant denominations broke away from the rigid hierarchal Roman Catholic Church. This time period, from the first century (beginning at Pentecost) to now, is known as the Church Age. Paul calls it when we were talking about deciphering the mysteries of prophecy, "the Dispensation of Grace." Ephesians 3:2 "If ye have heard of the dispensation of the grace of God which is given me to you-ward." The Church Age coincided and was overlaid with the time of the Gentiles period referenced above referring to gentile rule over Israel and Jerusalem. Church scholars classify the seven churches listed in Revelation 2 and 3 into seven eras of the church in history. The below list compares the two.

|   | chapter | city | Church Type | AD | Historical Era |
|---|---------|------|-------------|----|----------------|
| 1 | Rev 2:1-7 | Ephesus | The Loveless Church | 33-100 | Apostolic Church |
| 2 | Rev 2:8-11 | Smyrna | The Persecuted Church | 100-313 | Roman Persecuted Church |
| 3 | Rev 2:12-17 | Pergamos | The Compromising Church | 313-538 | Compromising Church |
| 4 | Rev 2:18-29 | Thyatira | The Corrupt Church | 538-1517 | Corrupt Church |
| 5 | Rev 3:1-6 | Sardis | The Dead Church | 1517-1755 | Reformation Chur |
| 6 | Rev 3:7-13 | Philadelphia | The Faithful Church | 1755-1844 | Missionary Mover |
| 7 | Rev 3:14-22 | Laodicea | The Lukewarm Church | 1844-present | Apostasy Church |

We looked at the seven eras of the Church Age above, the question of "do today's churches seem to represent the idea of the Laodicean lukewarm church?" I think a case can be argued that yes, they do. There are more concerned with offending man than offending God, and with traditional mainstream church attendance in decline, the "feel good" brand of Christianity is taking hold rather than living by conviction and repentance. Jesus Himself said in Matthew 10:32-33 "32 Therefore whoever confesses Me before men, him I will also confess before My Father who is in heaven. 33 But whoever denies Me before men, him I will also deny before My Father who is in heaven."

# Chapter 10

# "The Warning Signs"

Moving to our next thread, now we can look at what Peter and Paul say about what prophetic signs to keep a watch for at the end of days. When we looked at The Olivet Discourse above, we saw both physical signs and the moral state of man being in decline. Peter and Paul reinforce the latter thought and cite specific conditions concerning the attitudes of society just before Christ's return. Peter writes in 2 Peter 3:3-4 "3 Knowing this first, that there shall come in the last days scoffers, walking after their own lusts, 4 and saying, where is the promise of his coming? for since the fathers fell asleep, all things continue as they were from the beginning of the creation." Peter also talks about Jesus' return as a thief in the night, referring to those who do not study prophecy will be caught unawares or by surprise. 2 Peter 3:10-13 "10 But the day of the Lord will come as a thief in the night; in the which the heavens shall pass away with a great noise, and the elements shall melt with fervent heat, the earth also and the works that are therein shall be burned up. 11 Seeing then that all these things shall be dissolved, what manner of persons ought ye to be in all holy conversation and godliness, 12 Looking for and hasting unto the coming of the day of God, wherein the heavens being on fire shall be dissolved, and the elements shall melt with fervent heat? 13 Nevertheless we, according to his promise, look for new heavens and a new earth, wherein dwelleth righteousness." This thought about the earth dissolving by fire is reinforced by John in Revelation 21:1 "And I saw a new heaven and a new earth, for the first heaven and the first earth were passed away. And there was no more sea." Peter also warns against those who manipulate, alter or otherwise reshape the Bible to suit their own agenda. 2 Peter 3:14-16 (NIV) "14 So then, dear friends, since you are looking forward to this, make every effort to be found spotless, blameless and at peace with him. 15 Bear in mind that our Lord's patience means salvation, just as our dear brother Paul also wrote you with the wisdom that God gave him. 16 He writes the same way in all his letters, speaking in them of these matters. His letters contain some things that are hard to understand, which ignorant and unstable people distort, as they do the other Scriptures, to their own destruction."

Paul's warning list is a little longer. 2 Timothy 3:1-9 (NKJV) "¹But know this, that in the last days perilous times will come: ² For men will be lovers of themselves, lovers of money, boasters, proud, blasphemers, disobedient to parents, unthankful, unholy, ³ unloving, unforgiving, slanderers, without self-control, brutal, despisers of good, ⁴ traitors, headstrong, haughty, lovers of pleasure rather than lovers of God, ⁵ having a form of godliness but denying its power. And from such people turn away! ⁶ For of this sort are those who creep into households and make captives of gullible women loaded down with sins, led away by various lusts, ⁷ always learning and never able to come to the knowledge of the truth. ⁸ Now as Jannes and Jambres resisted Moses, so do these also resist the truth: men of corrupt minds, disapproved concerning the faith; ⁹ but they will progress no further, for their folly will be manifest to all, as theirs also was." If we look at the state of society, it is safe to say the conditions described are spot on for the world today. The foundation of any society is the family unit of one mother and one father. That has been radically altered. How many grandparents are raising a second generation of children because one or both parents are absentees for one reason or another? If the child is lucky enough, to have both parents in the home, married or not, both adults need to have full-time jobs to be able to pay for expenses. It used to be one parent, usually the father, worked outside the home while the other, usually the mother, stayed home to raise the children because the one salary was sufficient to carry the load. Not so today. Both parents need to work at least 40 hours, if not more, to be able to afford the necessities of life. Not to mention that in year's past families had 4-5 children or more as opposed to the 2-3 today.

People have fallen prey to the spirit of deception that Jesus warned against. Currently, there are many reasons people do not contemplate their eternal soul with regards to Christ. They are too involved in a great many distractions or diversions. A bunch of white noise if you will. Furthermore, lack of civility and respect toward one another are rampant. People are being demonized because they have an opposite opinion instead of acknowledging that the person on the other side of the argument has as much right to their opinion as you have to yours. There are loud angry visceral voices on both sides. The church used to be the center of attention for society. Now it's just one of several events that happen on the weekend and not even a priority. There is no sense of urgency. People seem to act as though they believe either they will not be held accountable for their sins or maybe there is always time later to make a decision for Christ. You might know of John Lennon's song "Imagine." It starts with the lyric, "Imagine there is no heaven or hell. No religion too." How bleak would life be if that were true. The first observation Romans 1:28-

32 "28 And even as they did not like to retain God in their knowledge, God gave them over to a reprobate mind, to do those things which are not convenient; 29 Being filled with all unrighteousness, fornication, wickedness, covetousness, maliciousness; full of envy, murder, debate, deceit, malignity; whisperers, 30 Backbiters, haters of God, despiteful, proud, boasters, inventors of evil things, disobedient to parents, 31 Without understanding, covenant breakers, without natural affection, implacable, unmerciful: 32 Who knowing the judgment of God, that they which commit such things are worthy of death, not only do the same, but have pleasure in them that do them." Does this sound like today's society? The second observation, when one begins life's journey the outlook is ahead and the attitude is invulnerable, immortal, and invincible. It's not until one has a few years life experience do they realize just how fragile, unpredictable, and precarious life can be. Jesus said in Luke 12:19-20 (NKJV) "19 And I will say to my soul, "Soul, you have many goods laid up for many years; take your ease; eat, drink, and be merry.'" 20 But God said to him, 'Fool! This night your soul will be required of you; then whose will those things be which you have provided?" With the number of high profile celebrity deaths, the indiscriminate randomness of mass killings across the world, the exploding opioid epidemic, and people dying at the hands of other men shows that none of us knows when our last day on earth will be. How many of them kissed their loved ones' goodbye as they left for their daily routine expecting to return but didn't. My first thought when these situations are reported is I hope for their sake they made peace with God. I wonder how many are surprised at the first thing they encounter in the next life is that they wake up in heaven or hell. They will either be in the arms of Jesus, or sadly, they will realize too late the folly of putting off thinking about their eternal soul. The unintended consequence of putting off taking the time to consider Christ's gift is eternal separation from Him. Once you die, there is no failsafe second chance at redemption or do over. Psalm 103:15-18 "15 As for man, his days are like grass; as a flower of the field, so he flourisheth. 16 For the wind passeth over it, and it is gone, and its place thereof shall know it no more. 17 But the mercy of the LORD is from everlasting to everlasting upon them that fear Him, and His righteousness unto children's children. 18 To such as keep His covenant, and to those who remember His commandments to do them." 1 Peter 1:22-24 "22 Seeing ye have purified your souls in obeying the truth through the Spirit unto unfeigned love of the brethren, see that ye love one another with a pure heart fervently: 23 Being born again, not of corruptible seed, but of incorruptible, by the word of God, which liveth and abideth for ever. 24 For all flesh is as grass, and all the glory of man as the flower of grass. The grass withereth, and the flower thereof falleth away." We are reminded once again that our time on earth is not only short

but also unpredictable. Time is a commodity that can never be renewed. We will look at what happens at death a little further on.

As bad as it is now it's nothing compared to how it's going to be in the Tribulation, which could be liked to craziness on steroids. As mentioned before, do some people think that if the Tribulation comes, they can always make a decision for Christ then. Well, they are playing against a stacked deck. There will be severe environmental global calamities or physical plague level afflictions, let alone the purges that will come from the Antichrist. There will be devastating consequences for the population of those left behind after the rapture and living during the Tribulation with day to day living. Paul expresses this condition as the earth groaning. Romans 8:22 (NIV) "We know that the whole creation has been groaning as in the pains of childbirth right up to the present time." As it's already been expressed the thought of people thinking they will have a second chance for salvation during the Tribulation, but what if they never get that chance? There are 3 points which we need to be aware that will take place in the first half of the Tribulation. 1) A quarter of the population will perish. Revelation 6:8 "And I looked, and behold a pale horse: and his name that sat on him was Death, and Hell followed with him. And power was given unto them over the fourth part of the earth, to kill with sword, and with hunger, and with death, and with the beasts of the earth." 2) The devastation will be so great men call out to the rocks to kill them, but God does not allow it. Revelation 9:6 "And in those days shall men seek death, and shall not find it; and shall desire to die, and death shall flee from them." 3) An additional third of those survivors will also perish. Revelation 9:15 "And the four angels were loosed, which were prepared for an hour, and a day, and a month, and a year, for to slay the third part of men." Just to give an idea of what these numbers mean if the Tribulation were to start today there are approximately 7.5 billion people in the world. According to the Pew Research Center's December 19, 2011, the number of people that self-identify as Christian is 32 % or 2.4 billion. If the Rapture were to happen and every self-claimed Christian were taken it would leave 5.1 billion people on earth. From there a quarter of those left (1.275) would be dead and leave 3.825 billion. A third of those (1.275) dead would leave a total of 2.55 billion. That's over half of the world population erased from the earth with in a relatively short period of time. These occur during the first half of the Tribulation and before the mid-point. The odds are not in favor of survival.

# Chapter 11

# "Be Not Deceived"

Faith is defined as trusting in God that He will do what He said He would do. Some people do not have faith because they are being deceived that their finite human mind can comprehend what the infinite mind of God created. Consequently, when they cannot understand something, they say there is no God, or it's God fault about whatever tragedy happened. Ironically, few people understand the process and the mechanics of an engine starting when the key is turned, yet they have more faith in that the engine will start than they do about trusting their futures and lives in the hands of the creator.

Dr. David Reagan explains that there are three primary areas of deception that Jesus, Peter, and Paul's lists fall under namely materialism, humanism, and hedonism.

- Materialism is the belief that fulfillment or joy can be found, bought or otherwise obtained from the accumulation of inanimate tangible objects. There is a popular bumper sticker that said "he who dies with the most toys wins!", which is the polar opposite of Jesus' message found in Mark 8:36 "For what will it profit a man, if he shall gain the whole world, and loses his own soul?" The allure of working towards the capture of a prize will ring hollow once it is achieved since those inanimate things offer no reciprocal sense of love. Then, it's on to the next shiny bauble. Matthew 6:19-21 "19 Lay not up for yourselves treasures upon earth, where moth and rust doth corrupt, and where thieves break through and steal: 20 But lay up for yourselves treasures in heaven, where neither moth nor rust doth corrupt, and where thieves do not break through nor steal:21 For where your treasure is, there will your heart be also." It's not a sin to have money, but it is a sin to lust or make it the god of your life. 1 Timothy 6:10 (NKJV) "For the love of money is a root of all kinds of evil, for which some have strayed from the faith in their greediness, and pierced themselves through with many sorrows." Matthew 6:24 "No one can serve two masters; for either he will hate the one, and love the other, or else he will hold to the one, and despise the other. Ye cannot serve God and mammon." "Mammon," according to Strong's #G3126, the word *"mamōnas"* means love of money in English. Luke 12:15 (NIV) "Then he said to them, "Watch out! Be on your guard against all kinds of greed; life does not consist in an abundance of possessions." The sense of fulfillment or joy can only be found in the source of love, God the Father Himself, and by extension, His Son Jesus Christ. John 15:9-11 (NKJV) "9 As the Father loved Me, I also have loved you; abide in My love. 10 If you keep My commandments, you will abide in My love, just as I have kept My Father's commandments and abide in His love. 11 "These things I have spoken to you, that My joy may remain in you, and that your joy may be full." John 16:33 "These things I have spoken to you, that in Me ye might have peace. In the world ye shall have tribulation, but be of good cheer, I have overcome the world."

- Humanism is the belief that mankind alone can solve any problem if we work hard or long enough for it. Atheism and Agnosticism fall under this category. King David warns us in Psalm 14:1 "The fool has said in his heart, "There is no God." They are corrupt, they have done abominable works, there is none that doeth good." We do not realize that sooner or later there are so many things we cannot control, especially when one gains a few years of life experience. We cannot control what happens to us, but we can control how we react. The 19th century philosopher Friedrich Nietzsche made the claim that "God is dead." He died in 1900 and let me assure you, he knows now that God certainly is not dead. Self-deception is included in this category. It is in our nature to deceive ourselves into thinking that we can hide anything from God. Jeremiah 17:9 "The heart is deceitful above all things, and desperately wicked; who can know it?" God can! There are a few ideas that are now commonly accepted but are biblically contradictory. In no particular order, God is known by many different names. Some say that Allah and Yahweh/Jehovah are the same God, sometimes referred to as Chrislam. Another is God is a God of love only, He really doesn't mean it when He says He will judge me. Still another, a prominent tv host has mistakenly announced that there are many paths to God where Jesus clearly said when we looked the new covenant, He is the ONLY way to God. John 14:6 (NIV) "Jesus answered, "I am the way and the truth and the life. No one comes to the Father except through me." Isaiah 19:3 (NKJV) "The spirit of Egypt will fail in its midst; I will destroy their counsel, and they will consult the idols and the charmers, the mediums, and the sorcerers." Ideas like psychics or mediums, palm readers, astrology, crystal power, the mother earth goddess, karma, fate, or chance are all types of false religions. Satan has deceived many others by planting thoughts like heaven and hell do not exist. All of these concepts are paving the way for acceptance of a one world religion and false prophet. 1 John 4:1 (NIV) "Dear friends, do not believe every spirit, but test the spirits to see whether they are from God, because many false prophets have gone out into the world." Before the dam bursts, it starts with a trickle, then a crack, then destruction.

- Hedonism is the outlook of anything that feels good goes, so long as it doesn't hurt anybody else. It's a belief system that is based on feelings, in particular pleasure, which, as we all know, are unreliable and undependable, particularly in times of crisis, can change dramatically. It's the love of the pleasures of the flesh. Galatians 5:19-21 "[19] Now the works of the flesh are manifest, which are these; Adultery, fornication, uncleanness, lasciviousness, [20] Idolatry, witchcraft, hatred, variance, emulations, wrath, strife, seditions, heresies, [21] Envyings, murders, drunkenness, revellings, and such like: of the which I tell you before, as I have also told you in time past, that they which do such things shall not inherit the kingdom of God." Having a knowledge of God but not letting His teachings affect one's thought or behavior is another track in this category. Having a sense of spiritualism but not a relationship. It's living by a moral code rather than being transformed by the word of God. True Christianity is based on one recognizing that he/she is a sinner and that only through confession comes forgiveness and through forgiveness comes redemption. Making a resolute choice and being dependent on the strength of God's word rather than our weak imperfections. Hebrews 11:1 "Now faith is the substance of things hoped for, the evidence of things not seen." We walk by knowledge and trust in God's word over feelings. Paul says it this way. 2 Corinthians 5:7 "For we walk by faith, not by sight." I like to think of true happiness or joy is as a glass of water. The water symbolizes our happiness or joy. God's law is like the glass in that it gives us a solid form in which can hold our happiness or joy. When filled we are surrounded by His strength. Without the glass, it is formless and slips through our fingers.

The deception of denial of His existence and attempts to displace God from His throne is working its way into the general population and churches across the world. There are some churches that preach a message of things other than the Gospel of Jesus' death and resurrection to pay for the forgiveness of sins and of His return. Paul warned us of them in 2 Timothy 4:3-4 (NIV) "3 For the time will come when people will not put up with sound doctrine. Instead, to suit their own desires, they will gather around them a great number of teachers to say what their itching ears want to hear. 4 They will turn their ears away from the truth and turn aside to myths." 1 Timothy 6:20-21 (NIV) "20 Timothy, guard what has been entrusted to your care. Turn away from godless chatter and the opposing ideas of what is falsely called knowledge, 21 which some have professed and in so doing have departed from the faith. Grace be with you all." Additionally, Paul wrote about A Great Falling Away or Apostasy that must take place before Christ returns. 2 Thessalonians 2:1-4 "1 Now we beseech you, brethren, by the coming of our Lord Jesus Christ, and by our gathering together unto him, 2 That ye be not soon shaken in mind, or be troubled, neither by spirit, nor by word, nor by letter as from us, as that the day of Christ is at hand. 3 Let no man deceive you by any means: for that day shall not come, except there come a falling away first, and that man of sin be revealed, the son of perdition; 4 Who opposeth and exalteth himself above all that is called God, or that is worshipped; so that he as God sitteth in the temple of God, shewing himself that he is God." The original word for "falling away" in Greek is Strong's #G646 "apostasia" or Anglicized Apostasy. This point is on our chart. The definition of Apostasy is not just falling way but also a defection. Satan's influence in the church is both subtle and blatant. When he is subtle, things like promoting unsound doctrine or practices expressly forbidden by God worms its way into a church. Satan's tempting of Adam and Eve is the first example of his subtleness. Isaiah writes Isaiah 1:16-17 (NKJV) "16 Wash yourselves, make yourselves clean; put away the evil of your doings from before My eyes. Cease to do evil, 17 Learn to do good; seek justice, rebuke the oppressor; defend the fatherless, plead for the widow." Micah 6:8 (NASB) "He has told you, O man, what is good; and what does the LORD require of you but to do justice, to love kindness, and to walk humbly with your God." Some churches are so involved with programs, membership drives, or social justice issues, and they are all important, but not to the exclusion of preaching the gospel. An example of blatant deception is anything from cults to Satan worship. It is reported that there are approximately over 2,500 cults in America. Those who are immersed or assimilated into a cult are often victimized. The leader has complete authority, usually paired with mind control (sometimes achieved through illegal drug use) and/or sexual dominance. Some also persuade their followers that the end of the world is at hand and they can assure their place in heaven by mass suicide. David Koresh and Jim Jones are more notable. Satan is also behind the increase of the occult or Satanic religion. September 2016 was a busy month as two events were touted for the promotion of Satan. A new Satanic temple world headquarters opened in

Salem, MA, and a replica of the 'Harbinger of Baal' Arch was erected in New York City. Wicca and witchcraft are all now considered to be acceptable "religions." However, the Bible says they are sins. 1 Samuel 15:23 "For rebellion is as the sin of witchcraft, and stubbornness is as iniquity and idolatry. Because thou hast rejected the word of the LORD, He hath also rejected thee from being king." There is also a rise in occult themed entertainment. Paul encourages the faithful not to waiver in the faith because the things listed must happen before Christ returns. As Daniel prophesized, it does seem as though the more knowledge we humans acquire, the more ignorant we become and less dependent on or concerned about the things of God. Satan knows that his time is short and he is working overtime to cause as much damage as possible. Revelation 12:12 "Therefore rejoice, ye heavens, and ye that dwell in them. Woe to the inhabiters of the earth and of the sea! for the devil is come down unto you, having great wrath, because he knoweth that he hath but a short time."

These lists above from Peter and Paul corroborates Jesus' warning of being deceived by false Christs or teachers. The dictionary defines deception as "to make someone believe something that is not true." The Bible says that Satan is the father of lies. John 8:44 (NIV) "You belong to your father, the devil, and you want to carry out your father's desires. He was a murderer from the beginning, not holding to the truth, for there is no truth in him. When he lies, he speaks his native language, for he is a liar and the father of lies." Satan's most effective weapons are not a sickness or severe troubles, although they are disastrous, they are lying and deception. He crafts it so close to the truth it is common for good people to misunderstand and be led astray. He deceived Adam and Eve and it cost them everything. Satan persuaded King David to obey him, and it was not some lustful desire, it was to take a census. The sin was not in the activity it was putting another god above God. 1 Chronicles 21:1 "And Satan stood up against Israel and provoked David to number Israel." Satan doesn't always use titillating flagrant temptations of taboo, sometimes his tricks are subtle and flattering. Delivered not in a shout but in a whisper. God's nature is to create something good but Satan's nature is to take that creation and twist it ever so slightly to pervert it. He knows the Bible better than you and me. He tried to trick Jesus in the desert by quoting scriptures. Matthew 4:7 "Jesus said unto him, "It is written again, 'thou shalt not tempt the LORD thy God.'" Luke 4:12 (NKJV) "And Jesus answered and said to him, "It has been said, 'You shall not tempt the LORD your God.'" The scripture Jesus was referring to was most likely Deuteronomy 6:16 (NKJV) "You shall not tempt the LORD your God as you tempted Him in Massah." Moreover, the prophet Isaiah warned about calling good evil and evil good. Isaiah 5:20 "Woe unto them that call evil good, and good evil; that put darkness for light, and light for darkness; that put bitter for sweet, and sweet for bitter!" Signs of this point everywhere. In a country that was founded on the basis of an individual's indisputable right to worship God, the unrelenting secular progressive agenda of removing any reference or acknowledgment of God is as strong now as it ever has been and is gaining ground. There is the erosion of civil discourse. If you have an opposite opinion of the prevailing agenda, it is branded as hate speech and legal action can be taken. With God's hand of protection being pushed aside, it provides Satan a temporary advantage to press his influence in the world. Then, when bad things do happen, people blame God for allowing the tragedy to happen, when all He did was give mankind what he wanted. Under the banner of "tolerance," this agenda has silently infiltrated the general subconscious promoting the acceptance of "alternative lifestyles," not to mention that laws have been passed at the highest level that clearly goes against God's law. The name or word of God has been removed from the school house, the court house, and main street. Anyone who expresses and promotes a Christian lifestyle is ridiculed and branded a nut job. Just ask Tim Tebow, Kim Davis, Roy Moore, Aaron and Melissa Klein, Tim Allen, David and Jason Benham, Christian Mingle, or Chip and Joanna Gaines. While the world does not understand why these people put their relationship to Jesus first, God does. The very idea of man thinking he can make God change his views on issues instead of us learning and following His path is pure deception. Galatians 6:7 "Be not deceived, God is not mocked; for whatsoever a man soweth, that he will also reap." Persecution is alive and well. In an effort to deflect or discredit the message, the messengers are targeted, make no mistake, Christianity is under attack. In the Middle East, people literally, put their lives in jeopardy when they publicly convert to Christ. If found out, they would be arrested and executed, usually by beheading. Yet, in Egypt, Iran, and Iraq people are coming to Christ in droves. On Palm Sunday 2017, Egyptian Christians were singled out and executed. Here in America in Huston TX, five pastors were subpoenaed to submit their sermons to city hall for approval in case they contradicted the LGBT agenda. In 2016, the California Senate Bill 1146 was introduced. It purports that Christian colleges who adhere to their interpretation of the Bible, and as such, have an opposite view on the LGBT agenda, may have their grants or government backed financial support be cut off. Professing Christians are thought of being less intelligent or having a mental illness. Sadly, the fear of offending someone is more prevalent than the fear of offending God. It causes some to remain silent when we are called to be salt and light. Matthew 5:13-16 (NIV) "[13] You are the salt of the earth. But if the salt loses its saltiness, how can it be made salty again? It is no longer good for anything, except to be thrown out and trampled underfoot. [14] "You are the light of the world. A town built on a hill cannot be hidden. [15] Neither do people light a lamp and put it under a bowl. Instead they put it on its stand, and it gives light to everyone in the house. ¹⁶ In the same way, let your light shine before others, that they may see your good deeds and glorify your Father in heaven." Mark 4:21-23 (NKJV) "²¹ Also He said to them, "Is a lamp brought to be put under a basket or under a bed? Is it not to be set on a lampstand? ²² For there is nothing hidden which will not be revealed, nor has anything been kept secret but that it should come to light. ²³ If anyone has ears to hear, let him hear." Luke 8:16-18 (NKJV) "¹⁶ No one, when he has lit a lamp, covers it with a vessel or puts it under a bed, but sets it on a lampstand, that those who enter may see the light. ¹⁷ For nothing is a secret that will not be revealed, nor anything hidden that will not be known and come to light. ¹⁸ Therefore take heed how you hear. For whoever has, to him more will be given; and whoever does not have, even what he seems to have will be taken from him."

Paul commands us to hold fast to the true way and to keep the good fight so that we may be counted worthy to ascend. 2 Thessalonians 1:4-6 (NIV) "⁴ Therefore, among God's churches we boast about your perseverance and faith in all the persecutions and trials you are enduring. ⁵ All this is evidence that God's judgment is right, and as a result you will be counted worthy of the kingdom of God, for which you are suffering. ⁶ God is just: He will pay back trouble to those who trouble you." 2 Thessalonians 2:13-15 "¹³ But we are bound to give thanks alway to God for you, brethren beloved of the Lord, because God hath from the beginning chosen you to salvation through sanctification of the Spirit and belief of the truth: ¹⁴ Whereunto he called you by our gospel, to the obtaining of the glory of our Lord Jesus Christ. ¹⁵ Therefore, brethren, stand fast, and hold the traditions which ye have been taught, whether by word, or our epistle." 1 Timothy 6:12 (NKJV) "Fight the good fight of faith, lay hold on eternal life, to which you were also called and have confessed the good confession in the presence of many witnesses." The Gospel of Jesus does set the bar high, but it is reachable. Matthew 7:14 "Because strait is the gate, and narrow is the way, which leadeth unto life, and few there be that find it." Those who are faithful are rewarded with life with Jesus in heaven for eternity. Paul also says accepting to follow Christ is a life changing experience. 2 Corinthians 5:17 "Therefore, if any man be in Christ, he is a new creature; old things are passed away; behold, all things are become new."

# Chapter 12

## "The Rapture"

So, what's on the horizon for the church or the bride of Christ? When we examined the Olivet Discourse, we talked about Jesus' Second Coming in two phases, (in the third question the disciples asked in Matthew 24) one unexpected and one calculable. We also talked about the coming of the Messiah at the end of the age to be visible and with power and great glory. But only after a seven year period known by several names including the Day of Wrath, Jacob's Trouble, and the Tribulation. We also talked about the earth and people going through such awful ecological, pandemic, and catastrophic calamities before Christ returns as a judge when we bookmarked the Jewish narrative.

Remember, according to Strong's #G1577 the term for the "church" is "ekklēsia." It is used 115 times in the New Testament. We looked at the historical Gentile eras with the seven churches listed in Revelation 2 and 3. After Revelation 3:22 the term "ekklēsia" is not mentioned again until Revelation 22:16 (NKJV) "I, Jesus, have sent My angel to testify to you these things in the churches. I am the Root and the Offspring of David, the Bright and Morning Star." The obvious questions are "why the gap?", "what happened to the church?", and "how did they get to heaven in the first place if they are to return with Christ?" In Revelation 19:6-8 and 14 "⁶ And I heard as it were the voice of a great multitude, and as the voice of many waters, and as the voice of mighty thunderings, saying, Alleluia: for the Lord God omnipotent reigneth. ⁷ Let us be glad and rejoice, and give honour to him: for the marriage of the Lamb is come, and his wife hath made herself ready. ⁸ And to her was granted that she should be arrayed in fine linen, clean and white: for the fine linen is the righteousness of saints." and "¹⁴ And the armies which were in heaven followed him upon white horses, clothed in fine linen, white and clean." Revelation 21:9 (NKJV) "Then one of the seven angels who had the seven bowls filled with the seven last plagues came to me and talked to me, saying, "Come, I will show you the bride, the Lamb's wife." The text clearly indicates it is the Bride of Christ, which we earlier established as the body of believers called the church that returns with Christ for the final battle between Christ the Conqueror vs. the Beast (Antichrist) and his earthly kings. If they are to return with Christ how or when did they get to heaven in the first place?

Bible scholars and theologians have coined the word Rapture for this event. Paul writes in 1 Thessalonians 4:17 "Then we which are alive and remain shall be "caught up" together with them in the clouds, to meet the Lord in the air: and so shall we ever be with the Lord." According to Strong's #G726 the original Greek word for "caught up" is "harpazo," which is defined as a quick, sudden seizure or quick snatch. As an example of "harpazo," is to be forcibly pulling somebody out of the way of an oncoming bus. St. Jerome's Vulgate Latin translation of "harpazo" to the Latin was "rapio." The term rapio was later Anglicized to Rapture. The most common argument opposing against this concept is that the word Rapture is not in the Bible. True and neither is the word Trinity yet there is a general acceptance among believers that it refers to the Father, Son, and the Holy Spirit. Furthermore, Christmas and Easter are not in the Bible either, but we celebrate these holidays yearly. The other passage Paul talks about the Rapture is 1 Corinthians 15:51-52 "[51] Behold, I shew you a mystery; we shall not all sleep, but we shall all be changed, [52] in a moment, in the twinkling of an eye, at the last trump: for the trumpet shall sound, and the dead shall be raised incorruptible, and we shall be changed."

The question of timing is a point of discussion or contention among students of prophecy. There are three main schools of thought with some minor delineations in each of those: Pre-Tribulation, Mid-Tribulation, and Post-Tribulation. These are defined just as they are simply labeled Pre-trib is before the Tribulation, Mid-trib is in the middle and Post-trib is at the end. For our purpose, we will stay with the one this author thinks is the most logical, Pre-Tribulation, for the following reasons;

- In Revelation 4:1 (NKJV) "After these things I looked, and behold, a door standing open in heaven. And the first voice which I heard was like a trumpet speaking with me, saying, "Come up here, and I will show you things which must take place after this." John is transported from earth to heaven by voice command by God. The same voice that called creation into being. This can be seen as an example of what we can expect when He gives the command to His church to join Him. 1 Thessalonians 4:16-17 "[16] For the Lord himself shall descend from heaven with a shout, with the voice of the archangel, and with the trump of God: and the dead in Christ shall rise first: [17] Then we which are alive and remain shall be caught up together with them in the clouds, to meet the Lord in the air: and so shall we ever be with the Lord." Colossians 3:4 "When Christ, who is our life, shall appear, then shall ye also appear with him in glory." Not to mention that we just looked at the fact that the church is not mentioned between chapters of Revelation 6-19.

- Revelation 3:10-11 (NKJV) "10 Because you (the church in Philadelphia) have kept My command to persevere, I also will keep you from the hour of trial which shall come upon the whole world, to test those who dwell on the earth. 11 Behold, I am coming quickly! Hold fast what you have, that no one may take your crown." This clearly gives those believers who remain faithful a measure of protection to keep us out of harm's way when judgment comes.

- When we ended the section of the end of days with the Jews, we learned that one of the names of that time was the Day of Wrath. We noted that it will affect the Jews and the Gentile unbelievers. There are more than a few scripture passages that God promises He will provide a way for believers to avoid the Day of Wrath. As we have already confirmed, God keeps His promises. 1 Thessalonians 1:9-10 "9 For they themselves shew of us what manner of entering in we had unto you, and how ye turned to God from idols to serve the living and true God; 10 And to wait for his Son from heaven, whom He raised from the dead, even Jesus, which delivered us from the wrath to come." Colossians 3:6-7 "6 For which things' sake the wrath of God cometh on the children of disobedience: 7 In the which ye also walked some time, when ye lived in them." Romans 1:18-21 "18 For the wrath of God is revealed from heaven against all ungodliness and unrighteousness of men, who hold the truth in unrighteousness; 19 because that which may be known of God is manifest in them; for God hath shewed it unto them. 20 For the invisible things of him from the creation of the world are clearly seen, being understood by the things that are made, even his eternal power and Godhead; so that they are without excuse: 21 Because that, when they knew God, they glorified him not as God, neither were thankful; but became vain in their imaginations, and their foolish heart was darkened." Revelation 6:16-17 "16 And said to the mountains and rocks, "Fall on us, and hide us from the face of him that sitteth on the throne, and from the wrath of the Lamb: 17 For the great day of his wrath is come; and who shall be able to stand?" Romans 5:8-9 "8 But God commendeth his love toward us, in that, while we were yet sinners, Christ died for us. 9 Much more then, being now justified by his blood, we shall be saved from wrath through him." John 3:36

"He that believeth on the Son hath everlasting life: and he that believeth not the Son shall not see life; but the wrath of God abideth on him." 1 Thessalonians 5:9 "For God hath not appointed us to wrath, but to obtain salvation by our Lord Jesus Christ."

The chart below shows the main differences between the Rapture and the Second Coming;

| | Rapture | | Second Coming |
|---|---|---|---|
| no warning | Matthew 24:36 (NKJV) "But concerning that day and hour no one knows, not even the angels of heaven, nor the Son, but the Father only." | warning | Matthew 24:14 (NKJV) "And this gospel of the kingdom will be preached in all the world as witness to all the nations, and then the end will come." |
| Christ comes only as far as the clouds. | 1 Thessalonians 4:17 "Then we which are alive and remain shall be caught up together with them in the clouds, to meet the Lord in the air: and so shall we ever be with the Lord." | Christ's foot touches the earth and splits the Mount of Olives in two. | Zechariah 14:4 "And his feet shall stand in that day upon the mount of Olives, which is before Jerusalem on the east, and the mount of Olives shall cleave in the midst thereof toward the east and toward the west, and there shall be a very great valley; and half of the mountain shall remove toward the north, and half of it toward the south." |

| | | | |
|---|---|---|---|
| The rapture is ushered in at the last trumpet. | 1 Corinthians 15:51-52 "⁵¹ Behold, I shew you a mystery; We shall not all sleep, but we shall all be changed, ⁵² In a moment, in the twinkling of an eye, at the last trump: for the trumpet shall sound, and the dead shall be raised incorruptible, and we shall be changed." | The second coming is ushered in with the great trumpet of God. | Matthew 24:31 (NKJV) "And He will send His angels with a great sound of a trumpet, and they will gather together His elect from the four winds, from one end of heaven to the other." |
| When Jesus comes to collect his bride, it will be as a thief in the night. | 1 Thessalonians 5:1-2 "¹ But of the times and the seasons, brethren, ye have no need that I write unto you. ² For yourselves know perfectly that the day of the Lord so cometh as a thief in the night." Revelation 16:15 (NKJV) "Behold, I am coming as a thief. Blessed is he who watches, and keeps his garments, lest he walk naked and they see his shame." | When Jesus returns to earth the second time, He will return the same way He ascended. Visibly and physically. | Acts 1:9-11 "⁹ And when he had spoken these things, while they beheld, he was taken up; and a cloud received him out of their sight. ¹⁰ And while they looked stedfastly toward heaven as he went up, behold, two men stood by them in white apparel; ¹¹ Which also said, Ye men of Galilee, why stand ye gazing up into heaven? this same Jesus, which is taken up from you into heaven, shall so come in like manner as ye have seen him go into heaven." |

| The rapture happens in the twinkling of an eye (faster than the speed of light reflecting in the eye) | 1 Corinthians 15:52a "In a moment, in the twinkling of an eye, at the last trumpet." | The second coming will take time as it will need to travel across the globe | Matthew 24:27 (NKJV) "For as the lightning comes from the east and flashes to the west, so also will the coming of the Son of Man be."<br><br>Revelation 1:7 "Behold, he cometh with clouds; and every eye shall see him, and they also which pierced him: and all kindreds of the earth shall wail because of him. Even so, Amen." |
|---|---|---|---|

# Chapter 13

# "Our Glorified New Bodies"

After the Bridegroom (Jesus) collects His Bride (the Church), we will then be called into the presence of God to be judged or better defined as rewarded to receive crowns (see the chart below for the 5 types of crowns) for our faithfulness during the Age of Grace or Church Age. This ceremony is called the Judgment Seat of Christ. Once collected, we shall cast those crowns before Him as a tribute. Matthew 16:27 "For the Son of Man shall come in the glory of His Father with His angels, and then He shall reward every man according to his works." Remember to keep in mind that John's writing of these sequences of events will be set at a future date. So, when the elders cast their crowns, we will take their lead and join in the ceremony. Revelation 4:9-11 "9 And when those beasts give glory and honour and thanks to him that sat on the throne, who liveth for ever and ever, 10 The four and twenty elders fall down before him that sat on the throne, and worship him that liveth for ever and ever, and cast their crowns before the throne, saying, 11 Thou art worthy, O Lord, to receive glory and honour and power: for thou hast created all things, and for thy pleasure they are and were created." The Bible identifies this event as the Judgment Seat of Christ. Romans 14:10-12 "10 But why dost thou judge thy brother? or why dost thou set at nought thy brother? for we shall all stand before the judgment seat of Christ. 11 For it is written, As I live, saith the Lord, every knee shall bow to me, and every tongue shall confess to God. 12 So then every one of us shall give account of himself to God." 2 Corinthians 5:10-11 "10 For we must all appear before the judgment seat of Christ; that every one may receive the things done in his body, according to that he hath done, whether it be good or bad. 11 Knowing therefore the terror of the Lord, we persuade men; but we are made manifest unto God; and I trust also are made manifest in your consciences." This event is sometimes called the Bema Seat. According to Strong's #G968 the Greek word "bema" translates to "judgment seat." It's important to point out that the judgment here is more of assessing reward for the type of service similar to an Olympian athlete being rewarded with either gold, silver, or bronze medals.

| Title | Bible Passage |
|---|---|
| Crown of Righteousness | 2 Timothy 4:8 (NIV) "Now there is in store for me the crown of righteousness, which the Lord, the righteous Judge, will award to me on that day, and not only to me, but also to all who have longed for his appearing." |
| Crown of Glory | 1 Peter 5:2-4 (NIV) "2 Be shepherds of God's flock that is under your care, watching over them—not because you must, but because you are willing, as God wants you to be; not pursuing dishonest gain, but eager to serve; 3 not lording it over those entrusted to you, but being examples to the flock. 4 And when the Chief Shepherd appears, you will receive the crown of glory that will never fade away." |
| | Isaiah 62:3 "Thou shalt also be a crown of glory in the hand of the LORD, and a royal diadem in the hand of thy God." |
| Imperishable Crown | 1 Corinthians 9:25 (NKJV) "And everyone who competes for the prize is temperate in all things. Now they do it to obtain a perishable crown, but we for an imperishable crown." |
| Crown of Rejoicing | 1 Thessalonians 2:19 "For what is our hope, or joy, or crown of rejoicing? Are not even ye in the presence of our Lord Jesus Christ at his coming ?" |
| Crown of Life | James 1:12 "Blessed is the man that endureth temptation: for when he is tried, he shall receive the crown of life, which the Lord hath promised to them that love Him." |
| | Revelation 2:10 (NKJV) "Do not fear any of those things which you are about to suffer. Indeed, the devil is about to throw some of you into prison, that you may be tested, and you will have Tribulation ten days. |

Be faithful until death, and I will give you the crown of life."

Those souls who will be caught up at the Rapture will have new glorified bodies as exemplified by Jesus Himself. 1 John 3:2-3 (NIV) "[2] Dear friends, now we are children of God, and what we will be has not yet been made known. But we know that when Christ appears, we shall be like him, for we shall see him as he is. [3] All who have this hope in him purify themselves, just as he is pure." It will have the properties of light and be luminous. Matthew 17:2 "And was transfigured before them: and his face did shine as the sun, and his raiment was white as the light." John 20:17 (NIV) "Jesus said, "Do not hold on to me, for I have not yet ascended to the Father. Go instead to my brothers and tell them, 'I am ascending to my Father and your Father, to my God and your God." Our current earthly bodies will be reconditioned to exist in heaven. Philippians 3:20-21 (NIV) "[20] But our citizenship is in heaven. And we eagerly await a Savior from there, the Lord Jesus Christ, [21] who, by the power that enables him to bring everything under his control, will transform our lowly bodies so that they will be like his glorious body." After Jesus came back from the grave, He was presumably in His glorified body. When He came to His disciples to prove to them, He was real and alive, He ate food. Luke 24:38-43 "[38] And he said unto them, "Why are ye troubled? and why do thoughts arise in your hearts? [39] Behold my hands and my feet, that it is I myself: handle me, and see; for a spirit hath not flesh and bones, as ye see me have. [40] And when he had thus spoken, he shewed them his hands and his feet. [41] And while they yet believed not for joy, and wondered, he said unto them, Have ye here any meat? [42] And they gave him a piece of a broiled fish, and of an honeycomb. [43] And he took it, and did eat before them." This implys that we will be able to eat. 1 Corinthians 15:42-45 "[42] So also is the resurrection of the dead. It is sown in corruption; it is raised in incorruption: [43] It is sown in dishonour; it is raised in glory: it is sown in weakness; it is raised in power: [44] It is sown a natural body; it is raised a spiritual body. There is a natural body, and there is a spiritual body. [45] And so it is written, the first man Adam was made a living soul; the last Adam was made a quickening spirit."

The last Adam (Jesus) became a life-giving spirit." 1 Corinthians 15:50-55 "[50] Now this I say, brethren, that flesh and blood cannot inherit the kingdom of God; neither doth corruption inherit incorruption. [51] Behold, I shew you a mystery; We shall not all sleep, but we shall all be changed, [52] In a moment, in the twinkling of an eye, at the last trump: for the trumpet shall sound, and the dead shall be raised incorruptible, and we shall be changed. [53] For this corruptible must put on incorruption, and this mortal must put on immortality. 54 So when this corruptible shall have put on incorruption, and this mortal shall have put on immortality, then shall be brought to pass the saying that is written, Death is swallowed up in victory. 55 O death, where is thy sting? O grave, where is thy victory?"

Additionally, we may have the ability to appear and disappear at will. John 20:19-20 (NIV) "19 On the evening of that first day of the week, when the disciples were together, with the doors locked for fear of the Jewish leaders, Jesus came and stood among them and said, "Peace be with you!" 20 After he said this, he showed them his hands and side. The disciples were overjoyed when they saw the Lord." Luke 24:28-31 "28 And they (the two on the road to Emmaus) drew nigh unto the village, whither they went: and He made as though He would have gone further. 29 But they constrained him, saying, "Abide with us: for it is toward evening, and the day is far spent. And He went in to tarry with them. 30 And it came to pass, as He sat at meat with them, He took bread, and blessed it, and brake, and gave to them. 31 And their eyes were opened, and they knew Him; and he vanished out of their sight." Luke 24:36-37 "36 And as they thus spake, Jesus himself stood in the midst of them, and saith unto them, Peace be unto you. 37 But they were terrified and affrighted, and supposed that they had seen a spirit." To fully understand and appreciate the transformation from earthly to heavenly bodies, we must look at what the Bible says about what happens to the body and the spirit or soul at death.

The Bible says that God knew us before we were even born. Psalm 139:13-14 (NIV) "13 For you created my inmost being; you knit me together in my mother's womb. 14 I praise you because I am fearfully and wonderfully made; your works are wonderful, I know that full well." Jeremiah 1:4-5 (NKJV) "4 Then the word of the LORD came to me, saying: 5 "Before I formed you in the womb I knew you; before you were born I sanctified you; I ordained you a prophet to the nations." The Bible also says there is a season for birth and one for death. Ecclesiastes 3:1-2 "1 To everything there is a season, and a time to every purpose under the heaven: 2 A time to be born, and a time to die; a time to plant, and a time to pluck up that which is planted." It also confirms that each of us will die. 1 Corinthians 15:22 "For as in Adam all die, even so in Christ all shall be made alive." Hebrews 9:27-28 "27 And as it is appointed unto men once to die, but after this the judgment: 28 So Christ was once offered to bear the sins of many; and unto them that look for him shall he appear the second time without sin unto salvation." Scholars believe the judgment mentioned here is the Great White Throne Judgment, after the Millennium and before Eternity.

The Bible says that for believers, their spirits are brought into Jesus' presence when they die. 2 Corinthians 5:6-8 "⁶ Therefore we are always confident, knowing that, whilst we are at home in the body, we are absent from the Lord: ⁷ For we walk by faith, not by sight: ⁸ We are confident, I say, and willing rather to be absent from the body, and to be present with the Lord." Jesus called that place Paradise when He was speaking with the thieves on the cross. Luke 23:39-43 (NIV) ³⁹ One of the criminals who hung there hurled insults at him: "Aren't you the Messiah? Save yourself and us!" ⁴⁰ But the other criminal rebuked him. "Don't you fear God," he said, "since you are under the same sentence? ⁴¹ We are punished justly, for we are getting what our deeds deserve. But this man has done nothing wrong." ⁴² Then he said, "Jesus, remember me when you come into your kingdom." ⁴³ Jesus answered him, "Truly I tell you, today you will be with me in paradise." Non-believers are sent to be tormented in a place called Hades. Luke 16:22-23 (NIV) "²² The time came when the beggar died and the angels carried him to Abraham's side. The rich man also died and was buried. ²³ In Hades, where he was in torment, he looked up and saw Abraham far away, with Lazarus by his side." It is thought that Hades is sort of an intermediate location before one is sent to hell, the lake of fire and brimstone, or bottomless pit. At death, our spirit transcends to the next life while our physical bodies remain on earth. This is known as the First Death. Ultimately though, at the end of time, every soul ever born will be summoned before God. Daniel 12:1-2 "¹ And at that time (the end of days) shall Michael stand up, the great prince which standeth for the children of thy people: and there shall be a time of trouble, such as never was since there was a nation even to that same time: and at that time thy people shall be delivered, every one that shall be found written in the book (the book of life). ² And many of them that sleep in the dust of the earth shall awake, some to everlasting life, and some to shame and everlasting contempt." John 5:28-29 "²⁸ Marvel not at this: for the hour is coming, in the which all that are in the graves shall hear his voice, ²⁹ And shall come forth; they that have done good, unto the resurrection of life; and they that have done evil, unto the resurrection of damnation." For the believers, the Rapture will rejoin the soul with the physical body and transform to the new glorified at which body we just looked. We will refer back to this discussion of glorified bodies and First Death at the time of the Millennium.

# Chapter 14

# "The Day of Wrath aka The Tribulation"

Getting back to what happens at the Rapture, we will remain in Heaven with Jesus for the next seven years while the wrath of God is poured out on earth. As was touched upon above in the Olivet Discourse, those who come to faith during the Tribulation will probably experience a painful death in one of two ways. They will be delivered and killed for His name's sake. Matthew 24:9-10 (NLKV) "9 Then they will deliver you up to Tribulation and kill you, and you will be hated by all nations for My name's sake. 10 And then many will be offended, will betray one another, and will hate one another." They and unbelievers may also fall victim of the natural disasters. Matthew 24:7 (NLKV) "For nation will rise against nation and kingdom against kingdom. And there will be famines, pestilences, and earthquakes in various places." Either way at the end of the Tribulation we who are with Jesus will be joined with those souls who die during the Tribulation. These later souls are the ones who will become known as the Tribulation Saints. Just before Christ physically returns to earth at the end of the Tribulation, He will invite all believers as His bride to the Marriage Supper of the Lamb in heaven. Revelation 19:6-9 "6 And I heard as it were the voice of a great multitude, and as the voice of many waters, and as the voice of mighty thunderings, saying, Alleluia: for the Lord God omnipotent reigneth. 7 Let us be glad and rejoice, and give honour to him: for the marriage of the Lamb is come, and his wife hath made herself ready. 8 And to her was granted that she should be arrayed in fine linen, clean and white: for the fine linen is the righteousness of saints. 9 And He saith unto me, Write, Blessed are they which are called unto the marriage supper of the Lamb. And He saith unto me, these are the true sayings of God." This celebration is paralleled to the third phase of the Ancient Jewish Marriage custom. We will then return with Christ to fight

Satan a final time. We will come back to this when we talk about the end of the Tribulation, Christ's Return, and the Millennium.

Before we go back to the beginning of the Day of Wrath or Tribulation period and whom it affects a few points need to be explained first. Bear in mind the timing of the following conditions may or may not transpire anywhere from before the Rapture through the beginning of the Tribulation. Prophecy scholars identify these events as prophetic for the later days or day of the Lord but are not corroborated in Revelation like some of Daniel's, Isaiah's and Jeremiah's prophecies. Supporting the belief that they are specific to the Jews. Remember that the most important factor for the end times is that Israel must be back and in control of their own state or country and, as we noted in the Fig Tree parable, those recalled people will be the Terminal generation.

- There is an incorrect understanding that the Rapture signifies the beginning of the Tribulation. In fact, according to Daniel 9:27a "And he shall confirm the covenant with many for one week:" the beginning of the clock for the seven year Tribulation does not start ticking until the Antichrist appears and confirms his peace treaty with Israel and her enemies. There may be and probably will be some time whether it be days, weeks or months between the Rapture and the start of the Tribulation.

- As we discussed in the Olivet Discourse, the reconstruction of Solomon's (3rd) Temple on the temple mount in Jerusalem is now being occupied by the Dome of the Rock, a Muslim mosque. Permission for the reconstruction of the temple could be offered as an olive branch to that conflict. It could begin before or after the beginning of the Tribulation but it has to be completed by the middle mark for the Abomination of Desolation to take place. Daniel 9:27b "and in the midst of the week he shall cause the sacrifice and the oblation to cease, and for the overspreading of abominations he shall make it desolate." Daniel 12:10-13 "[10] Many shall be purified, and made white, and tried; but the wicked shall do wickedly: and none of the wicked shall understand; but the wise shall understand. [11] And from the time that the daily sacrifice shall be taken away, and the abomination that maketh desolate set up, there shall be a thousand two hundred and ninety days. [12] Blessed is he that waiteth, and cometh to the thousand three hundred and five and thirty days. [13] But go thou thy way till the end be: for thou shalt rest, and stand in thy lot at the end of the days." Matthew

24:15a (NKJV) "Therefore when you see the 'abomination of desolation,' spoken of by Daniel the prophet." This interim between Rapture and Tribulation could give time to at least begin construction of the Temple.

- Jerusalem will be at the center of controversy for possession. Zechariah 12:2-3 (NKJV) "2 Behold, I will make Jerusalem a cup of drunkenness to all the surrounding peoples when they lay siege against Judah and Jerusalem. 3 And it shall happen in that day that I will make Jerusalem a very heavy stone for all peoples; all who would heave it away will surely be cut in pieces, though all nations of the earth are gathered against it." God will bring judgment to the nations on their treatment of His chosen people Israel. Joel 3:1-2 "1 For, behold, in those days, and in that time, when I shall bring again the captivity of Judah and Jerusalem, 2 I will also gather all nations, and will bring them down into the valley of Jehoshaphat, and will plead with them there for my people and for my heritage Israel, whom they have scattered among the nations, and parted my land." A "Two State Solution" between Israel and the so-called Palestinians has been put up for discussion several times with various political figures since 1948. In July of 2000, President Bill Clinton hosted Israeli prime minister Ehud Barak and Palestinian Authority chairman Yasser Arafat for a peace summit which ended without a deal. There have been several others floated and proposed, but failed to bring lasting peace. On December 6, 2017, President Trump announced the USA will recognize Jerusalem as Israel's capital city and move its official embassy there. Two days later, the following Friday, December 8, the fifteen member UN Security Council (the strongest governing agency for the UN) took a vote to denounce this declaration. The results were unanimous against with the US standing alone. As you might expect, the Muslim nations, and those who support them, erupted in violent protests across the globe. So much for a religion of "peace." Palestinians have absolutely no interest in coming to an agreement of living side-by-side with Israel. Since Israel's rebirth in 1948, they refuse to even acknowledge Israel's right to exist. They wished to simply exterminate the Israelis, just like the Nazis. Although the Israelis have offered the Palestinians land in exchange for peace, (i.e. the Gaza Strip, West Bank, and Golan Heights), yet the Palestinians continue to fire rockets into Israel from Gaza as recently reported. How can you negotiate in good faith with an adversary who does not even recognize your right to live? All past and future attempts to bring the Palestinians and Israel to live together side by side will fail. Until the Antichrist takes his place and acknowledges Israel's right to exist by confirming an accepted peace agreement. Furthermore, Islam allows lying and deception when dealing with the "enemy." It's called Taqiyya. As we just read in Joel any country, including the USA, puts their well-being in jeopardy if they force a condition to this conflict that involves Jerusalem or any part of Israel to be divided. Watching the evening world news, the stories that dominate are usually those concerning the Middle East.

- In order for the Antichrist to confirm a seven-year peace treaty, Israel must be in some form of conflict. Let's look to see if we can understand the historical basis of the ancestral family feud between the Arabs and the Hebrews. When we looked at Abraham and Hagar early on, we read that God would bless Ishmael to be the Father of many nations, collectively called Arabs, because he was of Abraham's seed. The catalyst of the rivalry was because Sarah didn't want Ishmael to receive the birthright blessing from Abraham so she forced Hagar and Ishmael to be banished from camp. Subsequently, after this event, God will test Abraham's faith by calling Abraham to Mt. Moriah to offer Isaac as an offering. When the test is passed God told Abraham that He would bless Isaac specifically to be the channel of God's plan. We need to make a distinction between an Arab and a Muslim. An Arab is a national designation like American, French, or English etc.... Muslim is a religious belief system like Protestantism, Catholic, or Jewish. Unlike the Hebrews whose existence can be traced back close to 6,000 years, the Muslim or Islamic faith was founded in the late 6th - early 7th century. The god "Allah" was one of many gods Muhammed had from which to choose to have a focal point for his political ambitions to control the population. At his death in 632 AD, this new religion went through a schism and produced two warring factions over who would take over for Muhamad; namely, the Sunnis (mostly in Iran) and the Shiites (just about every other Muslim). The only 2 things that they truly share are they both worship Allah and that they share a deep visceral hatred of the Jews. In 1979, the Islamic Revolution took place when it started with the ousting of the US backed Shah of Iran and the subsequent hostage taking of the US Embassy in Tehran. The government was taken over by Islamic religious zealots' extremists who now rule by Sharia Law. Fast forward to today, Iran's chief export is terrorism, but as we saw earlier, people who do evil things think that they are doing good. Iran is behind Syria, Hezbollah, and Hamas in finances, weapon supply, and philosophy. As troublesome as Hezbollah and Hamas are, Israel's major concern is Iran. Iran's tactic is to stall or delay to allow its pawns, Hamas, and Hezbollah, to move around the chess board to drag out any meaningful peace talks and to give time to set up a military offensive from Syria. It is only allowing Iran to take advantage of the time they need to either acquire or develop nuclear weapons. Lastly, Iran calls Israel the "little Satan" and the US the "Big Satan." Both the US and Israel are in Iran's cross hairs.

There are three Bible prophecies that most prophecy teachers say have yet to be fulfilled and that they are outside of the seven-year Day of Wrath period but specifically involve Israel. They are the Isaiah 17:1 Damascus destruction, the Psalm 83 war, and the Ezekiel 38 and 39 aka Gog/Magog war.

- Isaiah 17:1 (NKJV) "The burden against Damascus. "Behold, Damascus will cease from being a city, and it will be a ruinous heap." Damascus has been continually occupied since estimated at 630 BCE until today. With the civil war in Syria and the retaking of Aleppo, the largest city in Syria, Damascus could be the next center of conflict to show on our nightly news. How that will affect Israel is anybody's guess, but we should keep an eye out for it. The end of chapter seems to indicate that the destruction will be sudden and overnight. Isaiah 17:14 (NIV) "In the evening, sudden terror! Before the morning, they are gone! This is the portion of those who loot us, the lot of those who plunder us." It might not be in the public awareness, but there is a stockpile of chemical/biological weapons of mass destruction under Damascus right now. Should those canisters be broken one way or another it could render the area unfit for human or animal habitation.

- Psalm 83:4-8 "4 They have said, Come, and let us cut them off from being a nation; that the name of Israel may be no more in remembrance. 5 For they have consulted together with one consent: they are confederate against thee: 6 The tabernacles of Edom, and the Ishmaelites; of Moab, and the Hagarenes; 7 Gebal, and Ammon, and Amalek; the Philistines with the inhabitants of Tyre; 8 Assur also is joined with them: they have holpen the children of Lot. Selah." These ethnic groups are sometimes referred to as the "inner circle" as they border directly with Israel. Below are the nations as listed compared to the nations of today.

| Psalm 83 | Today Nations |
|---|---|
| The Tents of Edom | Palestinians (PLO) and Southern Jordan |
| The Ishmaelites | Saudi Arabia and Portions of Jordan |
| Moab | Palestinians (PLO) and Central Jordan |
| Hagrites | Northeast Jordan |
| Gebal | Lebanon (Hezbollah) |
| Ammon | Palestinians (PLO) and Northwest Jordan |
| Amalek | Sinai Arabs and Southern Israel |
| Philistia | Gaza (Hamas) |
| The Inhabitants of Tyre | Lebanon (Hezbollah) |
| Assyria | Southeast Turkey, Northwest Syria, Northeast Iraq (ISIS) |
| The Children of Lot | Jordan |

Of note, according to an Oct. 27, 2005, NY Times article, the sentiment of verse 4 was proclaimed by Iran's then President Mahmoud Ahmadinejad who reiterated in a speech he gave the day before at the World Without Zionism conference. He said, quote "As the Imam (Ayatollah Ruhollah Khomeini) said, Israel must be wiped off the map" unquote. This rhetoric can be traced back to at least 1979 when Ayatollah Khomeini had just assumed the leadership of the Islamic Revolution. Just for the sake of full disclosure, there are some who think this prophecy was fulfilled in the 1973 Yom Kippur War. Opponents to this argument say not all of the groups listed were involved in this conflict and most notably Egypt, who along with Syria spearheaded the attack, were not listed in Psalm 83. The point here is IF we were to see these groups come together to attack Israel, we should recognize it for what it is. A fulfillment of a specific prophecy for the State of Israel.

- Ezekiel 38 and 39 aka Gog/Magog war. First, let's see exactly what the Bible says. This is perhaps the most detailed prophecy in the Bible pertaining to the people of Israel. A natural question might be why? The answer might just be simply that when it comes to pass, Israel will know the return of the Messiah is at hand. We will examine several important points about this prophecy afterward.

Ezekiel 38:1-6 (NKJV) "¹ Now the word of the LORD came to me, saying, ² "Son of man, set your face against Gog, of the land of Magog, the prince of Rosh, Meshech, and Tubal, and prophesy against him, ³ and say, 'Thus says the Lord GOD: Behold, I am against you, O Gog, the prince of Rosh, Meshech, and Tubal. ⁴ I will turn you around, put hooks into your jaws, and lead you out, with all your army, horses, and horsemen, all splendidly clothed, a great company with bucklers and shields, all of them handling swords. ⁵ Persia, Ethiopia, and Libya are with them, all of them with shield and helmet; ⁶ Gomer and all its troops; the house of Togarmah from the far north and all its troop's many people are with you." Some translations have the names of Cush and Put included but not in the NKJV. The combatants in this coming conflict are sometimes referred to as the outer circle as they do not have direct border contact with Israel.

Ezekiel 38:7-9 (NKJV) "⁷ Prepare yourself and be ready, you and all your companies that are gathered about you; and be a guard for them. ⁸ After many days you will be visited. In the latter years, you will come into the land of those brought back from the sword and gathered from many people on the mountains of Israel, which had long been desolate; they were brought out of the nations, and now all of them dwell safely. ⁹ You will ascend, coming like a storm, covering the land like a cloud, you and all your troops and many peoples with you."

Ezekiel 38:10-13 (NKJV) "¹⁰ Thus says the Lord GOD: "On that day it shall come to pass that thought will arise in your mind, and you will make an evil plan: ¹¹ You will say, 'I will go up against a land of unwalled villages; I will go to a peaceful people, who dwell safely, all of them dwelling without walls, and having neither bars nor gates' ¹² to take plunder and to take booty, to stretch out your hand against the waste places that are again inhabited, and against a people gathered from the nations, who have acquired livestock and goods, who dwell in the midst of the land. ¹³ Sheba, Dedan, the merchants of Tarshish, and all their young lions will say to you, 'Have you come to take plunder? Have you gathered your army to take booty, to carry away silver and gold, to take away livestock and goods, to take great plunder?'

| Ezekiel 38:1-6 | | Today Nations |
|---:|:---:|:---:|
| Magog | } | Russia |
| Meshech | } | Turkey |
| Tubal | } | Turkey |
| Rosh | } | Russia |
| Persia | } | Iran |
| Ethiopia | } | Sudan |
| Libya | } | Libya |
| Gomer | } | Turkey |
| Togarmah | } | Turkey |
| Cush | } | Modern Day Ethiopia |
| Put | } | North Africa |
| Ezekiel 38:10-13 | | |
| Sheba | } | Saudi Arabia |
| Dedan | } | Saudi Arabia |
| Merchants of Tarshish | } | Spain/England? |
| Young Lions | } | USA ? |

Ezekiel 38:14-17 (NKJV) "14 Therefore, son of man, prophesy and say to Gog, 'Thus says the Lord GOD: "On that day when My people Israel dwell safely, will you not know it? 15 Then you will come from your place out of the far north, you and many peoples with you, all of them riding on horses, a great company, and a mighty army. 16 You will come up against My people Israel like a cloud, to cover the land. It will be in the latter days that I will bring you against My land, so that the nations may know Me, when I am hallowed in you, O Gog, before their eyes." 17 Thus says the Lord GOD: "Are you he of whom I have spoken in former days by My servants the prophets of Israel, who prophesied for years in those days that I would bring you against them?"

Ezekiel 38:18-23 (NKJV) "18 And it will come to pass at the same time when Gog comes against the land of Israel," says the Lord GOD, "that My fury will show in My face. 19 For in My jealousy and in the fire of My wrath I have spoken: 'Surely in that day there shall be a great earthquake in the land of Israel, 20 so that the fish of the sea, the birds of the heavens, the beasts of the field, all creeping things that creep on the earth, and all men who are on the face of the earth shall shake at My presence. The mountains shall be thrown down, the steep places shall fall, and every wall shall fall to the ground.' 21 I will call for a sword against Gog throughout all My mountains," says the Lord GOD. "Every man's sword will be against his brother. 22 And I will bring him to judgment with pestilence and bloodshed; I will rain down on him, on his troops, and on the many peoples who are with him, flooding rain, great hailstones, fire, and brimstone. 23 Thus I will magnify Myself and sanctify Myself, and I will be known in the eyes of many nations. Then they shall know that I am the LORD.'"

Ezekiel 39:1-10 (NKJV) "1 And you, son of man, prophesy against Gog, and say, 'Thus says the Lord GOD: "Behold, I am against you, O Gog, the prince of Rosh, Meshech, and Tubal; 2 and I will turn you around and lead you on, bringing you up from the far north, and bring you against the mountains of Israel. 3 Then I will knock the bow out of your left hand, and cause the arrows to fall out of your right hand. 4 You shall fall upon the mountains of Israel, you and all your troops and the peoples who are with you; I will give you to birds of prey of every sort and to the Beasts of the field to be devoured. 5 You shall fall on the open field; for I have spoken," says the Lord GOD. 6 "And I will send fire on Magog and on those who live in security in the coastlands. Then they shall know that I am the LORD. 7 So I will make My holy name known in the midst of My people Israel, and I will not let them profane My holy name anymore. Then the nations shall know that I am the LORD, the Holy One in Israel. 8 Surely it is coming, and it shall be done," says the Lord GOD. "This is the day of which I have spoken. 9 "Then those who dwell in the cities of Israel will go out and set on fire and burn the weapons, both the shields and bucklers, the bows and arrows, the javelins and spears; and they will make fires with them for seven years. 10 They will not take wood from the field nor cut down any from the forests because they will make fires with the weapons, and they will plunder those who plundered them and pillage those who pillaged them," says the Lord GOD.

Ezekiel 39:11-16 (NKJV) "11 It will come to pass in that day that I will give Gog a burial place there in Israel, the valley of those who pass by east of the sea; and it will obstruct travelers because there they will bury Gog and all his multitude. Therefore, they will call it the Valley of Hamon Gog. 12 For seven months the house of Israel will be burying them, in order to cleanse the land. 13 Indeed all the people of the land will be burying, and they will gain renown for it on the day that I am glorified," says the Lord God. 14 "They will set apart men regularly employed, with the help of a search party, to pass through the land and bury those bodies remaining on the ground, in order to cleanse it. At the end of seven months, they will make a search. 15 The search party will pass through the land; and when anyone sees a man's bone, he shall set up a marker by it, till the buriers have buried it in the Valley of Hamon Gog. 16 The name of the city will also be Hamonah. Thus they shall cleanse the land."'

Ezekiel 39:17-20 (NKJV) "17 And as for you, son of man, thus says the Lord God, 'Speak to every sort of bird and to every beast of the field: "Assemble yourselves and come; Gather together from all sides to My sacrificial meal Which I am sacrificing for you, A great sacrificial meal on the mountains of Israel, that you may eat flesh and drink blood. 18 You shall eat the flesh of the mighty, Drink the blood of the princes of the earth, Of rams and lambs, Of goats and bulls, All of them fatlings of Bashan. 19 You shall eat fat till you are full, and drink blood till you are drunk, At My sacrificial meal Which I am sacrificing for you. 20 You shall be filled at My table with horses and riders, with mighty men and with all the men of war," says the Lord God."

Ezekiel 39:21-29 (NKJV) "21 I will set My glory among the nations; all the nations shall see My judgment which I have executed and My hand which I have laid on them. 22 So the house of Israel shall know that I am the Lord their God from that day forward. 23 The Gentiles shall know that the house of Israel went into captivity for their iniquity; because they were unfaithful to Me, therefore I hid My face from them. I gave them into the hand of their enemies, and they all fell by the sword. 24 According to their uncleanness and according to their transgressions I have dealt with them, and hidden My face from them."' 25 "Therefore thus says the Lord God: 'Now I will bring back the captives of Jacob, and have mercy on the whole house of Israel; and I will be jealous for My holy name 26 after they have borne their shame, and all their unfaithfulness in which they were unfaithful to Me, when they dwelt safely in their own land and no one made them afraid. 27 When I have brought them back from the peoples and gathered them out of their enemies' lands, and I am hallowed in them in the sight of many nations, 28 then they shall know that I am the Lord their God, who sent them into captivity among the nations, but also brought them back to their land, and left none of them captive any longer. ²⁹ And I will not hide My face from them anymore; for I shall have poured out My Spirit on the house of Israel,' says the Lord GOD."

We will now highlight several important points about this coming conflict.

A. Gog is a title like Prince or President, not a country. Ezekiel 38:2a "Son of man, set your face against Gog, of the land of Magog, the prince of Rosh." In Ezekiel 38:6 and Ezekiel 39:2 states the coming enemies who will go up against Israel are from "the far north." In the Bible, all directions (north, east, and south west) are in a relative position from Jerusalem. IF this were applicable today, the far north from Jerusalem could be Russia and its leader is Vladimir Putin.

B. There has to be a reason the Magog/Meshech/Persian et al. coalition moves against Israel. Let's look at some specific requirements the Bible lists that cause the countries of the coalition to plot together their assault. Ezekiel 38:8 "In the latter years you will come into the land of those brought back from the sword and gathered from many people on the mountains of Israel, which had long been desolate; they were brought out of the nations, and now all of them dwell safely." Ezekiel 38:10-12 "¹⁰ You will make an evil plan: ¹¹ You will say, 'I will go up against a land of unwalled villages; I will go to a peaceful people, who dwell safely, all of them dwelling without walls, and having neither bars nor gates' ¹² to take plunder and to take booty." There are two points that need to be made here. They are "the land being long desolate," and "unwalled villages and living in safety." Point one, before the land area was reverted back to the Jews in 1948, the land was arid and desolate. According to some accounts, there were no trees or greenery of any kind as far as the eye could see in the pre-1948 Israel era. Also, the population of the inhabitants was very low, estimated of less than 700,000. As noted, before when we listed signs of the "latter day," two of those signs were the desert land of Israel blooming and that the Israelites being called home from the four corners of the earth called Aliyah. However, now that Israel is the agricultural envy of the Middle East, there must be something more that would cause this coalition to plan an invasion. It is natural gas and oil, the hook in the jaw if you will. Ezekiel 38:4 (NKJV) "I will turn you around, put hooks into your jaws, and lead you out." Within the last five years, an enormous underwater and underground gas reserve has been newly discovered off the coast of Israel and in the oil fields found in the Golan Heights. The gas fields are just a few miles from the unpredictable Syrian civil war. Russia and Iran are supporting the Assad regime not because they like him, but because they see Syria and Damascus as the strategic place it is. They will have a better position when they decide to pull the trigger against Israel. In recent months, both Russia and Iran have been building permanent bases in Syria. On January 20, 2018, Turkey invaded northern Syria. All a preliminary move to invade Israel. Israel has taken action by attacking the base. Russia and Iran have been trading partners in the past, but never before, until recently, have they been military partners. Thanks to Iranian cash reserves being released as part of the Iranian Nuclear Deal under President Obama, they now have funds which they are using to buy advanced missile systems from Russia. Point two, is the issue of "unwalled villages" and "living in safety." This could be a reference to Israel's ability to protect itself. The Israeli Defense Force (IDF) is considered to be in the top 20 of military capabilities in the world, according to a 2016 ranking from Global Firepower, are they living in safety? From a certain point of view perhaps. Safety is relative. The Ezekiel 38 and 39 war could not happen unless they consider themselves to be "living in safety." Consider this, if your definition of safety is the absence of any type of violent crime or attacks, then that cannot ever be until the Millennium. Until Jesus sets up His kingdom there will always be sin and evil in the world and no country, including Israel, will be exempt. More than a few Israeli citizens claim they are as safe today as they have ever been, even under the specter of rocket attacks by Hamas or Hezbollah or the Israeli/Palestine conflict. Certainly, an argument can be made that Jerusalem is safer than any major US city when crimes rates are compared. They are always in a state of vigilance, watchfulness, and preparedness which enhances their self-confidence they can defend themselves. The Jews are firm in their resolve that the atrocities of the Holocaust will never be repeated. Their chant is an oath and a rallying cry, "Never Forget, Never Again!"

C.  What is holding the Magog/Meshech/Persian et al coalition back from launching their offensive? Currently, the only thing keeping this coalition at bay is the fear of retaliation from the US. But, consider this, with the rapture event, the sphere of influence and military might of the USA and Europe could be drastically impaired with the sudden vanishing of millions of its citizens and soldiers. It is certainly in the realm of probability that this scenario is at least possible. Seemingly with Israel's' powerful allies gone, this coalition could decide to attack Israel. In Ezekiel 38:16 (NKJV) "You will come up against My people Israel like a cloud." Israel is clearly the target. When the Ezekiel 38 and 39 war begins, there will be only four countries that voice a protest and not send military aid to Israel when Russia/Iran attacks. Ezekiel 38:13 (NKJV) "Sheba, Dedan, the merchants of Tarshish, and all their young lions." Sheba and Dedan are universally believed to be Saudi Arabia, which has maintained open support for Israel these last few years, much to the anger of Iran and fanatical Islam. The identity of the "Merchants of Tarshish" and the "young lions" are more vague. There are several possibilities for Tarshish, but the common theme that runs through the possibilities is they are from the far west of Israel and on the Mediterranean Sea. They could be from the north coast of Africa, Spain or even Great Britain. One of the popular candidates for the "young lions" is the USA. IF so, this is the only place in the Bible where the USA is inferred in prophecy. The USA is the strongest economic and military country ever formed, so why is it conspicuous by its absence in the Bible and especially in latter-day writings? The obvious answer is the USA is either unwilling or unable to come to Israel's defense. Before we go on, please rest assured the following observations are not intended to either support or disparage any presidential administration. However, when viewed through the lens of Bible prophecy you can't help but notice the pendulum of political viewpoint regarding foreign policy as it swings either pro or anti-Israel. If the answer to the question of USA's absence in prophecy is its unwillingness, it could simply be because the level and commitment of support to Israel can waiver. One administration can be proactive and another not as much. It could be argued that our current president is more proactive as he authorized moving the USA's embassy from Tel Aviv to Jerusalem, something many before have promised to do but didn't because of the political fallout. Our past presidential administrations and state departments have insulted Israel in subtle and not so subtle ways. Most notably, then President Obama and Secretary of State Kerry are reported to have worked behind the scenes of orchestrating the members of the UN Security Council to vote 14-0 on December 23, 2016. The motion is to condemn Israel for developing the expansion settlements of their ancestral heritage land, Judea, and Samaria (West Bank). The motion also calls for Israel to place oversight for the old city, which includes the temple mount, the western (wailing) wall, and other holy sites for Christianity and Judaism over to Muslim control. The US used to be Israel's only country they could depend on for back up, but with this motion, the US effectively stabbed Israel in the back by supporting the "Palestinian" position. No country came to Israel's defense. Furthermore, there is an anti-Semitic movement called Boycott, Divest and Sanction Movement (BDS). It was initiated by Palestinians as a protest against the Israeli "occupation" of the West Bank. There are many companies in the US who agree with this movement. The world has distanced themselves from Israel just as predicted 2,800 years go by Israel's prophets. The answer to our question of why the USA is absent from Bible prophecy is we are unable to do so. It is foolish of us to trust Iran or North Korea to dismantle their nuclear arsenal. This will be explained in detail when we look at the second horse of the Apocalypse in chapter 17.

D.  Israel will be left alone to defend herself from the onslaught, but it is by God's hand they are protected. God will make His purpose known to the world and Israel that God's covenant with God's chosen people still stands. Ezekiel 38:16 and 23 (NKJV) "16 It will be in the latter days that I will bring you against My land, so that the nations may know Me." and "23 Thus I will magnify Myself and sanctify Myself, and I will be known in the eyes of many nations. Then they shall know that I am the LORD.'" Ezekiel 39:22 (NKJV) "So the house of Israel shall know that I am the LORD their God from that day forward." God will personally intervene and destroy Israel's attackers. Ezekiel 38:18-22 (NKJV) "18 That My fury will show in My face. 19 For in My jealousy and in the fire of My wrath I have spoken: 'Surely in that day there shall be a great earthquake in the land of Israel 20 so that the fish of the sea, the birds of the heavens, the beasts of the field, all creeping things that creep on the earth, and all men who are on the face of the earth shall shake at My presence. The mountains shall be thrown down, the steep places shall fall, and every wall shall fall to the ground.' 21 I will call for a sword against Gog throughout all My mountains," says the Lord GOD. "Every man's sword will be against his brother. 22 And I will bring him to judgment with pestilence and bloodshed; I will rain down on him, on his troops, and on the many peoples who are with him, flooding rain, great hailstones, fire, and brimstone." Like in the days of Moses and Pharaoh, God will cause the ground to open up and swallow Israel's enemies and call for the skies to unleash their calamities so that the Jews never have to lift a finger. God Almighty, Himself will destroy the invading armies via manipulating the earth's environment and what is called today friendly fire where soldiers erroneously fire upon their comrades.

E.  This war is sometimes confused with Armageddon. There are similarities in regards to the timing of the Rapture in relation to the Tribulation (Pre, Mid or Post Tribulation), but Ezekiel 39:9 (NKJV) "Then those who dwell in the cities of Israel will go out and set on fire and burn the weapons, and they will make fires with them for seven years." This length of time coincides with the length of time for the Tribulation. The text seems to corroborate the position that it occurs just before or just after the beginning of the Tribulation. Additionally, when His Millennial Kingdom on earth is created, we will not have a need for anything from the former seven years' time as all our needs will be met. Isaiah 51:3-4 (NKJV) "3 For the LORD will comfort Zion, He will comfort all her waste places; He will make her wilderness like Eden, and her desert like the garden of the LORD; Joy and gladness will be found in it, Thanksgiving and the voice of melody. 4 "Listen to Me, My people; and give ear to Me, O My nation: For the law will proceed from Me, and I will make My justice rest as a light of the peoples."

The players of the Gog/Magog war are definitely lining up as the stage is being set.

# Chapter 15

# "What's Next?"

So, now we have come full circle. Remember the purpose of this period is twofold, primarily for the Jews coming to faith and accepting that Jesus is the Messiah, and secondarily for the judgment of the Gentile world. During that time, all hell will break loose, literally. Only Jesus has the power to make things right, however, it's going to get worse before it gets better. Nonetheless, Christ will win in the end. Below is an overview of the Book of Revelation with important key verses. Let's take a moment to clarify an incorrect understanding of the term "Apocalypse." Nearly everyone, both the churched and unchurched, have heard the terms Armageddon, Rapture, Tribulation, and Apocalypse. However, many of both groups are uneducated on the correct meaning of those terms. Trust me they have nothing to do with vampires, zombies, or walking dead. Apocalypse is incorrectly identified as a horrible final event or war or a harbinger of doom. The correct definition of Apocalypse is a Greek term meaning "to reveal" or "to remove the curtain," a Revelation. Through John, God lays out His final seven-year plan to reclaim those souls left after in the Rapture, Jew, and Gentile. Notice below chart does not give specific definitions of the length of time each calamity takes. Some may take days, some might take weeks or months. The only time of note is the half way point (7 years split in half equals 3 ½ years each) at the abomination of desolation mentioned in Daniel 9:27, Matthew 24:15, and Revelation 13:5-7 "⁵ And there was given unto him a mouth speaking great things and blasphemies; and power was given unto him to "continue" forty and two months (second half 3 ½ years). ⁶ And he opened his mouth in blasphemy against God, to blaspheme His name, and His tabernacle, and them that dwell in heaven. ⁷ And it was given unto him to make war with the saints, and to overcome them: and power was given him over all kindreds, and tongues, and nations."

The first half is called the Tribulation and the second half is called the Great Tribulation. The Book of Revelation breaks down the first half of the Tribulation in chapters 6-11, where we see the arrival of the Four Horsemen of the Apocalypse (also the first 4 seals), followed by the remaining 3 of the 7 seals, after which point we have the sealing of the 144,000, the seven trumpets, and closing out the first half, the introduction of the two witnesses. Chapter 12 details the midpoint with the woman giving birth and the Dragon lying in wait to devour the child. The Great Tribulation begins the second half in chapter 13, detailing the Beasts of the Sea and of the Earth, the 144,000 once again, and ending with the final seven bowls including the gathering of Satan's forces at Armageddon in chapter 16. In chapters 17 through the 1st half of 19, speaks about the Scarlet Woman, mystery Babylon, the Final Battle, Christ's arrival as Messiah where He completes His final victory, and lastly, the Beast and the False Prophet being thrown into the lake of fire. The 2nd half of chapter 19 through chapter 22, we are given details about Satan being bound and cast into the lake of fire while we rule with Christ on earth for 1,000 years, aka the Millennium. It then closes out with God recasting the earth and heaven into a new earth and new heaven where we will live for eternity.

| CHAPTER | VERSES | TITLE | KEY VERSE (S) |
|---|---|---|---|
| 6 | 1-2 | First Seal: The Conqueror | "2 And I saw, and behold, a white horse. And he that sat on it had a bow, and a crown was given unto him, and he went forth conquering and to conquer." |
| | 3-4 | Second Seal: Conflict on Earth | "4 And there went out another horse that was red. And power was given to him that sat thereon to take peace from the earth, and that they should kill one another, and there was given unto him a great sword." |
| | 5-6 | Third Seal: Scarcity on Earth | "5 And when he had opened the third seal, I heard the third beast say, Come and see. And I beheld, and lo a black horse; and he that sat on him had a pair of balances in his hand." |

| | | | |
|---|---|---|---|
| | 7-8 | Fourth Seal: Widespread Death on Earth | "⁸ And I looked, and behold a pale horse: and his name that sat on him was Death, and Hell followed with him. And power was given unto them over the fourth part of the earth, to kill with sword, and with hunger, and with death, and with the beasts of the earth." |
| | 9-11 | Fifth Seal: The Cry of the Martyrs | "¹⁰ And they cried with a loud voice, saying, How long, O Lord, holy and true, dost thou not judge and avenge our blood on them that dwell on the earth? ¹¹ And white robes were given unto every one of them; and it was said unto them, that they should rest yet for a little season, until their fellow servants also and their brethren, that should be killed as they were, should be fulfilled." |
| | 12-17 | Sixth Seal: Cosmic Disturbances | "¹² And I beheld when he had opened the sixth seal, and, lo, there was a great earthquake; and the sun became black as sackcloth of hair, and the moon became as blood; " |
| | | | "¹⁶ And said to the mountains and rocks, Fall on us, and hide us from the face of him that sitteth on the throne, and from the wrath of the Lamb: ¹⁷ For the great day of His wrath is come; and who shall be able to stand?" |
| 7 | 1-8 | The Sealed of Israel | "⁴ And I heard the number of them which were sealed. And there were sealed an hundred and forty-four thousand of all the tribes of the children of Israel: " |
| | 9-17 | A Multitude from the Great Tribulation | "⁹ After this I beheld, and, lo, a great multitude, which no man could number, of all nations, and kindreds, and people, and tongues, stood before the throne, and before the Lamb, clothed with white robes, and palms in their hands; ¹⁰ And cried with a loud voice, saying, Salvation to our |

| | | | |
|---|---|---|---|
| | | | God which sitteth upon the throne, and unto the Lamb." |
| 8 | 1-6 | Seventh Seal: Prelude to the Seven Trumpets | "¹ And when He opened the seventh seal, there was silence in heaven for about half an hour." |
| | 7 | First Trumpet: Vegetation Struck | "⁷ The first angel sounded: and there followed hail and fire mingled with blood, and they were cast upon the earth. And a third part of the trees was burned up, and all green grass was burned up." |
| | 8-9 | Second Trumpet: The Seas Struck | "⁸ And the second angel sounded, and as it were a great mountain burning with fire was cast into the sea: and the third part of the sea became blood; ⁹ And the third part of the creatures which were in the sea, and had life, died; and the third part of the ships were destroyed." |
| | 10-11 | Third Trumpet: The Waters Struck | "¹¹ The name of the star is called Wormwood. And the third part of the waters became wormwood, and many men died from of the waters because they were made bitter." |
| | 12-13 | Fourth Trumpet: The Heavens Struck | "¹² And the fourth angel sounded: and a third part of the sun was smitten, and the third part of the moon, and a third part of the stars, so as the third of them were darkened, and the day shone not for a third part of it, and the night likewise." |

| | | | |
|---|---|---|---|
| 9 | 1-12 | Fifth Trumpet: The Locusts from the Bottomless Pit | "³ And there came out of the smoke locusts upon the earth: and unto them was given power, as the scorpions of the earth have power. ⁴ And it was commanded them that they should not hurt the grass of the earth, neither any green thing, neither any tree; but only those men which have not the seal of God in their foreheads. ⁵ And to them it was given that they should not kill them, but that they should be tormented five months: and their torment was as the torment of a scorpion, when he striketh a man. ⁶ And in those days shall men seek death, and shall not find it; and shall desire to die, and death shall flee from them." |
| | 13-21 | Sixth Trumpet: The Angels from the Euphrates | "¹⁴ Saying to the sixth angel which had the trumpet, Loose the four angels which are bound in the great river Euphrates. ¹⁵ And the four angels were loosed, which were prepared for an hour, and a day, and a month, and a year, for to slay the third part of men." |
| 10 | 1-7 | The Mighty Angel with the Little Book | "¹ And I saw another mighty angel come down from heaven, clothed with a cloud: and a rainbow was upon his head, and his face was as it were the sun, and his feet as pillars of fire: ² And he had in his hand a little book open: and he set his right foot upon the sea, and his left foot on the earth." |
| | 8-11 | John Eats the Little Book | "¹⁰ And I took the little book out of the angel's hand, and ate it up; and it was in my mouth sweet as honey: and as soon as I had eaten it, my belly was bitter. ¹¹ And he said unto me, thou must prophesy again before many peoples, and nations, and tongues, and kings." |

| | | | |
|---|---|---|---|
| 11 | 1-6 | The Two Witnesses | "³ And I will give power unto my two witnesses, and they shall prophesy a thousand two hundred and threescore days, clothed in sackcloth. ⁴ These are the two olive trees, and the two candlesticks standing before the God of the earth. ⁵ And if any man will hurt them, fire proceedeth out of their mouth, and devoureth their enemies: and if any man will hurt them, he must in this manner be killed. ⁶ These have power to shut heaven, that it rain not in the days of their prophecy: and have power over waters to turn them to blood, and to smite the earth with all plagues, as often as they will." |
| | 7-10 | The Witnesses Killed | "⁷ And when they shall have finished their testimony, the beast that ascendeth out of the bottomless pit shall make war against them, and shall overcome them, and kill them." |
| | 11-14 | The Witnesses Resurrected | "¹¹ And after three days and an half the spirit of life from God entered into them, and they stood upon their feet; and great fear fell upon them which saw them." |
| | 15-19 | Seventh Trumpet: The Kingdom Proclaimed | "¹⁵ And the seventh angel sounded; and there were great voices in heaven, saying, "The kingdoms of this world are become the kingdoms of our Lord, and of his Christ; and he shall reign for ever and ever." |
| 12 | 1-6 | The Woman, the Child, and the Dragon | "¹ And there appeared a great wonder in heaven; a woman clothed with the sun, and the moon under her feet, and upon her head a crown of twelve stars: ² And she being with child cried, travailing in birth, and pained to be delivered. ³ And there appeared another wonder in heaven; and behold a great red dragon, having seven heads and ten horns, and seven crowns upon his heads." |

|    |       |                           |                                                                                                                                                                                                                                                                                                                                                                                                                                                                                                                                                                                                                                                |
|----|-------|---------------------------|---|
|    | 7-12  | Satan Thrown Out of Heaven | "⁹ And the great dragon was cast out, that old serpent, called the Devil, and Satan, which deceiveth the whole world: he was cast out into the earth, and his angels were cast out with him." |
|    | 13-17 | The Woman Persecuted      | "¹³ And when the dragon saw that he was cast unto the earth, he persecuted the woman which brought forth the man child." |
| 13 | 1-10  | The Beast from the Sea    | "¹ And I stood upon the sand of the sea, and saw a beast rise up out of the sea, having seven heads and ten horns, and upon his horns ten crowns, and upon his heads the name of blasphemy." |
|    |       |                           | "⁸ And all that dwell upon the earth shall worship him, whose names are not written in the book of life of the Lamb slain from the foundation of the world." |
|    | 11-18 | The Beast from the Earth  | "¹¹ And I beheld another beast coming up out of the earth; and he had two horns like a lamb, and he spake as a dragon." and "¹⁶ And he causeth all, both small and great, rich and poor, free and bond, to receive a mark in their right hand, or in their foreheads: ¹⁷ And that no man might buy or sell, save he that had the mark, or the name of the beast, or the number of his name.¹⁸ Here is wisdom. Let him that hath understanding count the number of the beast: for it is the number of a man; and his number is Six hundred threescore and six (666)." |

| | | | |
|---|---|---|---|
| 14 | 1-5 | The Lamb and the 144,000 | "$^1$ And I looked, and, lo, a Lamb stood on the mount Sion, and with him an hundred forty and four thousand, having his Father's name written in their foreheads." and "$^4$ These are they which were not defiled with women; for they are virgins. These are they which follow the Lamb whithersoever he goeth. These were redeemed from among men, being the firstfruits unto God and to the Lamb." |
| | 6-13 | The Proclamations of Three Angels | "$^9$ And the third angel followed them, saying with a loud voice, If any man worship the beast and his image, and receive his mark in his forehead, or in his hand, $^{10}$ The same shall drink of the wine of the wrath of God, which is poured out without mixture into the cup of his indignation; and he shall be tormented with fire and brimstone in the presence of the holy angels, and in the presence of the Lamb." |
| | 14-16 | Reaping the Earth's Harvest | "$^{16}$ And he that sat on the cloud thrust in his sickle on the earth; and the earth was reaped." |
| | 17-20 | Reaping the Grapes of Wrath | "$^{20}$ And the winepress was trodden without the city, and blood came out of the winepress, even unto the horse bridles, by the space of a thousand and six hundred furlongs." |
| 15 | 1-18 | Prelude to the Bowl Judgments | "$^1$ And I saw another sign in heaven, great and marvellous, seven angels having the seven last plagues; for in them is filled up the wrath of God." and "$^7$ And one of the four beasts gave unto the seven angels seven golden vials full of the wrath of God, who liveth for ever and ever." |

| | | | |
|---|---|---|---|
| 16 | 1-2 | First Bowl: Loathsome Sores | "² And the first went, and poured out his vial upon the earth; and there fell a noisome and grievous sore upon the men which had the mark of the beast, and upon them which worshipped his image." |
| | 3 | Second Bowl: The Sea Turns to Blood | "³ And the second angel poured out his vial upon the sea; and it became as the blood of a dead man: and every living soul died in the sea." |
| | 4-7 | Third Bowl: The Waters Turn to Blood | "⁴ And the third angel poured out his vial upon the rivers and fountains of waters; and they became blood." |
| | 8-9 | Fourth Bowl: Men Are Scorched | "⁸ And the fourth angel poured out his vial upon the sun; and power was given unto him to scorch men with fire." |
| | 10-11 | Fifth Bowl: Darkness and Pain | "¹⁰ And the fifth angel poured out his vial upon the seat of the beast; and his kingdom was full of darkness; and they gnawed their tongues for pain, ¹¹ And blasphemed the God of heaven because of their pains and their sores, and repented not of their deeds." |
| | 12-16 | Sixth Bowl: Euphrates Dried Up | "¹² And the sixth angel poured out his vial upon the great river Euphrates; and the water thereof was dried up, that the way of the kings of the east might be prepared." |
| | | | "¹⁶ And he gathered them together into a place called in the Hebrew tongue Armageddon." |

|    |       |                                           |                                                                                                                                                                                                                                                                                                            |
|----|-------|-------------------------------------------|------------------------------------------------------------------------------------------------------------------------------------------------------------------------------------------------------------------------------------------------------------------------------------------------------------|
|    | 17-21 | Seventh Bowl: The Earth Utterly Shaken    | "17 And the seventh angel poured out his vial into the air; and there came a great voice out of the temple of heaven, from the throne, saying, It is done. 18 And there were voices, and thunders, and lightnings; and there was a great earthquake, such as was not since men were upon the earth, so mighty an earthquake, and so great." |
| 17 | 1-6   | The Scarlet Woman and the Scarlet Beast   | "3 So he carried me away in the spirit into the wilderness: and I saw a woman sit upon a scarlet coloured beast, full of names of blasphemy, having seven heads and ten horns. 4 And the woman was arrayed in purple and scarlet colour, and decked with gold and precious stones and pearls, having a golden cup in her hand full of abominations and filthiness of her fornication." |
|    | 7-18  | The Meaning of the Woman and the Beast    | "7 And the angel said unto me, Wherefore didst thou marvel? I will tell thee the mystery of the woman, and of the beast that carrieth her, which hath the seven heads and ten horns." |
| 18 | 1-8   | The Fall of Babylon the Great             | "2 And he cried mightily with a strong voice, saying, Babylon the great is fallen, is fallen, and is become the habitation of devils, and the hold of every foul spirit, and a cage of every unclean and hateful bird." |
|    | 9-20  | The World Mourns Babylon's Fall           | "9 And the kings of the earth, who have committed fornication and lived deliciously with her, shall bewail her, and lament for her, when they shall see the smoke of her burning, 10 Standing afar off for the fear of her torment, saying, Alas, alas that great city Babylon, that mighty city! for in one hour is thy judgment come." |

| | | | |
|---|---|---|---|
| | 21-24 | Finality of Babylon's Fall | "²¹ And a mighty angel took up a stone like a great millstone, and cast it into the sea, saying, Thus with violence shall that great city Babylon be thrown down, and shall be found no more at all." |
| 19 | 1-10 | Heaven Exults over Babylon | "⁷ Let us be glad and rejoice, and give honour to him: for the marriage of the Lamb is come, and his wife hath made herself ready. ⁸ And to her was granted that she should be arrayed in fine linen, clean and white: for the fine linen is the righteousness of saints. ⁹ And he saith unto me, Write, Blessed are they which are called unto the marriage supper of the Lamb. And he saith unto me, These are the true sayings of God." |
| | 11-16 | Christ on a White Horse | "¹¹ And I saw heaven opened, and behold a white horse; and he that sat upon him was called Faithful and True, and in righteousness he doth judge and make war." and "¹⁵ And out of his mouth goeth a sharp sword, that with it he should smite the nations: and he shall rule them with a rod of iron: and he treadeth the winepress of the fierceness and wrath of Almighty God. ¹⁶ And he hath on his vesture and on his thigh a name written, KING OF KINGS, AND LORD OF LORDS." |
| | 17-21 | The Beast and His Armies Defeated | "²⁰ And the beast was taken, and with him the false prophet that wrought miracles before him, with which he deceived them that had received the mark of the beast, and them that worshipped his image. These both were cast alive into a lake of fire burning with brimstone." |
| 20 | 1-3 | Satan Bound 1,000 Years | "¹ And I saw an angel come down from heaven, having the key of the bottomless pit and a great chain in his hand. ² And he laid hold on the dragon, that old serpent, which is the Devil, and Satan, and bound him a thousand years." |

| | 4-6 | The Saints Reign with Christ 1,000 Years | "⁴ And I saw thrones, and they sat upon them, and judgment was given unto them: and I saw the souls of them that were beheaded for the witness of Jesus, and for the word of God, and which had not worshipped the beast, neither his image, neither had received his mark upon their foreheads, or in their hands; and they lived and reigned with Christ a thousand years." |
|---|---|---|---|
| | 7-10 | Satanic Rebellion Crushed | "⁷ And when the thousand years are expired, Satan shall be loosed out of his prison, ⁸ And shall go out to deceive the nations which are in the four quarters of the earth, Gog, and Magog, to gather them together to battle: the number of whom is as the sand of the sea." |
| | 11-15 | The Great White Throne Judgment | "¹¹ And I saw a great white throne, and him that sat on it, from whose face the earth and the heaven fled away; and there was found no place for them. ¹² And I saw the dead, small and great, stand before God; and the books were opened: and another book was opened, which is the book of life: and the dead were judged out of those things which were written in the books, according to their works." |
| 21 | 1-8 | All Things Made New | "¹ And I saw a new heaven and a new earth: for the first heaven and the first earth were passed away; and there was no more sea." and "⁴ And God shall wipe away all tears from their eyes; and there shall be no more death, neither sorrow, nor crying, neither shall there be any more pain: for the former things are passed away." |

| | | | |
|---|---|---|---|
| | 9-21 | The New Jerusalem | "¹⁰ And he carried me away in the spirit to a great and high mountain, and shewed me that great city, the holy Jerusalem, descending out of heaven from God, ¹¹ Having the glory of God: and her light was like unto a stone most precious, even like a jasper stone, clear as crystal." |
| | 22-27 | The Glory of the New Jerusalem | "²² And I saw no temple therein: for the Lord God Almighty and the Lamb are the temple of it. ²³ And the city had no need of the sun, neither of the moon, to shine in it: for the glory of God did lighten it, and the Lamb is the light thereof." |
| 22 | 1-5 | The River of Life | "¹ And he shewed me a pure river of water of life, clear as crystal, proceeding out of the throne of God and of the Lamb." |
| | 6-11 | The Time Is Near | "⁷ Behold, I come quickly: blessed is he that keepeth the sayings of the prophecy of this book." and "¹⁰ And he saith unto me, Seal not the sayings of the prophecy of this book: for the time is at hand." |
| | 12-17 | Jesus Testifies to the Churches | "¹² And, behold, I come quickly; and my reward is with me, to give every man according as his work shall be. ¹³ I am Alpha and Omega, the beginning and the end, the first and the last." |
| | 18-19 | A Warning | "¹⁸ For I testify unto every man that heareth the words of the prophecy of this book, If any man shall add unto these things, God shall add unto him the plagues that are written in this book: ¹⁹ And if any man shall take away from the words of the book of this prophecy, God shall take away his part out of the book of life, and out of the holy city, and from the things which are written in this book (Book of Life)." |

| 20-21 | I Am Coming Quickly | "[20] He which testifieth these things saith, Surely I come quickly. Amen. Even so, come, Lord Jesus!" |

# Chapter 16

# "The One World Leader"

Before we unpack the Tribulation, the Day of the Lord, Day of Wrath of God, or Daniel's 70th week, as it is laid out in the Book of Revelation, we need to make clear that the person we call the Antichrist cannot appear until the Holy Spirit is moved out of the way. At the beginning of our discussion,, when we looked at the fourth point of why to study prophecy, the Holy Spirit has a finite period of ministry. 2 Thessalonians 2:5-8 (NKJV) "5 Do you not remember that when I was still with you I told you these things? 6 And now you know what is restraining, that he may be revealed in his own time. 7 For the mystery of lawlessness is already at work; only He who now restrains will do so until He is taken out of the way. 8 And then the lawless one will be revealed, whom the Lord will consume with the breath of His mouth and destroy with the brightness of His coming." The "Restrainer" mentioned in vs. 6 and 7 is the Holy Spirit, while the "lawless one" is the Antichrist. In this passage, Paul clearly states that the Holy Spirit/Restrainer must be moved out of the way for the Antichrist/Lawless one to appear. As we mentioned earlier, there probably may be a period of time between the Rapture event and the beginning of the Tribulation. The movement of the Restrainer out of the way is most likely to happen just before the beginning of the Tribulation when the Antichrist confirms his seven-year peace treaty. It is also important to note that there is a school of thought that suggests the Holy Spirit may still have work to do in the Tribulation, which is to bring people into conviction and repentance. Notice in vs 7 it says, "He is taken out of the way" not removed from the earth. In Acts 2, the Holy Spirit was sent to encourage and empower the new believers on Pentecost at the birth of the church. Nowhere is He recalled, not even at the Rapture. Acts 2:38-39 "38 Then Peter said unto them, Repent, and be baptized every one of you in the name of Jesus Christ for the remission of sins, and ye shall receive the gift of the Holy Ghost. 39 For the promise is unto you, and to your children, and to all that are afar off, even as many as the Lord our God shall call." Furthermore, during the whole period of the Tribulation, there will be a "multitude" of Jews and Gentiles who will now come to faith and accept Jesus as Messiah and Lord, many who of whom will eventually be martyred for their faith. Revelation 7:13-14 "¹³ And one of the elders answered, saying unto me, "What are these which are arrayed in white robes? and whence came they? ¹⁴ And I said unto him, Sir, thou knowest." And he said to me, "These are they which came out of great tribulation, and have washed their robes, and made them white in the blood of the Lamb." Revelation 20:4. "And I saw thrones, and they sat upon them, and judgment was given unto them: and I saw the souls of them that were beheaded for the witness of Jesus, and for the word of God, and which had not worshipped the beast, neither his image, neither had received his mark upon their foreheads, or in their hands; and they lived and reigned with Christ a thousand years." One last point about 2 Thessalonians 2:7 "For the mystery of lawlessness is already at work;" The mystery referred to is that nobody but God Himself knows the date of the Messiah's (second) coming., including Jesus, who knew His mission from a very early age. Luke 2:42 "And when He was twelve years old, they went up to Jerusalem after the custom of the Feast." He got separated from His parents and was later found in the temple teaching. Luke 2:48-50 "⁴⁸ And when they saw him, they were amazed: and His mother said unto him, Son, why hast thou thus dealt with us? behold, thy father and I have sought thee sorrowing. ⁴⁹ And He said unto them, "How is it that ye sought me? wist ye not that I must be about my Father's business? ⁵⁰ And they understood not the saying which He spake unto them."

Certainly, Satan does not know the date of Christ's return, even with all his knowledge of the scriptures. Satan has to have had agents in place ready to assume power over the course of history, Nimrod and the Tower of Babel, Pharaoh and the Egyptians, Haman and the Persian Empire, Nebuchadnezzar and the Babylonian Empire, The Kings of Assyria and the genocide of the ten northern tribes, Caesar and the Romans, Queen Isabella and King Ferdinand and the Spanish Inquisition, Hitler and the Holocaust, and finally, Stalin and the Purge. Let's consider this point. These emissaries of Satan all thought they were doing "good." They all thought they were eradicating a sub human genetically inferior race. They were totally deceived and manipulated. Satan can masquerade as anything he wishes, including an angel of light. 2 Corinthians 11:13-14 "¹³ For such are false apostles, deceitful workers, transforming themselves into apostles of Christ. ¹⁴ And no marvel; for Satan, himself is transformed into an angel of light." It is consistent that the future Antichrist may not yet know his identity or mission until the time is right for him to come forward to confirm the seven-year peace deal.

The idea of a one world leader, a one world government or a new world order is not so "new." The Bible tells us in Genesis 11 that the idea of a one world leader or government was attempted when the men at that time tried to make themselves equal to God by building the Tower of Babel. God couldn't destroy men again because of His covenant with Noah so he confused their speech. Genesis 11:8 "So the LORD scattered them abroad from thence upon the face of all the earth, and they left off to build the city." Since then, there have been many who have tried to conquer the known world, but have all failed. After World War II, the United Nations was created so that the countries of the world could come together economically and militarily to affect cooperation and defense. However, right from the start, their agenda was to form a one world global government. Several of its founders expressed just that idea. In 1945, Paul Henri Spaak, was the first elected chairman of the General Assembly of the United Nations. He is credited with the following quote: "We do not want another committee. We have too many already. What we want is a man of sufficient stature to hold the allegiance of all people and to lift us out of the economic morass in which we are sinking. Send us such a man and be he god or the devil we will receive him." According to Focus on Belgium (a state sponsored tourism and marketing website), "Spaak is one of the founding fathers of the European Union (EU)." Robert Muller was appointed for his first term as Assistant Secretary General in 1948. He is attributed with making the following quote: "We must move as quickly as possible to a one world government, a one world religion, under a one world leader." The Director of the UN World Health Organization Brock Chisum said in 1991 "To achieve a One World Government, it is necessary to remove from the mind of men their individualism, loyalty to family traditions, national patriotism, and religious dogmas." In 2009 the New York Times reported the then Pope Benedict "called for a reform of the United Nations so there could be a unified "global political body" that allowed the less powerful of the earth to have a voice, and he called on rich nations to help less fortunate ones." This sentiment is not exclusive to Europe.

Have you ever really looked at the back of a US dollar bill? On the left-hand side, where the Free Mason's all-seeing eye is, just under is the Latin phrase "Novus Ordo Seclorum," translated "New World Order." In 1990, George Bush Sr. delivered a speech before Congress at the beginning of the first Gulf war when Iraq invaded Kuwait. In it he said, "...What is at stake is more than one small country. It is a big idea, a new world order where diverse nations are drawn together in common cause to achieve the universal aspirations of mankind; peace and security, freedom, and the rule of law. Such is a world worthy of our struggle and worthy of our children's future." In a speech to the Kennedy Center in Washington DC, Bill Clinton stated, "And, after 1989, President Bush said, and it's a phrase that I use often myself, that we needed a New World Order." This phrase has been used by several presidents; most recently by President Obama when addressing the UN in September 2016. The ground work for a one world leader is being laid. Fast forward to November 11, 2018, France, and many other countries, commemorated the 100-year anniversary of the end of World War I. The French president Macron, declared that "patriotism is the exact opposite of nationalism." Additionally, the next day, German Chancellor Angela Merkel in a speech at the European Parliament, in agreement with Macron, announced that there should be "a real European (united) army." As another interesting item of note, with Great Britain leaving the EU (Brexit), we may be witnessing a reorganization of that part of the world's economic and political cooperation. The nightly news networks have no shortage of horrible news stories about the level of unrest and insecurity in Europe, South America, the Middle East, Africa, China, and the US. The world is desperate, and is looking for a leader who can bring peace and safety.

# Chapter 17

# "The Four Horsemen"

Let's get back to the beginning of the Tribulation. Since the seven seals, seven trumpets, and seven bowls are listed in the chart above, they will not be included them here. For the most part, they are self-explanatory. However, we will be looking at the key players and events during and Post-Tribulation. The first four seals to be opened are more commonly known as the Four Horsemen of the Apocalypse.

- The First Horse, the White Horse of the Conqueror. At some point in the not too distant future, there will be a last gentile person who accepts Christ before the command for the Rapture is issued. As millions of people (some suggest possibly including children) will suddenly disappear, without explanation, in the ensuing chaos and hysteria, and in close proximity to the Gog/Magog war, those people left behind will become exceedingly desperate as they look for a "savior." Empty churches will fill up with people frantically looking for an explanation or missing loved ones. People who have attended church all their lives, but never committed their lives to Christ, will be in the front rows. Almost certainty the world's economies will crash. Access to cash and the ability to buy goods, particularly food, will most undoubtedly be affected. People will go into survival mode owing to the utter devastation and economic chaos that ensues when millions of taxpayers suddenly vanish can only be imagined. Further, the sudden stoppage of the free flow of cash with millions no longer paying payroll or sales taxes, meeting mortgage payments, car loans, or credit cards. The Achilles heel is that there is a limited amount of backup supplies in the supply chain. It is estimated that within 72 hours stores will run out of inventory on store shelves. As people panic, they will try to grab or loot what they can as this scenario unfolds, they will become hysterical in the process. Today's problems of the country of Venezuela is a frighteningly real example. A counterfeit Christ will appear and seem to have all the answers, and as we know, the counterfeit clone's the genuine. We have already examined a couple of times Daniel 9:27 where the Antichrist will bring a seven-year peace treaty to start the Tribulation. He will bring a false sense of security as he assumes political power and control across the globe. The First Horse of the Apocalypse appears and will arrive on a White horse, a symbol of Kingship, to imitate Christ's return as the victor in chapter 19. Revelation 6:2 "And I saw, and behold a white horse: and he that sat on him had a bow; and a crown was given unto him: and he went forth conquering, and to conquer." Revelation 19:11 "And I saw heaven opened, and behold a white horse; and He that sat upon him was called Faithful and True, and in righteousness He doth judge and make war." Satan knows the scriptures and his intention is to deceive as many people as possible. Remember Jesus' and Paul's biggest warnings are against deception.

The chart below lists other names by which the Antichrist is known. Just a note the term "Antichrist" is only found in 1 John (2:18, 2:22, 4:3), and 2 John (1:7).

| NAME | REF | VERSE |
| --- | --- | --- |
| The Antichrist | 1 John 2:18 (NKJV) | "[18] Little children, it is the last hour; and as you have heard that the Antichrist is coming, even now many antichrists have come, by which we know that it is the last hour." |
| The Adversary and The Enemy | Psalm 74:10 | "[10] O God, how long shall the adversary reproach? Shall the enemy blaspheme Thy name forever?" |
| The Vile Person | Daniel 11:21 | "[21] And in his estate shall stand up a vile person, to whom they shall not give the honor of the kingdom; but he shall come in peaceably, and seize the kingdom by flatteries." |

| | | |
|---|---|---|
| The Willful King | Daniel 11:36 | "³⁶ And the king shall do according to his will; and he shall exalt himself, and magnify himself above every god, and shall speak marvellous things against the God of gods, and shall prosper till the indignation be accomplished: for that that is determined shall be done." |
| The Son of Perdition and the Man of Sin | 2 Thessalonians 2:3-4 | "³ Let no man deceive you by any means: for that day shall not come, except there come a falling away first, and that man of sin be revealed, the son of perdition; ⁴ Who opposeth and exalteth himself above all that is called God, or that is worshipped; so that he as God sitteth in the temple of God, shewing himself that he is God." |
| The Lawless One | 2 Thessalonians 2:8 (NIV) | "⁸ And then the lawless one will be revealed, whom the Lord will overthrow with the breath of His mouth and destroy with the splendor of His coming." |
| The Angel of the Bottomless Pit | Revelation 9:11 | "¹¹ And they had a king over them, which is the angel of the bottomless pit, whose name in Hebrew tongue is Abaddon, but in Greek tongue hath his name Apollyon." |
| The Beast Out of the Sea | Revelation 13:1 | "¹ And I stood upon the sand of the sea, and saw a beast rise up out of the sea, having seven heads and ten horns, and upon his horns ten crowns, and upon his heads the name of blasphemy." |

| The Beast | Revelation 19:19-20 | "¹⁹ And I saw the beast, and the kings of the earth, and their armies, gathered together to make war against him that sat on the horse, and against his army. ²⁰ And the beast was taken, and with him the false prophet that wrought miracles before him, with which he deceived them that had received the mark of the beast, and them that worshipped his image. These both were cast alive into a lake o fire burning with brimstone." |

There is a great deal of speculation as to who the Antichrist is, but it is just that, speculation. For those who will be raptured this issue is a moot point, and for those who are left behind, they may or may not recognize him for who he is. As we just mentioned above, it is quite possible the person may not even know his true identity until he is called (by Satan) to come forth. The Bible gives us a few clues as to what the Antichrist will be like initially and his characteristics. During the first half of the Tribulation, he will appear and deceive many as a man of peace, as we have discussed at length. Daniel 11:20-23 (NKJV) "²⁰ There shall arise in his place one who imposes taxes on the glorious kingdom; but within a few days he shall be destroyed, but not in anger or in battle. ²¹ And in his place shall arise a vile person, to whom they will not give the honor of royalty; but he shall come in peaceably, and seize the kingdom by intrigue. ²² With the force of a flood they shall be swept away from before him and be broken, and also the prince of the covenant. ²³ And after the league is made with him he shall act deceitfully, for he shall come up and become strong with a small number of people." He will have two faces,: one public and one private. His public face will be Pro-Israel, tolerant, politically correct, persuasive, charismatic, charming, and easily believed. His private hidden face will be devious, heavily involved with the occult, and a false sense of prosperity will follow him. Daniel 8:23-25 (NKJV) "²³ And in the latter time of their kingdom, when the transgressors are come to the full, a king of fierce countenance, and understanding dark sentences, shall stand up. ²⁴ And his power shall be mighty, but not by his own power: and he shall destroy wonderfully, and shall prosper, and practice, and shall destroy the mighty and the holy people. ²⁵ "Through his cunning, He shall cause deceit to prosper under his rule, and he shall exalt himself in his heart. He shall destroy many in their prosperity. He shall even rise against the Prince of princes, but he shall be broken without human means."

As the world reels in chaos, the Antichrist will seize the opportunity to take control, first through diplomacy, then through force. Every nation on earth, including the USA, then may willingly surrender their sovereignty to him. As we previously discussed in Daniel chapters 2 and 7, he will then reorganize the world's governments into 10 areas, assuming direct control of three of them. Daniel 7:19-20 (NKJV) "[19] Then I wished to know the truth about the fourth Beast, which was different from all the others, exceedingly dreadful, with its teeth of iron and its nails of bronze, which devoured, broke in pieces, and trampled the residue with its feet; [20] and the ten horns that were on its head, and the other horn which came up, before which three fell, namely, that horn which had eyes and a mouth which spoke pompous words, whose appearance was greater than his fellows." Daniel 7:21-25 (NKJV) "[21] I was watching, and the same horn was making war against the saints, and prevailing against them, [22] until the Ancient of Days came, and a judgment was made in favor of the saints of the Most High, and the time came for the saints to possess the kingdom. [23] "Thus he said: 'The fourth Beast shall be a fourth kingdom on earth, which shall be different from all other kingdoms, and shall devour the whole earth, trample it and break it in pieces. [24] The ten horns are ten kings who shall arise from this kingdom. And another shall rise after them; He shall be different from the first ones and shall subdue three kings. [25] He shall speak pompous words against the Most High, shall persecute the saints of the Most High, and shall intend to change times and law. Then the saints shall be given into his hand for a time and times and half a time." Most people are not aware that the UN has designated ten regions across the globe to track a wide variety of social, health, and economic indicators known as the Millennium Development Goal Indicators. Could this quite possibly be the genesis from where the Antichrist sets up his government? Perhaps, why re-invent the wheel?

He will solidify his authority with the help from the leader of a false religious leader called the False Prophet. The False Prophet will offer comfort and direction with his ultra-ecumenical council or a "new one world religion." It is a practical impossibility to rule the world forcibly. However, if you control the news outlets and administrations (one world government), money supply (one world currency), and belief system (one world religion) they will follow like sheep to the slaughter. Matthew 7:15 "Beware of False Prophets, which come to you in sheep's clothing, but inwardly they are ravenous wolves." As the new world's religious leader, the False Prophet will have and exert a vast influence over a chaotic world. Together with the Antichrist, they will quietly garner more and more control over the masses. He will demonstrate his influence more pronouncedly during the second half of the Tribulation. He will be possibly from Israel, but not absolutely. Revelation 13:11-12 "[11] And I beheld another beast coming up out of the earth; and he had two horns like a lamb, and he spake as a dragon. [12] And he exerciseth all the power of the first beast before him, and causeth the earth and them which dwell therein to worship the first beast, whose deadly wound was healed." The phrase "coming up out of the earth" is believed to be a reference to the land of Israel. This would help the False Prophet secure his role as *the* religious leader for the Jewish people. Remember Jesus warned of this. Matthew 24:24 (NKJV) "For false Christs and false prophets will rise and show great signs and wonders to deceive, if possible, even the elect."

A word of warning, neither one of these two will actually call themselves the False Prophet or the Antichrist. However, armed with information contained in the Bible, those who remain can recognize them for who they are if they have the resources and take the time to research. There will be many printed Bibles left and there is a wealth of information on line and YouTube, presumably if they are operational or unaltered.

Getting back to the Antichrist, his number will be 666. Revelation 13:18 "This calls for wisdom. Let the person who has insight calculate the number of the Beast, for it is the number of a man. That number is 666." Another tool to confirm his identity is a Hebrew practice of assigning a numeric value to Hebrew letter characters called Gematria. When the Antichrist does show, if the numeric values of the letters of his name were applied they would total 666.

He will come from a gentile world, probably Europe. Daniel 7:2-3 (NKJV) "[2] Daniel spoke, saying, "I saw in my vision by night, and behold, the four winds of heaven were stirring up the Great Sea. [3] And four great Beasts came up from the sea, each different from the other." He will come out of the Great Sea, a reference to the Mediterranean Sea. Sometimes this area is referred to as the Revived Roman Empire. More importantly, Daniel 9:26a (NIV) "After the sixty-two 'sevens,' the Anointed One will be put to death and will have nothing. The people of the ruler who will come will destroy the city and the sanctuary." This is perhaps the most telling of the Antichrist's lineage. As we discovered earlier, in 70 AD the Roman Empire sacked Jerusalem and the Temple and destroyed it so that no stone would stand on another. The "people of the ruler who will destroy the city and the sanctuary" is clearly the Roman Empire. At the height of the Roman era, their occupation covered the northern coast of Africa up through the Middle East, and across Asia Minor. The Roman Empire continued to extend all over Europe as far west as Spain, as far north as Germany and Great Britain. He could come from anywhere within those borders, and perhaps even the USA as we are extensions of Europe and England. Again, in the interest of full disclosure, there are those who suggest that lineage of the Antichrist might be Muslim. The Muslims preach their "savior", the Mahdi, will return to earth to rule and reign over all the earth. This Mahdi is also to come amidst great turmoil. This reason and their ancestral hatred of the Jews explain why they are so zealous in their commitment to implant the Muslim faith and Sharia law worldwide. However, there is a huge problem about the Antichrist being Muslim. It is inconceivable that after all the thousands of years of history of facing persecution, extinction, and subsequent rebirth, that the Jews would be willing to shake off their newly reacquired home land and accept the Muslim alternative.

The beginning of the second half of this period begins with the abomination of desolation foretold by Daniel 9:27 and Matthew 24:15 as reported earlier. This second half will be even more devastating than the first half. The Antichrist will show his true colors. In order for him to enter the temple to elevate himself as God, he will need to move his base of operations to Jerusalem. Daniel 11:45 (NKJV) "And he (the Antichrist) shall plant the tents of his palace between the seas and the glorious holy mountain (Mt. Zion in Jerusalem), yet he shall come to his end, and no one will help him." 2 Thessalonians 2:4 "Who opposeth and exalteth himself above all that is called God, or that is worshipped; so that he as God sitteth in the temple of God, shewing himself that he is God." With the arrival of Satan, he commands the Antichrist to persecute Israel. Revelation 12:13 "And when the dragon saw that he was cast unto the earth, he persecuted the woman which brought forth the man child." The "Dragon" is identified as Satan, the "woman" is symbolic of the nation of Israel, and "the male child" is Jesus. With Satan being expelled from heaven and taking residence on earth, he, the

Antichrist, and the False Prophet make up an entity known as the Unholy or Satanic Trinity in an obvious attempt to imitate God's Trinity. We will come back to this Unholy Trinity and their roles in the second half in a bit.

The Antichrist will also imitate the death and resurrection of Jesus. Revelation 13:3 (NKJV) "And I saw one of his heads as if it had been mortally wounded, and his deadly wound was healed. And all the world marveled and followed the beast." Revelation 13:12 (NKJV) "And he exercises all the authority of the first Beast in his presence and causes the earth and those who dwell in it to worship the first Beast, whose deadly wound was healed." After the counterfeit resurrection, the False Prophet will orchestrate the entire world by trickery to worship the Dragon and the Beast. Revelation 13:4-6 "4 And they worshipped the dragon which gave power unto the beast: and they worshipped the beast, saying, "Who is like unto the beast? who is able to make war with him? 5 And there was given unto him a mouth speaking great things and blasphemies; and power was given unto him to continue forty and two months. 6 And he opened his mouth in blasphemy against God, to blaspheme His name, and His tabernacle, and them that dwell in heaven." He will deceive many by performing miracles and signs of wonder. 2 Thessalonians 2:9-12 (NIV) "9 The coming of the lawless one will be in accordance with how Satan works. He will use all sorts of displays of power through signs and wonders that serve the lie, 10 and all the ways that wickedness deceives those who are perishing. They perish because they refused to love the truth and so be saved. 11 For this reason God sends them a powerful delusion so that they will believe the lie 12 and so that all will be condemned who have not believed the truth but have delighted in wickedness." His greatest trick will be to make an image speak. Revelation 13:14-15 "14 And deceiveth them that dwell on the earth by the means of those miracles which he had power to do in the sight of the beast; saying to them that dwell on the earth, that they should make an image to the beast, which had the wound by a sword, and did live. 15 And he had power to give life unto the image of the beast, that the image of the beast should both speak, and cause that as many as would not worship the image of the beast should be killed."

As a sign of allegiance and obedience, the world's population will be required to take a mark in their right hand or forehead. The Antichrist will take control of all business transactions, ( i.e., banking, grocery, shopping, buying gas for your car, etc....) Revelation 13:16-17 "[16] And he causeth all, both small and great, rich and poor, free and bond, to receive a mark in their right hand, or in their foreheads: [17] and that no man might buy or sell, save he that had the mark, or the name of the beast, or the number of his name." If you refuse you will be hunted and put to death by beheading without due process of law. Revelation 20:4 "And I saw thrones, and they sat upon them, and judgment was given unto them: and I saw the souls of them that were beheaded for the witness of Jesus, and for the word of God, and which had not worshipped the beast, neither his image, neither had received his mark upon their foreheads, or in their hands; and they lived and reigned with Christ a thousand years." !!WARNING!! The Bible also clearly and firmly says anyone who accepts that mark on the hand or forehead cannot enter the kingdom of heaven. Revelation 14:9-11 (NKJV) "[9] Then a third angel followed them, saying with a loud voice, "If anyone worships the Beast and his image and receives his mark on his forehead or on his hand, [10] he himself shall also drink of the wine of the wrath of God, which is poured out full strength into the cup of His indignation. He shall be tormented with fire and brimstone in the presence of the holy angels and in the presence of the Lamb. [11] And the smoke of their torment ascends forever and ever; and they have no rest day or night, who worship the Beast and his image, and whoever receives the mark of his name."

The systems necessary for the Antichrist to control the world's economies and implement a system by a "mark" will not mysteriously appear overnight. They are here. With the implementation of the Euro and Bitcoin, a one world currency is being shaped. The new "chip" Visa and MasterCard credit cards and the development of Radio Frequency Identification (RFID) devices, that are the size of a grain of rice, which can be placed subcutaneously into the skin of the forehead or right hand. The point of sale (POS) processing systems are in place today and are being used. The world is spiraling to becoming a cashless society. Some retailers and banks assess a fee for taking cash or checks. There has also been developed a "tech tattoo." This is something like a UPC bar code that can hold medical or financial data that is actually tattooed on one's skin. All of these technologies are dependent on internet connectivity with each other. As an item of note, in March 2014 control of the Internet was quietly transferred from the US to the UN. This could be significant in the future when tracking a person will be a priority. The individual privacy rights we enjoy today will be erased. Every card swipe, Google search or internet login leaves a digital footprint. If you are alive at this time and not taken the mark, you can and will be hunted down. The authorities use computer algorithms to forecast or predict your behavior and habits, making it just that much easier to find you. Lastly, according to Wikipedia, there are at least 15 countries, including England and the US, that have and utilize License Plate Reading technology. High Definition (HD) cameras are set up at key intersections to scan and record cars' license plates, usually without the knowledge of the driver, and flag cars at the discretion of law enforcement. Whether it is programmed for stolen cars, Amber Alert, or tolls all the systems can sort through a mountain of information almost instantaneously. Lastly, with the advancement and development of Facial Recognition Software, that is comparing your captured picture to a picture in a database file like your DMV or passport photos, it is used when searching for faces in high volume travel sites, such as airports, train hubs, or bus terminals. The FBI already uses this highly sophisticated technology to search for fugitives or criminals.

- The Second Horse, the Red Horse of War. Revelation 6:4 "And there went out another horse that was red: and power was given to him that sat thereon to take peace from the earth, and that they should kill one another: and there was given unto him a great sword." We have already discussed that the Ezekiel 38and39 war is most unlikely to happen here. However, what is more likely is a nuclear war. Zechariah 14:12 (NKJV) "And this shall be the plague with which the Lord will strike all the people who fought against Jerusalem: Their flesh shall dissolve while they stand on their feet, their eyes shall dissolve in their sockets, and their tongues shall dissolve in their mouths." This verse is a description of a nuclear blast. There are only a handful of countries that have nuclear intercontinental ballistic missiles and police each other by a principle called the Balance of Power which is supposed to keep each other in check. Five countries that have signed a Nonproliferation Treaty which are the USA, Russia, China, Great Britain, and France. There are an additional four countries and a fifth one looming that have nuclear warhead capabilities but have not signed any such agreement, Israel, Pakistan, India, North Korea, and Iran, who, with the signed "Nuclear Deal" of 2015, is on a path to acquire and develop them, if they do not already secretly have them. As we have already previously pointed out, with the armies and populations of the western powers decimated, who will there be to stop the rogue nations from launching the first strike? There are two phenomena associated with nuclear detonation, based on witnessing the results of the two atomic bombs dropped on Japan at the end of WW II, the first is an Electro Magnetic Pulse (EMP) and the second is called nuclear winter. An EMP has an effective range of 25 miles from detonation. It fries every electric circuit in that area leaving survivors with no phones, computers, transportation, electricity to run refrigeration, lights, or anything else that needs electricity to run. It'll be like stepping back into the 19th century. Nuclear winter effects destruction is complete within 1 mile with gradually decreasing damage as you move further from the center for about 3.5 miles. In addition, it contaminates the ground with so much radiation nothing will grow for years. Imagine hundreds of thousands of acres of prime farmland becoming useless for decades, not to mention the health crisis that would result from radiation poisoning. If the bombs would explode over populated cities, there would be total destruction that would affect everything, infrastructure, utilities (water, electricity, and gas), housing, and hospitals. Today's bombs are hundred times more powerful, and with multiple missiles launched you can only imagine the devastation. If you have followed the news, you will realize that the US has a clear and present danger of this from North Korea with their "testings." Just ask the people of Guam and Hawaii if we should be alert. This scenario leads into the next horse.

- The Third Horse, the Black Horse of Famine. Revelation 6:5-6 "5 And when he had opened the third seal, I heard the third beast say, Come and see. And I beheld, and lo a black horse; and he that sat on him had a pair of balances in his hand. 6 And I heard a voice in the midst of the four beasts say, A measure of wheat for a penny, and three measures of barley for a penny; and see thou hurt not the oil and the wine." The point here is that daily needs, such as a loaf of bread will cost a full day's wage. The rich will also be impacted, but not nearly as much. In short, with the middle class evaporating, as the saying goes, the rich get richer and the poor get poorer is prophetic.

- The Fourth Horse, the Pale Horse of Death. Revelation 6:8 "And I looked, and behold a pale horse: and his name that sat on him was Death, and Hell followed with him. And power was given unto them over the fourth part of the earth, to kill with sword, and with hunger, and with death, and with the beasts of the earth." According to Strong's #G5515, the original Greek word used for "pale" is "chloros," a more accurate translation is "green." It's where we get our word for "chlorophyll." The text seems to indicate that daily living will be unbelievably hard. With fruit and vegetables greatly inaccessible, and livestock unavailable, people will literally be starving to death, which could the beginning of an environmental nightmare. This will also undoubtedly lead to riots adding to the death toll.

Before we move on, a current topic needs to be addressed that is controversial. The following text states there will be indescribable ecological cosmic destruction the world has never seen before. Revelation 6:12-14 "[12] And I beheld when he had opened the sixth seal, and, lo, there was a great earthquake; and the sun became black as sackcloth of hair, and the moon became as blood; [13] And the stars of heaven fell unto the earth, even as a fig tree casteth her untimely figs, when she is shaken of a mighty wind. [14] And the heaven departed as a scroll when it is rolled together; and every mountain and island were moved out of their places." When we looked at the Olivet Discourse, we looked at the correlation of Mathew 24:7-8 and Revelation 6:5-8 and the birth pangs (increasing in frequency and intensity) of earthquakes as they will go into overdrive during the Tribulation. "Earthquakes" and "mountain and islands moving" could happen hand in hand. The Fukushima Daiichi atomic accident as a result of a tsunami generated by an underwater earthquake off the coast of Japan in 2015 is a prime example of what is likely to come. We touched upon these earlier too, but the Cascadia Fault Zones, the San Andreas Fault Zone, and the Yellowstone Caldera are all interconnected to the Ring of Fire. The Ring of Fire is the Pacific Tectonic plate that extends over the coasts of the countries that touch the Pacific Ocean. According to today's leading geologists, the three mentioned US areas are all overdue for an eruption. When they do erupt, islands like Hawaii, the South China Sea Islands, the Caribbean Islands, and possibly Puerto Rico and Cuba, could all be obliterated and sink into the sea. The western edge of the United States may also sink into the ocean and a new coast will emerge as coastal cities are laid waste.

# Chapter 18

# "A Way Out"

As in times before, God provides a way out to escape eternal death for His chosen people and those who will accept Christ during the Tribulation. To accomplish this, God will send two groups of His appointed evangelists. The first group are Jewish virgins, protected by God Almighty Himself, and a total of 144,000 who are sealed from harm. Revelation 7:4 "And I heard the number of them which were sealed, and there were sealed an hundred and forty-four thousand of all the tribes of the children of Israel." They will be sent out across the globe to preach the gospel of Christ as the Messiah. They reappear in the presence of God in Revelation 14:1-5 (NIV) "1 Then I looked, and there before me was the Lamb, standing on Mount Zion, and with him 144,000 who had his name and his Father's name written on their foreheads. 2 And I heard a sound from heaven like the roar of rushing waters and like a loud peal of thunder. The sound I heard was like that of harpists playing their harps. 3 And they sang a new song before the throne and before the four living creatures and the elders. No one could learn the song except the 144,000 who had been redeemed from the earth. 4 These are those who did not defile themselves with women, for they remained virgins. They follow the Lamb wherever he goes. They were purchased from among mankind and offered as first fruits to God and the Lamb. 5 No lie was found in their mouths; they are blameless." They are made up of 12,000 from each of the original tribes, including the 10 lost tribes captured by Assyria. They began their ministry at the start of the Tribulation period. Revelation 14 seems to indicate that they were somehow transported back to heaven as they were "purchased from among mankind." Through their work, there will be potentially millions who come to a saving knowledge of Christ. Revelation 7:14 "And I said unto him, Sir, thou knowest. And he said to me, "These are they which came out of great tribulation, and have washed their robes, and made them white in the blood of the Lamb." These 144,000 will be rewarded and remembered by all as the stars shining in the night sky. Daniel 12:3 "And they that be wise shall shine as the brightness of the firmament; and they that turn many to righteousness as the stars for ever and ever."

The second group are two Jewish witnesses. They were prophesied in Zechariah 4:11-14 "¹¹ Then answered I, and said unto him, "What are these two olive trees upon the right side of the candlestick and upon the left side thereof? ¹² And I answered again, and said unto him, "What be these two olive branches which through the two golden pipes empty the golden oil out of themselves? ¹³ And he answered me and said, "Knowest thou not what these be? And I said, No, my lord.¹⁴ Then said he, "These are the two anointed ones, that stand by the LORD of the whole earth." It is pretty universally agreed that one of them will be the return of Elijah. Malachi 4:5 "Behold, I will send you Elijah the prophet before the coming of the great and dreadful day of the LORD." The other one could be either Enoch or Moses. The case for Enoch Genesis 5:21-24 "²¹ And Enoch lived sixty and five years, and begat Methuselah: ²² And Enoch walked with God after he begat Methuselah three hundred years, and begat sons and daughters: ²³ And all the days of Enoch were three hundred sixty and five years: ²⁴ And Enoch walked with God: and he was not (vanished); for God took him (raptured)." Enoch and Elijah reached heaven but not through death. 2 Kings 2:11 "And it came to pass, as they (Elijah and Elisha) still went on, and talked, that, behold, there appeared a chariot of fire, and horses of fire, and parted them both asunder; and Elijah went up by a whirlwind into heaven." Could they still be alive and in heaven, ready to return? Maybe. The case for Moses. Moses is the other one most often suggested since Moses performed the several of the same plagues and wonders against Pharaoh and Egypt, particularly turning the water to blood, shutting off the rain, and calling fiery hail down from heaven which forced the Exodus. Also, according to Luke, Elijah and Moses joined Jesus on top of a mount for the transfiguration where the heavenly radiance covered all three participants showing the world that Jesus was from this world and the heavenly world. Luke 9:28-31 (NIV) "²⁸ About eight days after Jesus said this, he took Peter, John and James with him and went up onto a mountain to pray. ²⁹ As he was praying, the appearance of his face changed, and his clothes became as bright as a flash of lightning. ³⁰ Two men, Moses and Elijah, appeared in glorious splendor, talking with Jesus. ³¹ They spoke about his departure, which he was about to bring to fulfillment at Jerusalem." The two witnesses will have supernatural powers. They will bring Exodus like plagues as they hold back the rain for 3 ½ years as their length of service is only for the first half of the tribulation. Revelation 11:3-6 "³ And I will give power unto my two witnesses, and they shall prophesy a thousand two hundred and threescore days, clothed in sackcloth. ⁴ These are the two olive trees, and the two candlesticks standing before the God of the earth. ⁵ And if any man will hurt them, fire proceedeth out of their mouth, and devoureth their enemies: and if any man will hurt them, he must in this manner be killed. ⁶ These have power to shut heaven, that it rain not in the days of their prophecy: and have power over waters to turn them to blood, and to smite the earth with all plagues, as often as they will." Daniel 12:5-7 "⁵ Then I Daniel looked, and, behold, there stood other two, the one on this side of the bank of the river, and the other on that side of the bank of the river. ⁶ And one said to the man clothed in linen, which was upon the waters of the river, "How long shall it be to the end of these wonders? ⁷ And I heard the man clothed in linen, which was upon the waters of the river, when he held up his right hand and his left hand unto heaven, and swore by him that liveth for ever that it shall be for a time, times, and an half; and when he shall have accomplished to scatter the power of the holy people, all these things shall be finished." Just before the midpoint of the Tribulation, the Antichrist will convince the world that they are to blame for the world's ills and have the two killed. Their bodies will lie in the streets for three days for all the world to see. People will think the worst is over and celebrate with exchanges of gifts as if it was Christmas. Revelation 11:7-10 "⁷ And when they shall have finished their testimony, the beast that ascendeth out of the bottomless pit shall make war against them, and shall overcome them, and kill them. ⁸ And their dead bodies shall lie in the street of the great city, which spiritually is called Sodom and Egypt, where also our Lord was crucified. ⁹ And they of the people and kindreds and tongues and nations shall see their dead bodies three days and an half, and shall not suffer their dead bodies to be put in graves. ¹⁰ And they that dwell upon the earth shall rejoice over them, and make merry, and shall send gifts one to another; because these two prophets tormented them that dwelt on the earth." On the fourth day, God will breathe life back into them and they will ascend to heaven, witnessed by all and shown across the world on the internet and/or satellite TV. Revelation 11:11-12 "¹¹ And after three days and an half the spirit of life from God entered into them, and they stood upon their feet; and great fear fell upon them which saw them. ¹² And they heard a great voice from heaven saying unto them, Come up hither. And they ascended up to heaven in a cloud; and their enemies beheld them." The survivors of the Tribulation thus far were wrong to think that the worst was over, but the worst was not over, the worst was yet to come. The first half closes with more earthquakes and 7,000 people are killed before they realize the Antichrist's deceit. Revelation 11:13 "And the same hour was there a great earthquake, and the tenth part of the city (Jerusalem) fell, and in the earthquake were slain of men seven thousand: and the remnant were affrighted, and gave glory to the God of heaven."

# Chapter 19

# "It Goes From Bad to Worse"

Let's see how the Antichrist, the Jews, and the rest of the world are intertwined in the second half of the Tribulation. During the first half, the Jews will think they are finally safe from persecution or attack from the Arab/Muslim world. They will celebrate and claim they are finally at peace and living in security thanks to their new found political savior. Through the work of the Holy Spirit, the evangelism of the 144,000, and the two witnesses, the eyes of the Jews will be opened to seeing Jesus as the Messiah and that their current savior (the Antichrist) is a false Messiah. Daniel 7:25 (NIV) "He will speak against the Most High and oppress his holy people and try to change the set times and the laws. The holy people will be delivered into his hands for a time (1 year), times (2 years) and half a time (1/2 year)." Daniel 11:36-38 (NKJV) "36 The king (Antichrist) will do as he pleases. He will exalt and magnify himself above every god and will say unheard-of things against the God of gods. He will be successful until the time of wrath is completed, for what has been determined must take place. 37 He will show no regard for the gods of his ancestors or for the one desired by women, nor will he regard any god, but will exalt himself above them all. 38 Instead of them, he will honor a god of fortresses; a god unknown to his ancestors, he will honor with gold and silver, with precious stones and costly gifts." He will demand that he be worshipped as God above all Gods (the abomination of desolation). However, the Jews have been waiting and looking for thousands of years for signs of the return of their Messiah, and this guy isn't Him. They will not comply with this leader's demand.

Coupled with the abomination of desolation, as explained earlier, the second half of the Tribulation begins with the Dragon (Satan) being expelled from God's presence. Revelation 12:9 and 13 "9And the great dragon was cast out, that old serpent, called the Devil, and Satan, which deceiveth the whole world: he was cast out into the earth, and his angels were cast out with him." and "13 When the dragon saw that he had been hurled to the earth, he pursued the woman who had given birth to the male child." This is known as the time of Jacob's Troubles or Great Tribulation. Jeremiah 30:7 "Alas! For that day is great, so that none is like it; it is even the time of Jacob's trouble, but he shall be saved out of it." The Antichrist will begin implementing his plan to eradicate the Jews that will make Hitler's final solution look like child's play. God has promised to provide and protect the Jews by His own hand. Revelation 12:14-17 "¹⁴ And to the woman (Israel) were given two wings of a great eagle, that she might fly into the wilderness, into her place, where she is nourished for a time, and times, and half a time, from the face of the serpent. ¹⁵ And the serpent cast out of his mouth water as a flood after the woman, that he might cause her to be carried away of the flood. ¹⁶ And the earth helped the woman, and the earth opened her mouth, and swallowed up the flood which the dragon cast out of his mouth. ¹⁷ And the dragon was wroth with the woman, and went to make war with the remnant of her seed, which keep the commandments of God, and have the testimony of Jesus Christ." He will send them into the desert, like He did with Moses, and assign the Angel Michael to personally protect them. Daniel 12:1 "And at that time shall Michael stand up, the great prince which standeth for the children of thy people: and there shall be a time of trouble, such as never was since there was a nation even to that same time: and at that time thy people shall be delivered, every one that shall be found written in the book." Some suggest they will go to Petra in Jordan, where God will supernaturally supply food and water for the final 3 1/2 years, like He did in Moses' era. Jeremiah 30:7 ends with, "he shall be saved out of it." The promise of protection is also found in Joel 2:32 "And it shall come to pass, that whosoever shall call on the name of the LORD shall be delivered: for in mount Zion and in Jerusalem shall be deliverance, as the LORD hath said, and in the remnant whom the LORD shall call." In some translations there is a place called Bozrah, which is located in ancient Edom, but it is now in ruins; this is also suggested as the resting place of the Jews. Micah 2:12-13 "¹² I will surely assemble, O Jacob, all of thee; I will surely gather the remnant of Israel; I will put them together as the sheep of Bozrah, as the flock in the midst of their fold: they shall make great noise by reason of the multitude of men. ¹³ The breaker is come up before them: they have broken up, and have passed through the gate, and are gone out by it: and their king shall pass before them, and the LORD on the head of them." There is light at the end of the tunnel. Matthew 10:22 "And ye shall be hated of all men for my name's sake: but he (any surviving believer, Jew or Gentile) that endureth to the end shall be saved." Luke 21:12-19 (NIV) "¹² But before all this, they will seize you and persecute you. They will hand you over to synagogues and put you in prison, and you will be brought before kings and governors, and all on account of my name. ¹³ And so you will bear testimony to me. ¹⁴ But make up your mind not to worry beforehand how you will defend yourselves. ¹⁵ For I will give you words and wisdom that none of your adversaries will be able to resist or contradict. ¹⁶ You will be betrayed even by parents, brothers and sisters, relatives and friends, and they will put some of you to death. ¹⁷ Everyone will hate you because of me. ¹⁸ But not a hair of your head will perish. ¹⁹ Stand firm, and you will win life."

We have looked extensively at the Antichrist's hatred of the Jews. As the Antichrist turns on the Jews, he also begins to kill those gentiles who refuse to take the Mark of the Beast, mostly because of their new-found commitment to Christ. Remember that the second purpose of the Tribulation is to bring the Gentile nations into judgment, so there must be some, probably many who accept the mark. Isaiah 2:17 "The loftiness of man shall be bowed down, and the haughtiness of men shall be brought low. The LORD alone will be exalted in that day." As the Antichrist tightens his grasp on other countries, they start to refuse to cooperate, particularly as God's judgments ratchet up and the Antichrist's abilities appear to decline. The Antichrist ill then enlist the help of the Dragon (Satan) and the False Prophet by calling for three evil spirits from the lake of fire. Revelation 16:13-14 "¹³ And I saw three unclean spirits like frogs come out of the mouth of the dragon, and out of the mouth of the beast, and out of the mouth of the false prophet. ¹⁴ For they are the spirits of devils, working miracles, which go forth unto the kings of the earth and of the whole world, to gather them to the battle of that great day of God Almighty." Add to that the final seven bowls of judgment, and the devastation and destruction will suddenly be so great such that the world has never seen. Revelation 15:6-8 "⁶ And the seven angels came out of the temple, having the seven plagues, clothed in pure and white linen, and having their breasts girded with golden girdles. ⁷ And one of the four beasts gave unto the seven angels seven golden vials full of the wrath of God, who liveth for ever and ever. ⁸ And the temple was filled with smoke from the glory of God, and from his power; and no man was able to enter into the temple, till the seven plagues of the seven angels were fulfilled."

As we wrap up the final moments of the bloodiest part of the Tribulation, the end of chapter 14 talks about reaping the harvest and the grapes of wrath. Revelation 14:17-20 "¹⁷ And another angel came out of the temple which is in heaven, he also having a sharp sickle. ¹⁸ And another angel came out from the altar, which had power over fire; and cried with a loud cry to him that had the sharp sickle, saying, "Thrust in thy sharp sickle, and gather the clusters of the vine of the earth; for her grapes are fully ripe. ¹⁹ And the angel thrust in his sickle into the earth, and gathered the vine of the earth, and cast it into the great winepress of the wrath of God. ²⁰ And the winepress was trodden without the city, and blood came out of the winepress, even unto the horse bridles (4-5 feet), by the space of a thousand and six hundred furlongs (6 miles)." It is impossible to conceive how many people will need to die to fill this amount, but when we detail Armageddon, it will soon become clear. First, we will examine the name, which is only found in one verse in the entire Bible. Revelation 16:16 "And He gathered them together into a place in the Hebrew tongue, Armageddon." The area of "Megiddo" is in northern Israel. 78 miles north of Jerusalem. Armageddon is perhaps the most familiar battle that has never been fought, but it is also the most misunderstood too. The battle is not a single conflict but is rather has several stages.

Remember, when we looked at the second purpose of the Tribulation, we learned that the Antichrist's time to rule is limited. Daniel 11:35 "And some of them of understanding shall fall, to try them, and to purge, and to make them white, even to the time of the end: because it is yet for a time appointed." This means the Antichrist's efforts will be effective, but short lived. Earlier we looked at 2 Thessalonians 2:4 (NIV) "He will oppose and will exalt himself over everything that is called God or is worshiped, so that he sets himself up in God's temple, proclaiming himself to be God." In his delusion of grandeur, the Antichrist will claim that he is God and demand the world worship him. However, not all of the world will comply. They will also not repent of their sinful ways. Revelation 9:20-21 "[20] And the rest of the men which were not killed by these plagues yet repented not of the works of their hands, that they should not worship devils, and idols of gold, and silver, and brass, and stone, and of wood: which neither can see, nor hear, nor walk: [21] Neither repented they of their murders, nor of their sorceries, nor of their fornication, nor of their thefts." The Kings of the North and the Kings of the South will join forces and move against the Antichrist. Daniel 11:40-43 (NKJV) "[40] At the time of the end the king of the South shall attack him; and the king of the North shall come against him like a whirlwind, with chariots, horsemen, and with many ships; and he shall enter the countries, overwhelm them, and pass through. [41] He shall also enter the Glorious Land, and many countries shall be overthrown; but these shall escape from his hand: Edom, Moab, and the prominent people of Ammon. [42] He shall stretch out his hand against the countries, and the land of Egypt shall not escape. [43] He shall have power over the treasures of gold and silver, and over all the precious things of Egypt; also the Libyans and Ethiopians shall follow at his heels." The Bible does not clearly say who these two kings are, but, remember that all directions are in relationship to Israel. It does not say the far north, so it is probably not Russia, though it may be Turkey, Syria, Iraq, Iran, or what is left of them after the Ezekiel 38 and 39 war. The Kings of the South are mostly agreed by prophecy teachers as Egypt and possibly parts of Africa.

While the Antichrist is deals with these two, he hears about another flank being attacked by the Kings of the East. Daniel 11:44 (NKJV) "But news from the east and the north shall trouble him; therefore he shall go out with great fury to destroy and annihilate many." Most prophecy teachers believe this king is China, at least if not by herself alone, then as the head of a coalition. Since China's population is currently estimated at over a billion people, they have the numbers to reach a two hundred million army. Revelation 9:16 "And the number of the army of the horsemen were two hundred thousand thousand: and I heard the number of them." Their uniforms are described in detail and they match the Chinese color scheme of their army. Revelation 9:17 "And thus I saw the horses in the vision, and them that sat on them, having breastplates of fire, and of jacinth, and brimstone: and the heads of the horses were as the heads of lions; and out of their mouths issued fire and smoke and brimstone." God prepares a highway by having the great river Euphrates dry up for this army to have access. Revelation 16:12 "And the sixth angel poured out his vial upon the great river Euphrates; and the water thereof was dried up, that the way of the kings of the east might be prepared."

Just before the Antichrist is about to launch his counterstrike, his time is up. The last of the seven bowls are poured out, and God announces "it is done." Revelation 16:17-21 "[17] And the seventh angel poured out his vial into the air; and there came a great voice out of the temple of heaven, from the throne, saying, "It is done." [18] And there were voices, and thunders, and lightnings; and there was a great earthquake, such as was not since men were upon the earth, so mighty an earthquake, and so great. [19] And the great city was divided into three parts, and the cities of the nations fell: and great Babylon came in remembrance before God, to give unto her the cup of the wine of the fierceness of his wrath. [20] And every island fled away, and the mountains were not found. [21] And there fell upon men a great hail out of heaven, every stone about the weight of a talent: and men blasphemed God because of the plague of the hail; for the plague thereof was exceeding great." Again, God uses earthquakes and hail stones that weigh 75 pounds as the instruments of His punishment. As the text says, God will remember Babylon specifically. However, before Babylon is dealt with, John's narrative of events in the Tribulation is put on pause. He says his spirit was taken to the desert where he saw a woman in scarlet, sitting on a scarlet beast drunk on the blood of the saints. Revelation 17:1-6 "[1] And there came one of the seven angels which had the seven vials, and talked with me, saying unto me, "Come hither; I will shew unto thee the judgment of the great whore that sitteth upon many waters: [2] With whom the kings of the earth have committed fornication, and the inhabitants of the earth have been made drunk with the wine of her fornication." [3] So he carried me away in the spirit into the wilderness: and I saw a woman sit upon a scarlet coloured beast, full of names of blasphemy, having seven heads and ten horns. ⁴ And the woman was arrayed in purple and scarlet colour, and decked with gold and precious stones and pearls, having a golden cup in her hand full of abominations and filthiness of her fornication: ⁵ And upon her forehead was a name written, MYSTERY, BABYLON THE GREAT, THE MOTHER OF HARLOTS AND ABOMINATIONS OF THE EARTH. ⁶ And I saw the woman drunken with the blood of the saints, and with the blood of the martyrs of Jesus: and when I saw her, I wondered with great admiration." Prophecy scholars teach the rest of the chapter basically explains that the woman is representative of a religious system that led people away from the Gospel of Christ, which ultimately leads them to perdition or the bottomless pit.

Babylon is then brought to account for her part in the conspiracy to overthrow God from His earthly throne of being Sovereign Lord. Revelation 18:1-3 "¹ And after these things I saw another angel come down from heaven, having great power; and the earth was lightened with His glory. ² And he cried mightily with a strong voice, saying, Babylon the great is fallen, is fallen, and is become the habitation of devils, and the hold of every foul spirit, and a cage of every unclean and hateful bird. ³ For all nations have drunk of the wine of the wrath of her fornication, and the kings of the earth have committed fornication with her, and the merchants of the earth are waxed rich through the abundance of her delicacies." John is told that God's people are called out of Babylon before she faces severe punishment in Revelation 18:8 "Therefore shall her plagues come in one day, death, and mourning, and famine; and she shall be utterly burned with fire: for strong is the Lord God who judgeth her." Those who enjoyed living a life of luxury in Babylon, will turn away from her on a dime. Revelation 18:9-10 "⁹ The kings of the earth who committed fornication and lived luxuriously with her will weep and lament for her, when they see the smoke of her burning, ¹⁰ standing at a distance for fear of her torment, saying, 'Alas, alas, that great city Babylon, that mighty city! For in one hour your judgment has come." The final verses portray the absolute destruction of Babylon so that they will be the ones remembered no more, not Israel. Revelation 18:21 "And a mighty angel took up a stone like a great millstone, and cast it into the sea, saying, "Thus with violence shall that great city Babylon be thrown down, and shall be found no more at all." If the woman in chapter 17 is a religious system, Babylon represents a political or governmental system. According to a commentary on www.Bible.org, Babylon was a code for the early church to identify Rome so they wouldn't get caught speaking negatively about their oppressors and then subjected to severe punishment. Remember Rome was occupying the land of Israel and a good portion of the known world when John was on the Isle of Patmos when he wrote the Book of Revelation. It would stand to reason that Babylon could be a yet to be assembled government formation could be the Revived Roman Empire. The beginning of chapter 19 John is still in the spirit and hears the angels of heaven praising God for His victory over corrupted Babylon. Revelation 19:1-2 "¹ And after these things I heard a great voice of much people in heaven, saying, Alleluia; Salvation, and glory, and honour, and power, unto the Lord our God: ² For true and righteous are his judgments: for he hath judged the great whore, which did corrupt the earth with her fornication, and hath avenged the blood of his servants at her hand."

# Chapter 20

# "The Return of the King"

Earlier, we briefly mentioned the joining of the Raptured Saints and the Tribulation Saints when we talked about what the church can expect during the end of the Tribulation. Both groups are now considered as one when they are invited to the Marriage Supper of the Lamb as the Bride of Christ, which happens here. Revelation 19:6-9 "[6] And I heard as it were the voice of a great multitude, and as the voice of many waters, and as the voice of mighty thunderings, saying, Alleluia: for the Lord God omnipotent reigneth. [7] Let us be glad and rejoice and give honour to him: for the marriage of the Lamb is come, and his wife hath made herself ready. [8] And to her was granted that she should be arrayed in fine linen, clean and white: for the fine linen is the righteousness of saints. [9] And He saith unto me, Write, "Blessed are they which are called unto the marriage supper of the Lamb." And He saith unto me, "These are the true sayings of God."

Returning back to John's account, he writes that Christ will appear with His army, clothed in white linen riding on a white horse. It will be the shortest battle ever fought. However, we will not need to actually fight as Satan will be destroyed by the power of God's voice command. Revelation 19:11-16 "[11] And I saw heaven opened and behold a white horse; and He that sat upon him was called Faithful and True, and in righteousness He doth judge and make war. [12] His eyes were as a flame of fire, and on His head were many crowns; and He had a name written, that no man knew, but He himself. [13] And He was clothed with a vesture dipped in blood: and His name is called The Word of God. [14] And the armies which were in heaven followed Him upon white horses, clothed in fine linen, white and clean. [15] And out of His mouth goeth a sharp sword, that with it He should smite the nations: and He shall rule them with a rod of iron: and He treadeth the winepress of the fierceness and wrath of Almighty God. [16] And He hath on his vesture and on His thigh a name written, KING OF KINGS, AND LORD OF LORDS." This is the loud, unmistakable event that all people on earth will see and every knee shall bow that we talked about when we looked at Jesus' answer to the questions of what will be the sign of the end of the age. His answer was recorded in at least two places in the gospel, Matthew 24:27-31 and Luke 21:27-28. Particularly in Matthew 24:30 (NKJV) "Then the sign of the Son of Man will appear in heaven, and then all the tribes of the earth will mourn, and they will see the Son of Man coming on the clouds of heaven with power and great glory." Revelation 1:7 "Behold, He cometh with clouds; and every eye shall see Him, and they also which pierced Him: and all kindreds of the earth shall wail because of Him. Even so, Amen." Jude also emphasizes Christ's return when he mentions those who died in Christ to judge and make all things right. Jude 14-15 "14 And Enoch also, the seventh from Adam, prophesied of these, saying, Behold, the Lord cometh with ten thousands of His saints, 15 To execute judgment upon all, and to convince all that are ungodly among them of all their ungodly deeds which they have ungodly committed, and of all their hard speeches which ungodly sinners have spoken against Him." Christ will come back with His "saints" and His "angels." Zechariah 14:4-5 "4 And His feet shall stand in that day upon the mount of Olives, which is before Jerusalem on the east, and the mount of Olives shall cleave in the midst thereof toward the east and toward the west, and there shall be a very great valley; and half of the mountain shall remove toward the north, and half of it toward the south. 5 And ye shall flee to the valley of the mountains; for the valley of the mountains shall reach unto Azal: yea, ye shall flee, like as ye fled from before the earthquake in the days of Uzziah king of Judah: and the LORD my God shall come, and all the saints with thee." 2 Thessalonians 1:10 (NKJV) "When He comes, in that Day, to be glorified in His saints and to be admired among all those who believe because our testimony among you was believed." 1 Thessalonians 3:13 (NKJV) "So that He may establish your hearts blameless in holiness before our God and Father at the coming of our Lord Jesus Christ with all His saints." 2 Thessalonians 1:9-10 (NKJV) "9 These shall be punished with everlasting destruction from the presence of the Lord and from the glory of His power, 10 when He comes, in that Day, to be glorified in His saints and to be admired among all those who believe, because our testimony among you was believed." 2 Thessalonians 1:7 (NKJV) "And to give you who are troubled rest with us when the Lord Jesus is revealed from heaven with His mighty angels." Matthew 25:31 "When the Son of Man shall come in His glory, and all the holy angels with Him, then shall He sit upon the throne of His glory."

This seven year period of utter devastation and destruction will culminate when Jesus physically returns and takes control. The armies of the Antichrist and False Prophet are beaten and the birds of the air are called to a great feast on the bodies of the defeated. Revelation 19:17-18 "17 And I saw an angel standing in the sun; and he cried with a loud voice, saying to all the fowls that fly in the midst of heaven, Come and gather yourselves together unto the supper of the great God; ¹⁸ That ye may eat the flesh of kings, and the flesh of captains, and the flesh of mighty men, and the flesh of horses, and of them that sit on them, and the flesh of all men, both free and bond, both small and great." The Antichrist and False Prophet are then captured, bound, and thrown into hell. Revelation 19:19-20 "¹⁹ And I saw the beast, and the kings of the earth, and their armies, gathered together to make war against him that sat on the horse, and against his army. ²⁰ And the beast was taken, and with him the false prophet that wrought miracles before him, with which he deceived them that had received the mark of the beast, and them that worshipped his image. These both were cast alive into a lake of fire burning with brimstone." Christ does this like we just saw with the armies of Satan, with His voice. Revelation 19:21 "And the remnant were slain with the sword of Him that sat upon the horse, which sword proceeded out of His mouth: and all the fowls were filled with their flesh." Christ then has Satan seized and bound. He is then relegated to Hades for 1,000 years. Revelation 20:1-3 "¹And I saw an angel come down from heaven, having the key of the bottomless pit and a great chain in his hand. ² And he laid hold on the dragon, that old serpent, which is the Devil, and Satan, and bound him a thousand years, ³ And cast him into the bottomless pit, and shut him up, and set a seal upon him, that he should deceive the nations no more, till the thousand years should be fulfilled: and after that he must be loosed a little season." We will come back to the last sentence after we examine the Millennium.

After dealing with the Unholy Trinity, God turns His attention to the business of restoring His creation and setting up His governmental administration and holy laws of worship. This regime will last for 1,000 years. This is another example of an accepted term by theologians, church historians, and biblical scholars for a concept where the term used does not exist in the Bible, the Millennium. It is a combination of the words "mille" (thousand) and "annum" (year). Revelation 20:4-6 "⁴ And I saw thrones, and they sat upon them, and judgment was given unto them: and I saw the souls of them that were beheaded for the witness of Jesus, and for the word of God, and which had not worshipped the beast, neither his image, neither had received his mark upon their foreheads, or in their hands; and they lived and reigned with Christ a thousand years. ⁵ But the rest of the dead lived not again until the thousand years were finished. This is the first resurrection. ⁶ Blessed and holy is he that hath part in the first resurrection: on such the second death (see Rev 20:14 below) hath no power, but they shall be priests of God and of Christ, and shall reign with him a thousand years (the Millennium)."

# Chapter 21

# "The Millennium"

If Christ's return is the blessed hope, Titus 2:13 "Looking for that blessed hope, and the glorious appearing of the great God and our Saviour Jesus Christ," then the Millennium is the prize. Philippians 3:14 "I press toward the mark for the prize of the high calling of God in Christ Jesus." We will rule and reign with Him as kings and priests over those people living on earth who still are in their human body as they did not die nor were taken in the rapture. Revelation 1:6 (NKJV) "And has made us kings and priests to His God and Father, to Him be glory and dominion forever and ever. Amen." Revelation 5:10 "And hast made us unto our God kings and priests: and we shall reign on the earth." They still have a mortal life to live. If the Raptured saints and Tribulation saints, which returned with Christ at the Second Coming, are to rule and reign with Him the obvious question is "to whom do we reign over?" We can find our answers in the Old Testament prophecies about the restoration of the planet's eco-systems, the restoration of mankind and what they can expect from God's provisions, and Christ's edicts for His law and rules of worship.

Before we go on to examine the Millennium, there is an important distinction that needs to be made about the first and second resurrection and the first and second death which was just mentioned in Revelation 20:5-6. The first and second resurrection is for believers only. If you recall, at the Rapture the physical bodies of those who are taken will transform from our current physical corruptible bodies to new glorified incorruptible bodies. We shall have the same type of body Jesus had after He rose from the grave and will have when He returns. 1 John 3:2-3 (NIV) "2 Dear friends, now we are children of God, and what we will be has not yet been made known. But we know that when Christ appears, we shall be like Him, for we shall see Him as He is. 3 All who have this hope in him purify themselves, just as he is pure." This is the first resurrection. Bible scholars believe that the Tribulation Saints will get their glorified bodies at the Second Coming as both groups will then be returning with Christ. It will be in this form that the Raptured Saints and Tribulation Saints will rule and reign in the Millennium. Remember that the Tribulation saints are those who die in faith or are martyred specifically for their refusal to take the mark of the beast and were killed between the Rapture and the end of the Tribulation. However, there will be many people who refused to take the mark and evaded capture and survived to fulfill Jesus' prophecy of Matthew 24:13 "But he who endures to the end shall be saved." In addition, there will still be many Jewish people who fled into the desert beginning at the half way point of the Tribulation where God will protect and provide for them. Those believers who come to faith after the Rapture, those who survive during the Tribulation, and those who are born and remain alive up until the 1,000 years are over will be involved in the Second Resurrection if their names are found when the Book of Life is opened at the Great White Throne Judgement. We will explore the Great White Throne Judgement after we examine more closely what we can expect and how the earth is restored in the Millennium.

Regarding the first and second death, earlier we talked about what happens at death for the spirit and bodies when a person dies in the natural body. This is the first death. As we learned earlier at what happens at death, all deceased unbelievers since Adam and through the Tribulation will reside in Hades until the end of the Millennium. They will eventually be brought before God, where the Book of Life will be opened and if their name is not found there, they will be judged and sentenced to the lake of fire (hell) at the Great White Throne Judgment. This is the Second death mentioned in vs 6 and is only for unbelievers. Additionally, the unbelievers will not go into the Millennium. This topic will be examined in greater depth when we explore the restoration of mankind shortly.

We will now look at what the Bible says about what to expect in the Millennium. There are four main categories to examine: the Restoration of the Land, the Restoration of Mankind, the Absolute Authority of Jesus' Rule, and the Temple and Worship Laws.

- Restoration of the land. After seven years of cataclysmic disasters, the earth will be in ruins. With the voice command of God, He will renovate and restore the earth like it was in the Garden of Eden. Isaiah 51:3 "For the LORD shall comfort Zion: He will comfort all her waste places; and He will make her wilderness like Eden, and her desert like the garden of the LORD; joy and gladness shall be found therein, thanksgiving, and the voice of melody." Acts 3:21 "Whom heaven must receive until the times of restoration of all things, which God hath spoken by the mouth of all His holy prophets since the world began." The land will be able to support farming to provide food for the inhabitants of this time. Isaiah 4:2 (NIV) "In that day the Branch of the LORD will be beautiful and glorious, and the fruit of the land will be the pride and glory of the survivors in Israel." Isaiah 35:6-7 "⁶ Then shall the lame man leap as an hart, and the tongue of the dumb sing: for in the wilderness shall waters break out, and streams in the desert. ⁷ And the parched ground shall become a pool, and the thirsty land springs of water: in the habitation of dragons, where each lay, shall be grass with reeds and rushes." Joel 2:19 and 22 "¹⁹ Yea, the LORD will answer and say unto his people, Behold, I will send you corn, and wine, and oil, and ye shall be satisfied therewith: and I will no more make you a reproach among the heathen." and "²² Be not afraid, ye beasts of the field: for the pastures of the wilderness do spring, for the tree beareth her fruit, the fig tree and the vine do yield their strength." There will be such peace that even the animals will live in peace so that the lamb will be able to lie down with the wolf free from fear of being prey. Isaiah 11:6-7 "⁶ The wolf also shall dwell with the lamb, and the leopard shall lie down with the kid; and the calf and the young lion and the fatling together; and a little child shall lead them. ⁷ And the cow and the bear shall feed; their young ones shall lie down together: and the lion shall eat straw like the ox." Ezekiel 34:25 "And I will make with them a covenant of peace, and will cause the evil beasts to cease out of the land: and they shall dwell safely in the wilderness, and sleep in the woods." Children will be able to play by poisonous snake dens and not be afraid of being bitten. Isaiah 11:8 (NIV) "The infant will play near the cobra's den, and the young child will put its hand into the viper's nest." It is from these people who survive the Tribulation and the children they produce will need to farm for sustenance and repopulate the earth.

- Restoration of mankind. As we just touched upon, only the believers will enter the Millennium. Psalm 1:1-3 "¹ Blessed is the man that walketh not in the counsel of the ungodly, nor standeth in the way of sinners, nor sitteth in the seat of the scornful. ² But his delight is in the law of the LORD; and in His law doth he meditate day and night. ³ And he shall be like a tree planted by the rivers of water, that bringeth forth his fruit in his season; his leaf also shall not wither; and whatsoever he doeth shall prosper." Since Adam, God has always wanted a personal loving one on one relationship with each and every person born. The choice to participate is totally up to the individual. With Moses we learned how the concept of obedience brings blessing and disobedience brings judgment. And when judgment was called for, even then God provided a way back with His sacrifice of His only son to pay a debt He did not owe. In a word, He wanted us to have restoration (as before Adam sinned). In the truest sense of the word, God wanted to take His best creation, which had become corrupted and full of decay, and restore it to its original condition. Psalm 23:3 "He restoreth my soul; He leadeth me in the paths of righteousness for His name's sake." Psalm 51:7 (ERV) "Remove my sin and make me pure. Wash me until I am whiter than snow!" Ezekiel 20:37-38 (ERV) "37 I will judge you guilty and punish you according to the agreement. 38 I will remove all those who turned against me and sinned against me. I will remove them from your homeland. They will never again come to the land of Israel. Then you will know that I am the LORD." Isaiah 35:8-9 (NIV) "8 And a highway will be there; it will be called the Way of Holiness; it will be for those who walk on that Way. The unclean will not journey on it; wicked fools will not go about on it. 9 No lion will be there, nor any ravenous beast; they will not be found there. But only the redeemed will walk there." Jeremiah 31:31-34 "31 Behold, the days come, saith the LORD, that I will make a new covenant with the house of Israel, and with the house of Judah: 32 Not according to the covenant that I made with their fathers in the day that I took them by the hand to bring them out of the land of Egypt; which my covenant they brake, although I was an husband unto them, saith the LORD: 33 But this shall be the covenant that I will make with the house of Israel; After those days, saith the LORD, I will put my law in their inward parts, and write it in their hearts; and will be their God, and they shall be my people. 34 And they shall teach no more every man his neighbour, and every man his brother, saying, Know the LORD: for they shall all know me, from the least of them unto the greatest of them, saith the LORD: for I will forgive their iniquity, and I will remember their sin no more." Isaiah 1:18 (NIV) "Come now, and let us reason together," says the LORD, "Though your sins are like scarlet, they shall be as white as snow; though they are red like crimson, they shall be as wool." Joel 3:12 (NKJV) "Let the nations be wakened, and come up to the Valley of Jehoshaphat; for there I will sit to judge all the surrounding nations." Acts 17:31 "Because he hath appointed a day, in the which he will judge the world in righteousness by that man whom he hath ordained; whereof he hath given assurance unto all men, in that he hath raised him from the dead." When we looked at the Olivet discourse in Matthew 25:31-46 it talked about the separating of sheep/believers and goats/unbelievers. It clearly says in vs 34 "34 Then the King will say to those on His right hand (sheep), 'Come, you blessed of My Father, inherit the kingdom prepared for you from the foundation of the world." In vs 41 and 46 "41 Then He will also say to those on the left hand (goats), 'Depart from Me, you cursed, into the everlasting fire prepared for the devil and his angels:" and "⁴⁶ And these will go away into everlasting punishment, but the righteous into eternal life." God will usher believers into the Millennium and unbelievers will be sent to Hades, as just mentioned again, for the duration of the Millennium. As physical earthly beings, like we are now, those peoples still in their natural body who enter the Millennium will be responsible for repopulating the earth with children. Only married people will have the sex required to build the families as children will be produced. Matthew 22:30 "For in the resurrection they (returning saints with Christ) neither marry nor are given in marriage, but are as the angels of God in heaven." Zechariah 8:4-5 (NKJV) "⁴ Thus says the LORD of hosts: 'Old men and old women shall again sit in the streets of Jerusalem, Each one with his staff in his hand Because of great age. ⁵ The streets of the city shall be full of boys and girls playing in its streets." Earthly needs of food and water will be met and we will want for nothing. The Millennial people will work the land and enjoy the fruits of their labors. Micah 4:4 (NIV) "Everyone will sit under their own vine and under their own fig tree, and no one will make them afraid, for the LORD Almighty has spoken." Isaiah 35:6b "⁶ᵇ For in the wilderness shall waters break out, and streams in the desert." Isaiah 65:21-23 (NKJV) "²¹ They shall build houses and inhabit them; they shall plant vineyards and eat their fruit. ²² They shall not build and another inhabit; they shall not plant and another eat; for as the days of a tree, so shall be the days of My people, And My elect shall long enjoy the work of their hands. ²³ They shall not labor in vain, nor bring forth children for trouble; for they shall be the descendants of the blessed of the LORD, and their offspring with them." Long life and good health will be reinstated. There will be no illness or disease. Isaiah 35:5-6a "⁵ Then the eyes of the blind shall be opened, and the ears of the deaf shall be unstopped. ⁶ Then the lame shall leap like a deer and the tongue of the dumb sing." A person could die at 100 years old and his life span would be thought of like a child's. Isaiah 65:20 (NKJV) "No more shall an infant from there live but a few days, nor an old man who has not fulfilled his days; For the child shall die one hundred years old, But the sinner being one hundred years old shall be accursed." Micah 4:6-7 (NIV) "⁶ In that day," declares the LORD, "I will gather the lame; I will assemble the exiles and those I have brought to grief. ⁷ I will make the lame my remnant, those driven away a strong nation. The LORD will rule over them in Mount Zion from that day and forever." The instruments of war that were used will be reshaped into farming tools. The study of war will no longer be needed or studied. Isaiah 2:4 (NKJV) "He shall judge between the nations, and rebuke many people; they shall beat their swords into plowshares, and their spears into pruning hooks; nation shall not lift up sword against nation, neither shall they learn war any more." Micah 4:3 (NIV) "He will judge between many peoples and will settle disputes for strong nations far and wide. They will beat their swords into plowshares and their spears into pruning hooks. Nation will not take up sword against nation, nor will they train for war anymore." Everybody will be treated and thought of as equal by those who will have authority over them. Isaiah 32:1 (NKJV) "Behold, a king will reign in righteousness, and princes will rule with justice." There will be no second class citizens or third world countries. Hunger will be gone, disease will be gone, hurt feelings of betrayal will be gone. People will treat each other with courtesy and respect. The world will finally find peace. Isaiah 35:10 "And the ransomed of the LORD shall return, and come to Zion with songs and everlasting joy upon their heads. They shall obtain joy and gladness, and sorrow and sighing shall flee away." Deceit towards your neighbor or pride of any kind will not be tolerated, while humbleness will be the standing order of the day. Zephaniah 3:11-13 (NKJV) "11 In that day you shall not be shamed for any of your deeds in which you transgress against Me; For then I will take away from your midst those who rejoice in your pride, and you shall no longer be haughty In My holy mountain. 12 I will leave in your midst a meek and humble people, and they shall trust in the name of the LORD. 13 The remnant of Israel shall do no unrighteousness and speak no lies, nor shall a deceitful tongue be found in their mouth; for they shall feed their flocks and lie down, and no one shall make them afraid." As a result of Jesus' righteousness, the nation of Israel specifically and the world by extension will experience prosperity like never before. Jeremiah 23:5-6 "5 Behold, the days come, saith the LORD, that I will raise unto David a righteous Branch, and a King shall reign and prosper, and shall execute judgment and justice in the earth. 6 In his days Judah shall be saved, and Israel shall dwell safely: and this is his name whereby he shall be called, THE LORD OUR RIGHTEOUSNESS." Jeremiah 33:14-16 "14 Behold, the days come, saith the Lord, that I will perform that good thing which I have promised unto the house of Israel and to the house of Judah. 15 In those days, and at that time, will I cause the Branch of righteousness to grow up unto David; and he shall execute judgment and righteousness in the land. 16 In those days shall Judah be saved, and Jerusalem shall dwell safely: and this is the name wherewith she shall be called, The Lord our righteousness."

- Jesus' rule and authority will be absolute. Isaiah 9:6-7 "⁶ For unto us a Child is born, unto us a Son is given; and the government will be upon His shoulder. And His name will be called Wonderful, Counselor, Mighty God, Everlasting Father, Prince of Peace. ⁷ Of the increase of His government and peace there will be no end, upon the throne of David and upon His kingdom, to order it and establish it with judgment and justice from henceforth, even for ever. The zeal of the LORD of hosts will perform this." Daniel 7:14 (NKJV) "Then to Him was given dominion and glory and a kingdom, that all peoples, nations, and languages should serve Him. His dominion is an everlasting dominion, which shall not pass away, And His kingdom the one which shall not be destroyed." Daniel 7:27 (NKJV) "Then the kingdom and dominion, and the greatness of the kingdoms under the whole heaven, shall be given to the people, the saints of the Most High. His kingdom is an everlasting kingdom, and all dominions shall serve and obey Him." He will rule with a rod of iron. Revelation 12:5 "And she brought forth a man child, who was to rule all nations with a rod of iron: and her child was caught up unto God, and to his throne." Revelation 2:27 (NKJV) "He shall rule them with a rod of iron; they shall be dashed to pieces like the potter's vessels' as I also have received from My Father;" This phrase means once He makes a verdict, there will be no appeal or amnesty. Everyone will know the rules and be subject to punishment if they break one. Remember how, at the very beginning, we talked about God's consistency in keeping His word; otherwise, how could we feel safe to trust His word or judgment? As we just mentioned, those saints who return with Christ at the end of the Tribulation will rule and reign as kings and priests. As kings, those saints who return will serve as something like a mayor, a governor, or some other position of authority. They will have jurisdiction over the people who make it through the Tribulation. God's regent over the earth will be Jesus. King David will also return to take his place over Israel. Jeremiah 30:8-9 "⁸ For it shall come to pass in that day, saith the LORD of hosts, that I will break his yoke from off thy neck, and will burst thy bonds, and strangers shall no more serve themselves of him: ⁹ But they shall serve the LORD their God, and David their king, whom I will raise up unto them." Ezekiel 34:23-24 "²³ And I will set up one shepherd over them, and he shall feed them, even my servant David; he shall feed them, and he shall be their shepherd. ²⁴ And I the LORD will be their God, and my servant David a prince among them; I the LORD have spoken it." Ezekiel 37:24 "And David my servant shall be king over them; and they all shall have one shepherd: they shall also walk in my judgments, and observe my statutes, and do them." Hosea 3:5 "Afterward shall the children of Israel return, and seek the LORD their God, and David their king; and shall fear the LORD and his goodness in the latter days." The nation of Israel will be considered the pinnacle of earthly nations. Jesus will then set up His Capital and Temple in Jerusalem, and all the worlds' governments will submit their sovereignty in favor of God's kingship and send emissaries to pay homage and praise to Jesus the King. Luke 1:32-33 "32 He shall be great, and shall be called the Son of the Highest: and the Lord God shall give unto him the throne of his father David: 33 And he shall reign over the house of Jacob forever; and of his kingdom there shall be no end." Daniel 2:44 "And in the days of these kings shall the God of heaven set up a kingdom, which shall never be destroyed: and the kingdom shall not be left to other people, but it shall break in pieces and consume all these kingdoms, and it shall stand forever." All the nations of the world must then make a pilgrimage to bring Him honor and glory as tribute. Psalm 46:10 "Be still, and know that I am God; I will be exalted among the nations, I will be exalted in the earth!" Any nation that does not will be judged and punished for not doing so. Isaiah 2:2-3 (NKJV) "2 Now it shall come to pass in the latter days That the mountain of the LORD's house Shall be established on the top of the mountains, and shall be exalted above the hills; and all nations shall flow to it. 3 Many people shall come and say, "Come, and let us go up to the mountain of the LORD, to the house of the God of Jacob; He will teach us His ways, and we shall walk in His paths." For out of Zion shall go forth the law, and the word of the LORD from Jerusalem." He will rule from Jerusalem. Joel 3:14-17 "14 Multitudes, multitudes in the valley of decision: for the day of the LORD is near in the valley of decision. 15 The sun and the moon shall be darkened, and the stars shall withdraw their shining. 16 The LORD also shall roar out of Zion, and utter his voice from Jerusalem; and the heavens and the earth shall shake: but the LORD will be the hope of his people, and the strength of the children of Israel. 17 So shall ye know that I am the LORD your God dwelling in Zion, my holy mountain: then shall Jerusalem be holy, and there shall no strangers pass through her anymore." Zechariah 2:10-13 (NKJV) "10 Sing and rejoice, O daughter of Zion! For behold, I am coming and I will dwell in your midst," says the LORD. "11 Many nations shall be joined to the LORD in that day, and they shall become My people. And I will dwell in your midst. Then you will know that the LORD of hosts has sent Me to you. 12 And the LORD will take possession of Judah as His inheritance in the Holy Land, and will again choose Jerusalem. 13 Be silent, all flesh, before the LORD, for He is aroused from His holy habitation!" Failure to do so will cause the rain not to fall in that country. When Jesus enters the city, He will enter through the Golden Gate aka the Eastern Gate. Ezekiel 44:1-2 "¹ Then he brought me back the way of the gate of the outward sanctuary which looketh toward the east; and it was shut. ² Then said the LORD unto me; This gate shall be shut, it shall not be opened, and no man shall enter in by it; because the LORD, the God of Israel, hath entered in by it, therefore it shall be shut." In 1541, the Ottoman Sultan Suleiman the Magnificent had the gate walled up so that the coming messiah could not enter the city. However, Jesus will open the gate and enter when He moves His capital to Jerusalem. The nation of Israel will get back ALL the land promised to Abraham, not just the sliver of land they have today. Genesis 15:18-21 "¹⁸ In the same day the LORD made a covenant with Abram, saying, "Unto thy seed have I given this land, from the river of Egypt unto the great river, the river Euphrates: ¹⁹ The Kenites, and the Kenizzites, and the Kadmonites, ²⁰ And the Hittites, and the Perizzites, and the Rephaims, ²¹ And the Amorites, and the Canaanites, and the Girgashites, and the Jebusites."

- The last topic may be the most important. There will be only one religion, Messianic Judaism. If we recall, the whole purpose of the Tribulation, Day of the Lord, or Daniels's 70ᵗʰ week was to solidify Jesus' role as Messiah for the Jews and the world. Remember that the eyes of Israel would be opened to see Jesus as Messiah. Isaiah 35:5 "Then the eyes of the blind shall be opened, and the ears of the deaf shall be unstopped." In the Millennium, life will be centered around worship in God's Millennial Temple and Jesus as High Priest. Hebrews 9:11 (NKJV) "But Christ came as High Priest of the good things to come, with the greater and more perfect tabernacle not made with hands, that is, not of this creation." There will be an emphasis on living in righteousness or holiness. Isaiah 4:3-5 "³ And it shall come to pass that he who is left in Zion and remains in Jerusalem will be called holy everyone who is recorded among the living in Jerusalem. ⁴ When the Lord has washed away the filth of the daughters of Zion, and purged the blood of Jerusalem from her midst, by the spirit of judgment and by the spirit of burning, ⁵ then the LORD will create above every dwelling place of Mount Zion, and above her assemblies, a cloud and smoke by day and the shining of a flaming fire by night. For over all the glory there will be a covering." Isaiah 62:1-2 "¹ For Zion's sake will I not hold my peace, and for Jerusalem's sake I will not rest, until the righteousness thereof go forth as brightness, and the salvation thereof as a lamp that burneth. ² And the Gentiles shall see thy righteousness, and all kings thy glory: and thou shalt be called by a new name, which the mouth of the LORD shall name." Zechariah 8:3 (NIV) "This is what the LORD says: "I will return to Zion and dwell in Jerusalem. Then Jerusalem will be called the Faithful City, and the mountain of the LORD Almighty will be called the Holy Mountain." Zechariah 13:1 "In that day there shall be a fountain opened to the house of David and to the inhabitants of Jerusalem for sin and for uncleanness." Zechariah 14:20 "In that day shall there be upon the bells of the horses, HOLINESS UNTO THE LORD; and the pots in the LORD's house shall be like the bowls before the altar." Micah 4:1-2 "¹ But in the last days it shall come to pass, that the mountain of the house of the LORD shall be established in the top of the mountains, and it shall be exalted above the hills; and people shall flow unto it. ² And many nations shall come, and say, Come, and let us go up to the mountain of the LORD, and to the house of the God of Jacob; and he will teach us of his ways, and we will walk in his paths: for the law shall go forth of Zion, and the word of the LORD from Jerusalem." Jesus will serve as High Priest, and as mentioned before, while the saints who return with Christ will serve as priests. Hebrews 2:17 "Wherefore in all things it behoved him to be made like unto his brethren, that he might be a merciful and faithful High Priest in things pertaining to God, to make reconciliation for the sins of the people." Hebrews 3:1-2 (NKJV) "¹ Therefore, holy brethren, partakers of the heavenly calling, consider the Apostle and High Priest of our confession, Christ Jesus, ² who was faithful to Him who appointed Him, as Moses also was faithful in all His house." Hebrews 4:14-16 "¹⁴ Seeing then that we have a great high priest, that is passed into the heavens, Jesus the Son of God, let us hold fast our profession. ¹⁵ For we have not an high priest which cannot be touched with the feeling of our infirmities; but was in all points tempted like as we are, yet without sin. ¹⁶ Let us therefore come boldly unto the throne of grace, that we may obtain mercy, and find grace to help in time of need." As priests, the saints will have the responsibility of performing worship services. Psalm 100:1-5 "¹ Make a joyful noise unto the LORD, all ye lands. ² Serve the LORD with gladness: come before his presence with singing. ³ Know ye that the LORD he is God: it is he that hath made us, and not we ourselves; we are his people, and the sheep of his pasture. ⁴ Enter into his gates with thanksgiving, and into his courts with praise: be thankful unto him, and bless his name. ⁵ For the LORD is good; his mercy is everlasting; and his truth endureth to all generations." Psalm 145:10-13 "¹⁰ All thy works shall praise thee, O LORD; and thy saints shall bless thee. ¹¹ They shall speak of the glory of thy kingdom, and talk of thy power; ¹² To make known to the sons of men his mighty acts, and the glorious majesty of his kingdom. ¹³ Thy kingdom is an everlasting kingdom, and thy dominion endureth throughout all generations." There will be music for worship. Ezekiel 40:44 (NKJV) "Outside the inner gate were the chambers for the singers in the inner court, one facing south at the side of the northern gateway, and the other facing north at the side of the southern gateway." The yearly cycle of temple worship including the Feasts of the Lord, the Ten Commandments, the law of Sabbath, and sacrifices will be observed. Zechariah 14:17-19 (NKJV) "¹⁷ And it shall be that whichever of the families of the earth do not come up to Jerusalem to worship the King, the Lord of hosts, on them there will be no rain. ¹⁸ If the family of Egypt will not come up and enter in, they shall have no rain; they shall receive the plague with which the Lord strikes the nations who do not come up to keep the Feast of Tabernacles. ¹⁹ This shall be the punishment of Egypt and the punishment of all the nations that do not come up to keep the Feast of Tabernacles." Everybody will worship God as we were meant to in thought, word, and deed. Isaiah 66:23 (NKJV) "And it shall come to pass That from one New Moon to another, and from one Sabbath to another, all flesh shall come to worship before Me," says the Lord." Sacrifices will include the offerings of first fruits and animals. Deuteronomy 26:1-2 (NKJV) "¹ And it shall be, when you come into the land which the Lord your God is giving you as an inheritance, and you possess it and dwell in it, ² that you shall take some of the first of all the produce of the ground, which you shall bring from your land that the Lord your God is giving you, and put it in a basket and go to the place where the Lord your God chooses to make His name abide." Isaiah 56:1-8 "¹ Thus saith the Lord, "Keep ye judgment, and do justice: for my salvation is near to come, and my righteousness to be revealed. ² Blessed is the man that doeth this, and the son of man that layeth hold on it; that keepeth the sabbath from polluting it, and keepeth his hand from doing any evil. ³ Neither let the son of the stranger, that hath joined himself to the Lord, speak, saying, the Lord hath utterly separated me from his people: neither let the eunuch say, Behold, I am a dry tree. "⁴ For thus saith the Lord unto the eunuchs that keep my sabbaths, and choose the things that please me, and take hold of my covenant; ⁵ Even unto them will I give in mine house and within my walls a place and a name better than of sons and of daughters: I will give them an everlasting name, that shall not be cut off. ⁶ Also the sons of the stranger, that join themselves to the Lord, to serve him, and to love the name of the Lord, to be his servants, every one that keepeth the sabbath from polluting it, and taketh hold of my covenant; 7 Even them will I bring to my holy mountain, and make them joyful in my house of prayer: their burnt offerings and their sacrifices shall be accepted upon mine altar; for mine house shall be called an house of prayer for all people. 8 The Lord GOD, which gathereth the outcasts of Israel saith, Yet, will I gather others to him, beside those that are gathered unto him." The people of Israel were called originally to be kings and priests to God. Exodus 19:5-6 "5 Now therefore, if ye will obey my voice indeed, and keep my covenant, then ye shall be a peculiar treasure unto me above all people: for all the earth is mine: 6 And ye shall be unto me a kingdom of priests, and an holy nation. These are the words which thou shalt speak unto the children of Israel." But as we know, they did not. Even when God sent them his messengers, the prophets, they killed them rather than repent and seek forgiveness. In the Millennium the nation of Israel will be reinstated as the channel of blessing they were intend to be. Zechariah 8:7-8 (NKJV) "7 Thus says the LORD of hosts: 'Behold, I will save My people from the land of the east and from the land of the west; 8 I will bring them back, and they shall dwell in the midst of Jerusalem. They shall be My people and I will be their God, in truth and righteousness." Zechariah 8:11-13 (NKJV) "11 But now I will not treat the remnant of this people as in the former days,' says the LORD of hosts. 12 'For the seed shall be prosperous, the vine shall give its fruit, the ground shall give her increase, and the heavens shall give their dew I will cause the remnant of this people to possess all these. 13 And it shall come to pass that just as you were a curse among the nations, O house of Judah and house of Israel, so I will save you, and you shall be a blessing. Do not fear, let your hands be strong." As we read before, some of those who return with Christ will be priests and Jesus will be the high priest. God will cleanse and sanctify those priests who are called to serve. Ezekiel 37:23 "Neither shall they defile themselves any more with their idols, nor with their detestable things, nor with any of their transgressions: but I will save them out of all their dwelling places, wherein they have sinned, and will cleanse them: so shall they be my people, and I will be their God."

- In addition to Ezekiel's war of Gog/Magog in chapters 38 and 39, Ezekiel is chosen to also describe the exact dimensions and sacraments for a New Millennial Holy Temple in chapters 40-48. Ezekiel 43:7-9 (NKJV) "7 And He said to me, "Son of man, this is the place of My throne and the place of the soles of My feet, where I will dwell in the midst of the children of Israel forever. No more shall the house of Israel defile My holy name, they nor their kings, by their harlotry or with the carcasses of their kings on their high places. 8 When they set their threshold by My threshold, and their doorpost by My doorpost, with a wall between them and Me, they defiled My holy name by the abominations which they committed; therefore I have consumed them in My anger. 9 Now let them put their harlotry and the carcasses of their kings far away from Me, and I will dwell in their midst forever." Remember the Third Temple had to be built for the Antichrist to make his abomination of desolation toward the beginning of the Tribulation. Somehow it will be destroyed. It could be as a result of a natural event like an earthquake or the result of attack. The main point is God's purity will not allow himself to occupy a space that has been defiled, therefore, a Millennial Temple must be built. The floor plan is different to that of Solomon's temple or Moses' Tabernacle. Ezekiel 43:10-12 (NKJV) "10 Son of man, describe the temple to the house of Israel, that they may be ashamed of their iniquities; and let them measure the pattern. 11 And if they are ashamed of all that they have done, make known to them the design of the temple and its arrangement, its exits and its entrances, its entire design and all its ordinances, all its forms and all its laws. Write it down in their sight, so that they may keep its whole design and all its ordinances, and perform them. 12 This is the law of the temple: the whole area surrounding the mountaintop is most holy. Behold, this is the law of the temple." The cycle of the Feasts of the Lord will be restored and observed. Ezekiel 45:18-25 (NKJV) "18 Thus says the Lord GOD: "In the first month, on the first day of the month, you shall take a young bull without blemish and cleanse the sanctuary. 19 The priest shall take some of the blood of the sin offering and put it on the doorposts of the temple, on the four corners of the ledge of the altar, and on the gateposts of the gate of the inner court. 20 And so you shall do on the seventh day of the month for everyone who has sinned unintentionally or in ignorance. Thus you shall make atonement for the temple. 21 "In the first month, on the fourteenth day of the month, you shall observe the Passover, a Feast of seven days; unleavened bread shall be eaten. 22 And on that day the prince shall prepare for himself and for all the people of the land a bull for a sin offering. 23 On the seven days of the Feast he shall prepare a burnt offering to the LORD, seven bulls and seven rams without blemish, daily for seven days, and a kid of the goats daily for a sin offering. 24 And he shall prepare a grain offering of one ephah (bushel) for each bull and one ephah for each ram, together with a hin (about 5.5 qts) of oil for each ephah. 25 "In the seventh month, on the fifteenth day of the month, at the

Feast, he shall do likewise for seven days, according to the sin offering, the burnt offering, the grain offering, and the oil."

Below is a breakdown of the Millennial Temple's construction as told to Ezekiel.

| | | |
|---|---|---|
| Ezekiel 40 | 1-5 | A New City, a New Temple |
| | 6-16 | The Eastern Gateway of the Temple |
| | 17-19 | The Outer Court |
| | 20-23 | The Northern Gateway |
| | 24-27 | The Southern Gateway |
| | 28-37 | Gateways of the Inner Court |
| | 38-43 | Where Sacrifices Were Prepared |
| | 44-46 | Chambers for Singers and Priests |
| | 47-49 | Dimensions of the Inner Court and Vestibule |
| Ezekiel 41 | 1-4 | Dimensions of the Sanctuary |
| | 5-11 | The Side Chambers on the Wall |
| | 12 | The Building at the Western End |
| | 13-26 | Dimensions and Design of the Temple Area |
| Ezekiel 42 | 1-14 | The Chambers for the Priests |
| | 15-20 | Outer Dimensions of the Temple |
| Ezekiel 43 | 1-12 | The Temple, the Lord's Dwelling Place |
| | 13-17 | Dimensions of the Altar |
| | 18-27 | Consecrating the Altar |
| Ezekiel 44 | 1-3 | The East Gate and the Prince |
| | 4-9 | Those Admitted to the Temple |
| | 10-31 | Laws Governing Priests |
| Ezekiel 45 | 1-5 | The Holy District |
| | 6-8 | Properties of the City and the Prince |
| | 9-17 | Laws Governing the Prince |
| | 18-25 | Keeping the Feasts |
| Ezekiel 46 | 1-15 | The Manner of Worship |
| | 16-18 | The Prince and Inheritance Laws |
| | 19-24 | How the Offerings Were Prepared |

At the end of the 1,000 years, Satan is freed for a short time where he will make one last futile attempt to deceive as many as possible and gather an army to come against Jerusalem and Israel one last time only to be totally destroyed before they even launch their attack. Satan will be recaptured and sent directly to the everlasting lake of fire for all eternity never to be able to mislead anybody again. Revelation 20:7-10 "7 And when the thousand years are expired, Satan shall be loosed out of his prison, 8 And shall go out to deceive the nations which are in the four quarters of the earth, Gog, and Magog, to gather them together to battle: the number of whom is as the sand of the sea. 9 And they went up on the breadth of the earth, and compassed the camp of the saints about, and the beloved city: and fire came down from God out of heaven, and devoured them. 10 And the devil that deceived them was cast into the lake of fire and brimstone, where the beast and the false prophet are, and shall be tormented day and night for ever and ever." Jeremiah 50:3-5 "3 For out of the north there cometh up a nation against her, which shall make her land desolate, and none shall dwell therein: they shall remove, they shall depart, both man and beast. 4 In those days, and in that time, saith the LORD, the children of Israel shall come, they and the children of Judah together, going and weeping: they shall go, and seek the LORD their God. 5 They shall ask the way to Zion with their faces thitherward, saying, Come, and let us join ourselves to the LORD in a perpetual covenant that shall not be forgotten." As a special note, most prophecy scholars agree the Gog/Magog mentioned in Revelation 20:8 is not the Gog/Magog of Ezekiel 38 and 39 as vs 8 only mentions one of the three main participants that form the coalition to come against Israel in Ezekiel's account.

Life during the Millennium will be enriching and fulfilling as God always intended it to be. However, it is still each person's responsibility to confess with their mouths and ask for salvation. Romans 10:9-13 (NIV) "9 If you declare with your mouth, "Jesus is Lord," and believe in your heart that God raised him from the dead, you will be saved. 10 For it is with your heart that you believe and are justified, and it is with your mouth that you profess your faith and are saved. 11 As Scripture says, "Anyone who believes in him will never be put to shame." 12 For there is no difference between Jew and Gentile the same Lord is Lord of all and richly blesses all who call on him, 13 for, "Everyone who calls on the name of the Lord will be saved." As we previously talked about, the people who made the transition from the Tribulation, through the second coming and enter the Millennium will all be believers. Furthermore, they will have children who will still have man's spirit of rebellion in them. Nowhere in the Bible does it say that God removes that spirit during the Millennium. The children born during this time will not have a frame of reference for them to know how badly mankind behaved or the level of punishment for that behavior. It will be up to their parents to remember and teach them, but as anybody who has had children can tell you, a child always thinks they know more than their parents. What makes it even more tragic is even with all the blessings of God there will be some that refuse to surrender their lives to Christ because of the hubris of man. The very sin of self-pride that infected Adam and Eve in the first place. Regrettably, there will be some who will fall for Satan's scheme and lose their mortal life, as well as their eternal life in the second death, as mentioned above. Proverbs 16:18 "Pride goeth before destruction, and an haughty spirit before a fall."

This brings us to God's last action on this earth, which we have referenced a couple of times, the Great White Throne Judgement. Revelation 20:11-15 "[11] And I saw a great white throne, and him that sat on it, from whose face the earth and the heaven fled away; and there was found no place for them. [12] And I saw the dead, small and great, stand before God; and the books were opened: and another book was opened, which is the book of life: and the dead were judged out of those things which were written in the books, according to their works. [13] And the sea gave up the dead which were in it; and death and hell delivered up the dead which were in them: and they were judged every man according to their works. [14] And death and hell were cast into the lake of fire. This is the second death.[15] And whosoever was not found written in the Book of Life was cast into the lake of fire." The text clearly states all of mankind (since Adam) will be brought before God to be judged. This trial will be simple as the only evidence for the defense or criteria will be the Book of Life. It will be opened and the names read, if your name is found there you will be allowed entrance to heaven, if not, the only option is the lake of fire or hell. It is the great equalizer. Whatever good works one may have performed, or what station, or celebrity one may have held will not carry any weight. Acts 10:34-35 "[34] Then Peter opened his mouth, and said, of a truth I perceive that God is no respecter of persons: [35] But in every nation he that feareth him, and worketh righteousness, is accepted with Him." God loves each person equally. God does not love you any less than He loves Billy Graham or Mother Teresa, nor does He love you any more than the vilest criminal, the deepest destitute, or slave to addiction. He loves all equally so much so that He sacrificed His Son to pay our price for redemption. The only opportunity to get your name listed in the Book of Life is in this life. Daniel 7:9-11 (NKJV) "[9] I watched till thrones were put in place, and the Ancient of Days was seated; His garment was white as snow, and the hair of His head was like pure wool. His throne was a fiery flame, its wheels a burning fire. [10] A fiery stream issued and came forth from before Him. A thousand thousands ministered to Him; ten thousand times ten thousand stood before Him. The court was seated, and the books were opened. [11] "I watched then because of the sound of the pompous words which the horn was speaking; I watched till the beast was slain, and its body destroyed and given to the burning flame."

This is where one of Daniel's prophetic visions comes into play. Daniel 12:1-2 "1 And at that time shall Michael stand up, the great prince which standeth for the children of thy people: and there shall be a time of trouble, such as never was since there was a nation even to that same time: and at that time thy people shall be delivered, every one that shall be found written in the book (of life). 2 And many of them that sleep in the dust of the earth shall awake, some to everlasting life, and some to shame and everlasting contempt."

To clarify, some teachers suggest that only the unbelievers will be judged at the Great White Throne Judgment. They point out that believers were judged at the Judgement Seat of Christ (Bema Seat) after the Rapture or at the separating of the sheep and goats at the start of the Millennium. There are two problems with this theory. One, if we recall, at the Judgement Seat of Christ was an assessment and reward of your type of service and faithfulness. Later the separation of sheep/believers and goats/unbelievers at the beginning of the Millennium was to allow the returning saints re-entry to earth. Neither one was to allow advancement to heaven. Two, the point of view does not address the issue of God judging believers, living or passed, who come to a saving knowledge of Christ during the 1,000 years. Furthermore, the Revelation 20:11-15 above passage says in vs 12 "and I saw the dead, small and great, standing before God." And in vs 13 "and they were judged, each one according to his works." The text does not list any exemptions. What is more likely is that their presence at this judgment for those saints in both previous judgments will be merely a formality. They will be invited to enter paradise, but they do need to present themselves. Those whose names are not in the Book of Life will finally realize the full extent of horror and folly of their actions like we saw with the rich man in Hades. Matthew 13:41-43 "41 The Son of man shall send forth his angels, and they shall gather out of his kingdom all things that offend, and them which do iniquity; 42 And shall cast them into a furnace of fire: there shall be wailing and gnashing of teeth. 43 Then shall the righteous shine forth as the sun in the kingdom of their Father. Who hath ears to hear, let him hear." Matthew 13:49-50 "49 So shall it be at the end of the world: the angels shall come forth, and sever the wicked from among the just, 50 And shall cast them into the furnace of fire: there shall be wailing and gnashing of teeth." Matthew 7:21-23 "21 Not everyone that saith unto me, Lord, Lord, shall enter into the kingdom of heaven; but he that doeth the will of my Father which is in heaven. 22 Many will say to me in that day, Lord, Lord, have we not prophesied in thy name? and in thy name have cast out devils? and in thy name done many wonderful works? 23 And then will I profess unto them, I never knew you: depart from me, ye that work iniquity." Luke 13:22-30 (NKJV) "22 And He went through the cities and villages, teaching, and journeying toward Jerusalem. 23 Then one said to Him, "Lord, are there few who are saved?" And He said to them, ²⁴ "Strive to enter through the narrow gate, for many, I say to you, will seek to enter and will not be able. ²⁵ When once the Master of the house has risen up and shut the door, and you begin to stand outside and knock at the door, saying, 'Lord, Lord, open for us,' and He will answer and say to you, 'I do not know you, where you are from,' ²⁶ then you will begin to say, 'We ate and drank in Your presence, and You taught in our streets.' ²⁷ But He will say, 'I tell you I do not know you, where you are from. Depart from Me, all you workers of iniquity.' ²⁸ There will be weeping and gnashing of teeth when you see Abraham and Isaac and Jacob and all the prophets in the kingdom of God, and yourselves thrust out. ²⁹ They will come from the east and the west, from the north and the south, and sit down in the kingdom of God. ³⁰ And indeed there are last who will be first, and there are first who will be last."

# Chapter 22

# "Eternity, the Choice is Yours"

As we are closing in on the end of John's vision, God is telling him about the end of His master plan. He will reclaim and re-establish His rightful place as the Most High Almighty God. After God presides as the Supreme Judge over the traitor Satan, He will wipe the slate clean. He will begin with clearing away the infected sinful earth and replace it with a new earth and a new heaven. Revelation 21:1 "And I saw a new heaven and a new earth: for the first heaven and the first earth were passed away; and there was no more sea." Conceivably this is the time Jesus referred to when He promised to be with us in Matthew 28:20 to be with us "until the end of the age."

Revelation 21:4 "And God shall wipe away all tears from their eyes; and there shall be no more death, neither sorrow, nor crying, neither shall there be any more pain: for the former things are passed away." Unbelievers are not the only ones who will mourn and be moved to tears at the unbelievers' fate. Believers watching from heaven will shed tears after watching family, friends, and loved ones being summarily sentenced to everlasting torment. It is consistent and plausible that Jesus too will weep at the profound sadness of the sight of believers like He did when He came to Lazarus's funeral or as he did when He was looking over the city of Jerusalem and saw in advance the coming destruction of God's chosen city. John 11:33-35 "33 When Jesus therefore saw her weeping, and the Jews also weeping which came with her, he groaned in the spirit, and was troubled. 34 And said, "Where have ye laid him? They said unto him, Lord, come and see. 35 Jesus wept." Luke 19:41-44 (NIV) "41 As he approached Jerusalem and saw the city, he wept over it 42 and said, "If you, even you, had only known on this day what would bring you peace—but now it is hidden from your eyes. 43 The days will come upon you when your enemies will build an embankment against you and encircle you and hem you in on every side. 44 They will dash you to the ground, you and the children within your walls. They will not leave one stone on another, because you did not recognize the time of God's coming to you." Additionally, Jesus has a singularly unique perspective of the cost of salvation, namely His sacrifice, and the senseless wasted lives of unbelievers because they did not accept His offer.

Continuing on. Revelation 21:2-3 "2 And I John saw the holy city, new Jerusalem, coming down from God out of heaven, prepared as a bride adorned for her husband. 3 And I heard a great voice out of heaven saying, Behold, the tabernacle of God is with men, and he will dwell with them, and they shall be his people, and God himself shall be with them, and be their God." Revelation 21:9-21 gives details of the New Jerusalem. It has twelve gates made of precious stones and jewels symbolizing the twelve tribes of Israel. It has twelve fountains symbolizing the twelve apostles also made of precious stones and jewels. The end of the chapter tells of the glory of God Himself, who will provide light for the people to see by. The same glory that was shown in the Holy of Holies in the Tabernacle of Moses and the Solomon's Temple. Revelation 21:23 "And the city had no need of the sun, neither of the moon, to shine in it: for the glory of God did lighten it, and the Lamb is the light thereof." Only those souls whose name was listed in the Lamb's Book of Life will be able to drink from the water fountain of life and eat from the tree of life for all eternity. Revelation 22:1-5 (NKJV) "1 And he showed me a pure river of water of life, clear as crystal, proceeding from the throne of God and of the Lamb. 2 In the middle of its street, and on either side of the river, was the tree of life, which bore twelve fruits, each tree yielding its fruit every month. The leaves of the tree were for the healing of the nations. 3 And there shall be no more curse, but the throne of God and of the Lamb shall be in it, and His servants shall serve Him. 4 They shall see His face, and His name shall be on their foreheads. 5 There shall be no night there: They need no lamp nor light of the sun, for the Lord God gives them light. And they shall reign forever and ever."

The books of Genesis and Revelation mirror each other in the Bible as bookends in the sense that God opens and closes them by declaring His authority. Genesis 1:1 "In the beginning God created the heaven and the earth." Revelation 1:8 "I am Alpha and Omega, the beginning and the ending, saith the Lord, which is, and which was, and which is to come, the Almighty." Revelation 22:13 "I am Alpha and Omega, the beginning and the end, the first and the last." From the beginning of creation and man to the Great White Throne Judgement and the New Jerusalem. John is admonished to share what he saw and reinforce that Jesus will return. It's a question of when, not if. Revelation 22:10 "And he saith unto me, Seal not the sayings of the prophecy of this book: for the time is at hand." Revelation 22:12 "And, behold, I come quickly; and my reward is with me, to give every man according as his work shall be." Revelation 22:20 (NKJV) "He who testifies to these things says, "Surely I am coming quickly." Amen. Even so, come, Lord Jesus!"

So that's it. Bible and prophecy scholars refer to the fulfillment of multiple signs in relatively close proximity to each other and not just a sign here or there as a convergence. Namely, the rebirth of the nation of Israel and the city of Jerusalem, ethnic conflicts, ecological upheaval, the formation of an anti-Israel coalition, the apathy of people to search and prioritize Godly thoughts, persecution of the faithful, both subtle and violent. In addition, technology has advanced to the point that we now have instantaneous global telecommunication, it would take less than three days to fly around the world, computers have influenced and infiltrated to such an extent that business and tracking systems are already developed to take financial control of all transactions and move to a cashless society. Research for this book on prophecy could not have been done as easily without the invention of the internet. Though there are other details that may have been left out, those that we did explore conclusively describes God's complex, complete, expertly thought out plan with every variable accounted for in His master plan. The only issue is how will you respond? Every person's salvation is left to the individual's choice. Your parents, spouse, or any other person cannot do it for you. A non-choice is a default no choice. You must proactively choose to accept. It all boils down to a simple choice, acceptance or rejection? If you consider yourself a Christian, I hope you will come away with a renewed excitement about the impending return of our Lord. If you read through this book and still come away disbelieving in God's plan you can make that choice. If you come away and have realized just how much God loves you or need to reconnect with Him, there are four Bible promises that will guide you to Him.

1. Admit that you are a sinner. Romans 3:23 "For all have sinned and come short of the glory of God."

2. Believe in your heart that Jesus died for your sins. Acts 16:31 (NKJV) "So they said, "Believe on the Lord Jesus Christ, and you will be saved, you and your household." John 3:16 "For God so loved the world that He gave his only begotten Son, that whosoever believeth in him should not perish, but have everlasting life."

3. Confess with your mouth Jesus is Lord. Romans 10:9-13 (NKJV) "9 That if you confess with your mouth the Lord Jesus and believe in your heart that God has raised Him from the dead, you will be saved. 10 For with the heart, one believes unto righteousness, and with the mouth, confession is made unto salvation. 11 For the Scripture says, "Whoever believes in Him will not be put to shame." 12 For there is no distinction between Jew and Greek, for the same Lord over all is rich

to all who call upon Him. ¹³ For "whoever calls on the name of the LORD shall be saved."

4. Receive the Gift of Salvation. Ephesians 2:8 "⁸ For by grace are ye saved through faith; and that not of yourselves: it is the gift of God." Acts 4:12 (NIV) "Salvation is found in no one else, for there is no other name under heaven given to men by which we must be saved." Romans 3:24 "Being justified freely by His grace through the redemption that is in Christ Jesus."

As I watch this world spiraling out of control, my belief of His soon appearing becomes more firm. This world is not our home! When you see the news through the lens of Bible prophecy if the signs of Jacob's trouble are materializing in Israel now, how much closer are we to the rapture? We are indeed the terminal generation.

Romans 15:5-6 (NIV) "⁵ May the God who gives endurance and encouragement give you the same attitude of mind toward each other that Christ Jesus had, ⁶ so that with one mind and one voice you may glorify the God and Father of our Lord Jesus Christ."

Numbers 6:24-26 (NKJV) "²⁴ The LORD bless you and keep you; ²⁵ The LORD make His face shine upon you and be gracious to you; ²⁶ The LORD lift up His countenance upon you, and give you peace."

Please visit www.thetapestyofprophecy.org for the following free downloads

- Full color pdf page of Israel God's Prophetic Time Piece (pgs 8 & 9).

- A Power Point presentation with companions notes in word.doc for use at your church or organization.

# Bible/Prophecy Scholars* and Resources

Dr. David Jeremiah, https://www.davidjeremiah.org or http://www.shadowmountain.org

Perry Stone, https://www.perrystone.org

John Hagee, https://www.jhm.org

Dr David Regan and Nathan Jones, http://christinprophecy.org

Jack Hibbs, https://reallifewithjackhibbs.org

Amir Tsarfati, http://beholdisrael.org

JD Farag, https://calvarychapelkaneohe.com

Bill Salus, http://www.prophecydepotministries.net

Gary Stearman, https://prophecyinthenews.com

Joel Rosenberg, http://www.joelrosenberg.com

Dr. Ron Rhodes, http://ronrhodes.org

Dr. Mark Hitchcock, http://marklhitchcock.com

Jan Markell, https://olivetreeviews.org

Mark Biltz, http://elshaddaiministries.us

Ann Graham Lotz, http://www.annegrahamlotz.org

Dr. Andy Woods, https://slbc.org

John Haller, http://fbchapel.com

Greg Laurie, https://www.harvest.org

Dr. Charles Stanley, https://www.fba.org

Don Stewart, http://www.educatingourworld.com

https://www.gotquestions.org

Strong's Concordance, http://www.eliyah.com/lexicon.html

https://www.Biblegateway.com

http://Biblehub.com

http://arewelivinginthelastdays.com

---

* Please note the above people and ministries mentioned should not be considered as an endorsement from them nor as an all inclusive list. They are just listed for the convenience of the reader who wishes to research information in more depth.

# The Tapestry of Prophecy
# Bulk Order Form

Please send _____ copies of the Tapestry of Prophecy at $_____ ea. to;

Name of Pastor/leader
_____

Name of church/organization
_____

Address, ST, ZIP
_____

For every 10 copies ordered, an additional 1 will be included for the pastor/leader's use free. That's 11 for the price of 10. These type of sales to ministry or other organizations are to be shipped at no charge. Please allow 2-4 weeks for delivery.

Enclosed is a check for $_____ to;

The Tapestry of Prophecy
219 Doreen St.
New Bedford, MA   02745

Maranatha!!

www.ingramcontent.com/pod-product-compliance
Lightning Source LLC
Chambersburg PA
CBHW021403290426
44108CB00010B/372